"Paris loves lovers."

—COLE PORTER

For Ethan, Ripley, and Zachary: l'amour fou.

IN LOVE IN FRANCE

A TRAVELER'S GUIDE

to the Most Romantic Destinations in the Land of Amour

RHONDA CARRIER

PHOTOGRAPHY BY

CONRAD WILLIAMS

First published in the United States of America in 2009 by
Rizzoli International Publications, Inc.
300 Park Avenue South, New York, NY 10010
www.rizzoliusa.com

Photo credits:
Cover: © Peter Cade/ Iconica/Getty Images
Page 42: Hôtel du Petit Moulin © Christophe Bielsa
Page 43 (top): courtesy of Hôtel Caron de Beaumarchais
Page 43 (bottom): courtesy of Hôtel du Jeu de Paume
Page 157: courtesy of Grand Hôtel de l'Abbaye
Page 170: courtesy of Château Les Crayères

2009 2010 2011 2012 2013 / 10 9 8 7 6 5 4 3 2 1

Design by Susi Oberhelman

ISBN-13: 978-0-7893-2032-2

Library of Congress Control Number: 2009930296

Printed in China

CONTENTS

INTRODUCTION

It's early morning, a summer morning. The city is glowing with golden light but the air is still chilly. There's barely a soul around. I've just stepped off a train from Vienna, a love affair behind me, over. Crossing the road to a pâtisserie, I buy an almond croissant, then I stand outside and plunge my teeth into its gooey innards, braced for the sugar rush.

I'm not unhappy. I'm in Paris again, and with that knowledge comes that sense of potential, the feeling that anything is possible—something that is not true of every capital. I finish the croissant as I watch the street-cleaners spraying the roads, making them glisten as another day begins.

DIARY, 1988

That was twenty years—half a lifetime—ago, and yet that feeling of exhilaration as I stepped off the train and into another world still fizzes in my veins as I relive it in my mind. Paris is like that: one hit and you're hooked.

This book is my love letter to a city that I fell in love with the *idea* of, before I ever saw it. Visiting Paris as a teenager and then living in its Montparnasse district as a student only deepened my passion for the place. Like any love affair, it's had its ups and downs. Try finding a taxi at rush hour in the rain when you've got a train to catch, and you'll know what I mean. But as far as affairs go, this one has outlasted the others in my life to date.

Yet all these years and countless stays both long and short later, I wonder if I really know Paris—if anybody ever does. Paris, like a certain kind of woman, resists you even as she seems to submit to your advances. Standing at the top of the Eiffel Tower, for instance, and admiring the way the city unfurls to the horizon, the way she spreads herself invitingly around you, you may think that you know her. But as with the most elusive of lovers, you'll find that you can't ever get to the bottom of her. Her mystery lives on, in countless clandestine squares, alleys, and gardens, and in her most obscure nooks and crannies. Paris offers up countless charms but withholds many more; hence, perhaps, her endless fascination for so many people.

For I'm not alone. Paris is one of the world's great destinations for lovers, and a classic honeymoon setting at that. It would be hard *not* to feel romantically inclined here, given the sumptuous and often decadent hotels offering all kinds of enticements to those with love on their minds, the beautiful and intimate restaurants serving the most aphrodisiac of classic French dishes, and the gorgeous architecture that invites you to simply wander, aimlessly, hand in hand, outside of time and the responsibilities of day-to-day existence.

But Paris is also oversubscribed, and thus I've tried to point you in the direction of some of its lesser-known treasures: charming little museums that will open their doors just for you; tranquil, overgrown gardens where you probably won't encounter another soul; art-house cinemas where you might be lucky enough to enjoy a private screening of a classic Parisian movie from decades long past.

Of course, there's no escaping the obvious sights, like the Louvre, for instance. I've scrutinized these better-known aspects of Paris from a quirky, romantic angle, seeking out tidbits of information that you won't find in the conventional guidebooks. From seeing groundbreaking works of art to shopping for the sexiest shoes, you'll get under the skin of Paris in a way that few visitors ever do.

In spite of its green spaces, Paris offers a resolutely urban experience, deriving its character from its buildings and its inhabitants, present and past. There's the sense that every street (and every street name for that matter) have a story to tell. Artists and their works, their lives, and their loves, suffuse the city, and define it; having taken their inspiration from it, they've given something back and left their muse forever changed.

This is also true of the areas surrounding Paris, including the Loire Valley and the Champagne region, to each of which I have devoted a chapter. Within easy reach of the capital,

both areas are replete with culture, whether it is a castle once fought over by queens, an artist's hideaway, or a prestigious wine house. The sensuality of these regions is inherent in the landscape itself, from rolling vineyards full of ripe fruit where some of the world's most prized vintages are produced, to vast royal hunting forests where stags rut and wild boars roam.

The landscape is also one of the main draws of northern France. Normandy is characterized by fertile orchards where apples are grown for luscious desserts and fiery liqueurs, and by vast swatches of deserted shore from which you can watch fishermen go about their business. Brittany ups the ante, with its glistening oyster beds and its craggy coast of pink rocks, which stretch into turquoise bays or to more turbulent waters presided over by wind-lashed lighthouses.

But for the true flavor of the great French outdoors, head to the south, located within an easy express train or plane ride of Paris. Here, white-gold beaches, hills topped by precariously balanced villages, and waving fields of lavender have long inspired artists and writers to set up homes on the Côte d'Azur or in its undulating backcountry. In the neighboring Bouches du Rhône, wild white horses, pink flamingos, bullfighting arenas, and flamenco rhythms bespeak the fiery Romani region of the Camargue, while the city of Marseille is a white-hot slice of North Africa transported to the European continent.

In all of France, north, south, and in between, food and drink are intrinsic to the appreciation of life. As a teenager staying with French friends, I was impressed more than anything else by the long, lazy lunches, the hours spent at the table, chatting, breaking bread, enjoying simply prepared but wonderful local and seasonal food. Here, it seems to me, resides the greatest sensuality of the French people. For a healthy, hearty appetite for good cuisine goes hand in hand with the love of sex and a passion for life itself.

Hence, if much of this book seems preoccupied, *obsessed* even, with eating and drinking, whether it is the haute cuisine served up in Michelin-starred restaurants or the best places to stock up on great breads and cold fare for picnics by the sea, I offer no apologies. Indeed, at the end of this book, I offer some of my favorite French recipes, some of which were garnered from the French people who have shared their lives with me over the years.

Which brings me neatly back to art. In France, and especially in Paris, there's the sense that everyone is an artist, or an artist of the everyday. Rituals and rhythms are paramount here, raising the seemingly banal to the level of the sacred. This spirit is what I hope to convey to you in the following pages, as I take you by the hand on a journey through the places that have stolen my heart.

This book has been a partnership between me and my husband, Conrad Williams, whose images throughout these pages evoke the Paris I love—a Paris of chance encounters and secret spaces in which anything might happen, if you're of the mind to let it.

HEART OF PARIS

1ST AND 2ND:

Le Louvre, Les Halles, La Bourse

Mon manège à moi c'est toi.

You are my merry-go-round.

—EDITH PIAF

No one who comes to Paris can resist the lure of the **Musée du Louvre**, one of the world's greatest museums. Indeed, far from housing the undiscovered, Paris's aptly named 1st arrondissement, which occupies the most central section of the Rive Droite, or Right Bank, comprises both this most visited of cultural repositories and **Les Halles**, where the city's charming food market of old has sadly been replaced by a concrete mall that acts as a magnet for listless teenagers and aimless tourists. But amid the famous sights and artworks to be savored—including a large number of open-air nudes that may get your libido soaring—are surprising pockets of privacy offering low-key enjoyment. Among the district's hotels and restaurants, meanwhile, you'll find enclaves of unadulterated luxury and decadence that are crying out to be shared by lovers.

North from here, the 2nd arrondissement is less frequented by visitors, and perhaps by Parisians themselves, and for good reason: it's home to **La Bourse**, Paris's stock exchange, and largely the preserve of suited businessmen. But you could do much worse than to stray into this neighborhood for a little window-shopping in some of the city's most delightful and quintessentially Parisian arcades, to sample some luscious pâtisseries, or to stay in a hotel with a genuine royal connection.

LOOKING FOR LOVE IN THE LOUVRE

The ideal time to come to this most famous of museums is in the evening, when I. M. Pei's modern steel and glass Pyramide and the Hall Napoléon beneath it, which constitute the main entrance and lobby, are illuminated from the inside—a glorious sight. It's also utterly enchanting to wander through the Louvre's courtyards after dark, when they are artfully lit. In fact, you can combine an evening walk through the grounds with a tour of the museum, as the Louvre is open until 10 p.m. on Wednesdays and Fridays.

Though everyone who comes to Paris *must* visit the Louvre, a former royal palace and prison that became an art museum after the Revolution, you're deluded if you think you'll ever have the place to yourself—no matter what the season or hour. However, safe in the knowledge that 99 percent of other visitors are making a beeline for Leonardo da Vinci's overrated *Mona Lisa,* steer your lover in the direction of some lesser-known but perhaps more enjoyable—and certainly more romantic—works.

These include a fifteenth-century wool and silk tapestry depicting "the gift of the heart," a knight's declaration of love to his lady; Rubens's *The Village Fête*, a painting of a seventeenth-century Flemish fair replete with sensual goings-on; and a table decorated with scenes of pastoral love between shepherds and shepherdesses that belonged to Louis

XV's mistress Madame du Barry (see p. 126). Then there's an eighteenth-century pocket watch featuring the characters Pierrot and Columbine, the object of his desire, from the Italian commedia dell'arte; and Jean-Antoine Watteau's eighteenth-century dreamlike *Pèlerinage à l'île de Cythère*, or *Pilgrimage to Cythera*, which shows couples setting out for the goddess Aphrodite's island, and *Le faux-pas*, a regency seduction scene. Lastly, check out Jean-Honoré Fragonard's seventeenth-century *Le verrou*, or *The Bolt*, a vision of amorous libertinage full of symbols of high passion; a Greek terracotta of a nuptial scene; and the "Sarcophagus of the Spouses," which features an Etruscan couple facing eternity together. You can also ask the information desk for a copy of "I Love You—Love in the Louvre Collections," a thematic trail that is easily completed in about an hour and a half, or just print it out from the museum's Web site ahead of time.

These works aside, it's almost obligatory to pay homage to the naked and armless Aphrodite, known as the Venus de Milo. One of the most famous of ancient Greek sculptures, she is thought to have been carved by Alexandros, a sculptor of Antioch along the Maeander River in about 150 BC, and depicts Aphrodite, the Greek goddess of sexual love and beauty, whom the Greeks associated with the sea (*aphros* is Greek for "foam"). Known as Venus by the ancient Romans and associated with the planet, she makes another appearance in the Louvre in the Botticelli fresco *Venus and the Three Graces Presenting Gifts to a Young Woman*, which may have been commissioned by the Florentine Tornabuoni dynasty to mark the marriage of one of its members. In this piece, the goddess is depicted placing a gift in a cloth vessel held out by the bride.

Although not an overtly romantic painting to look at, another famous work depicting marriage is Veronese's *Wedding Feast at Cana*, the event at which Jesus is said to have performed the miracle of turning water into wine in order to gain the faith of his disciples. Some Christians have taken the story as evidence that Jesus approved of marriage and earthly celebrations. This interpretation would have come as a relief to Napoléon I, who wed Archduchess Marie Louise of Austria in 1810—you can see a necklace and pair of emerald and diamond earrings that he gave her for the occasion on display at the Louvre.

Napoléonic-style decor is one of the attractions of the stylish **Café Marly**, perhaps the Louvre's best option if you're in need of replenishment. This café affords gorgeous views of the courtyard, especially from its terrace, but you can also enjoy artwork viewable through its interior glass walls onto certain galleries. Its Sunday brunches are particularly decadent: champagne and orange juice, scrambled eggs, butter-laden brioches, and *pains aux chocolat* or *aux raisins*.

After you've refueled, you might want to head to the **Musée des Arts Décoratifs**, squirreled away in the northwest wing of the Louvre's Pavillon de Marsan. This revamped museum is a tranquil place in which to wander and to admire mainly French furniture, fabrics, wallpaper, tapestries, ceramics and glassware, objets d'art, religious paintings, and more, dating from the Middle Ages to the present. One of the highlights is the 1875 boudoir of the red-headed courtesan Lucie Delabigne, who is said to have inspired Émile Zola's character Nana (see p. 120). Lucy's giant bronze bed is a real eye-opener. Designed for a *lit de parade*, it allowed her to show herself off to her best advantage. In *Nana*, Zola describes the bed as: ". . . a bed such as had never been seen before, a throne, an altar where Paris would come to admire her sovereign nudity. It would be made of gold and repoussé silver, like a giant jewel, with roses flung up on a silver trellis, and at the head a garland of flowers would hang, bespying the voluptuous goings-on in the shadow of the curtains."

OPEN-AIR SCULPTURE, A BLUR OF WATER LILIES, AND SEXY SHOPPING

Stepping out from the west end of the Louvre is like continuing your museum visit, as there are also many sculptures in the **Jardin des Tuileries**. Paris's most central park is an excellent place to meet or to stroll with a lover past fountains, through formal gardens, and alongside a boating lake. Extending as far as the Place de la Concorde, it dates from the sixteenth century, when it was laid out for Catherine de Médicis—now recognized as one of the greatest French queens—as the grounds for the Palais des Tuileries.

The palace is long gone, but come for a walk, as many Parisians do, on a crisp winter's morning to fully appreciate this public space at its least crowded. Make sure to seek out the eighteen female figures sculpted by Aristide Maillol, which were bequeathed to the gardens by his model and muse, Dina Vierny. The latter met the artist when she was just fifteen and he was seventy-three, after he wrote to her, "Mademoiselle, it is said that you look like a Maillol and a Renoir." Upon setting eyes on the voluptuous young woman, he confirmed that she looked like one of his works come alive, and insisted that it was her body that he had been sculpting all along.

Vierny went on to model for Matisse and Bonnard, among others, but she remained true to Maillol, to the extent that after his death, she set up a private museum dedicated to him (see p. 61). Among the Maillol sculptures gracing the Tuileries are *Les trois nymphes* or *The Three Nymphs*, *Baigneuse à la draperie* or *Bather with Drapery*, *Jeune fille allongée* or *Young Girl Lying Down*, and *L'air*; they're located in the Jardin du Carrousel section of the park. If you're feeling young at heart, there's an actual carousel just beyond—one of many charming, traditional merry-go-rounds in Paris.

VAN CLEEF & ARPELS
Van Cleef & Arpels

If the weather isn't your friend, there are two museums worth slipping into at the Place de la Concorde end of the gardens. One, the beautiful **Musée de l'Orangerie**, was chosen and arranged by Claude Monet to display the majority of his famous paintings of water lilies (see p. 174). As its name suggests, the building was once used for the cultivation of oranges, lemons, and other exotic fruits. The massive *Nymphéas* occupy two stunning oval galleries; entering them is indeed a bit like moving into a dreamy underwater world, and, in fact, they've been described as the perfect antidote to "overworked nerves." The remainder of the building contains works by Paul Cézanne, Pierre-Auguste Renoir, Pablo Picasso (see p. 34), Henri Matisse (see pp. 194–195), and Amadeo Modigliani (see p. 114), among others.

There's contemporary art and photography across the Tuileries in the **Musée du Jeu de Paume**, but if you're suffering from cultural overload (or foot-ache), it's only a few steps to **Rodolphe Ménudier** (14 rue de Castiglione), purveyor of seriously sexy shoes for men and women. Within this sleek boutique filled with glossy black display units that form a strange counterpoint to all the weathered stonework you've been looking at, you'll find glamorous stiletto heels for the ladies, and winkle picker–style suede boots and animal-skin shoes for their beaux.

If your feet aren't aching too much, you might be enticed to head to the **Slow Club** (130 rue de Rivoli), where you can dance the night away. If it was good enough for Miles Davis, then it's probably good enough for you, too, particularly if you are connoisseurs of New Orleans–style and traditional jazz. Located in the medieval vaults of a former banana-ripening warehouse, it's low-key and intimate, with atmospheric acoustics. Or foodie couples might be tempted by the culinary workshops offered by the **Ritz Escoffier School** at the world-renowned Hôtel Ritz Paris on Place Vendôme. Auguste Escoffier, one of history's most illustrious chefs, invented the peach Melba and other classics. Good workshops for couples to take together are "Truffles," "Pairing Food and Wine," and "Cocktails." If you're worried that your French isn't up to the task, you can request an on-the-spot translation by an assistant.

Or you could just sample cocktails at the Hôtel Ritz's famous **Bar Hemingway**, where concoctions such as Picasso martinis—gin and Noilly Prat—are served with good tapas. If you're feeling reckless after cocktails, take your credit card for a short stroll north of Place Vendôme, to **Van Cleef & Arpels** (3 rue de la Paix). This legendary Parisian jeweler creates fantasy pieces based upon themes ranging from dragonflies and butterflies to snowflakes and *A Midsummer Night's Dream*—complete with fairies, sprites, and woodland creatures. Its marketing materials declare that its raison d'être is the "supremacy of love" and the search to express it, so it may as well be your first stop if all the romance of the 1st arrondissement has inspired you to propose. Or if you've already planned to get hitched in town, as well as diamond engagement rings, there are classic flat wedding bands (for him and her). Prince Rainier of Monaco gave Grace Kelly a Van Cleef & Arpels pearl necklace on their engagement in 1955, and the princess was often seen wearing VC&A pieces. If you're in Paris at Christmastime, it's worth heading this way for the fairy-tale window displays alone.

A PALACE FOR THE PEOPLE

Opposite the Louvre, there rises an elegant private mansion that was built for Cardinal de Richelieu and is now known as the **Palais-Royal**, home to the Ministry of Culture. You might think that it's not the kind of place that bears much exploration, but it conceals a surprise: tranquil gardens hidden within surrounding arcades built at the behest of Louis XIV's cousin, Louis Philippe Joseph d'Orléans, later the Duke of Orléans, to house shops, cafés, theaters, and apartments in order to raise funds to pay off debts and rebuild the Opéra, which had burned down. The arcades were a popular place for trysts and remain the perfect spot to wander with a lover. Home to Le Grand Véfour (see p. 26), one of the city's best restaurants, and the Comédie-Française (the state theater set up for the playwright Molière), they still house an array of shops selling all manner of quaint things, from old stamps and musical boxes to modern scents.

The square in front of the Palais-Royal is home to the charming **Louvre des Antiquaires**, an antiques emporium housing 250 vendors over three levels, in the chocolate-box building that was once home to the Grands Magasins du Louvre. This is the place for a leisurely Sunday browse, where you'll find everything from old postcards of the city to sparkling jewelry and one-off table decorations. There's also a tea room where you can go to debate what to spend your money on or to inspect your purchases.

There's more shopping of an altogether racier sort off the Palais-Royal. Here, you'll find **Cadolle** (255 rue St-Honoré), founded by Herminie Cadolle, the inventor of the modern brassiere, who drew her inspiration for the intimate garment from the engineering of the Eiffel Tower. Dubbed "the secret address of the world's most seductive women," the shop is now run by her great-great-granddaughter, Poupie ("Doll") Cadolle. Cadolle continues to sell the most sumptuous of custom-made, hand-finished lingerie, including wonderful, flattering corsets that have caught the eyes of Coco Chanel, Marlene Dietrich, the Duchess of Windsor, and Mata Hari, and continue to draw an elite clientele, including French movie stars and the dancers of the Crazy Horse cabaret club (see p. 66). The shop's most popular items include full-length nightgowns confected

HOME IS WHERE THE HEART IS

It must have been an act of love that inspired the owner of an apartment at 9 rue Beaujolais to vacate it upon reading in an interview that the sensualist novelist Colette, having moved fourteen times since leaving her husband Willy, said that she would never move again if only she could live in the Palais-Royal. A plaque now marks the apartment where the writer lived for seventeen years. Among other things, it was here that she hid her much-loved third and last husband, Jewish pearl dealer Maurice Goudeket, during World War II. The pair remained inseparable until her death in 1954, when he wrote a book about his great love.

If you're unfamiliar with Colette's work, good places to start are *Chéri* and *The Last of Chéri*, both set in Paris, about two lovers, one a courtesan, whose affair is challenged by the stark realities of life.

FANTAISIES .
Chantal T

from Lyon silk and Calais lace, and a house perfume. You will need to make an appointment before arriving.

On the same street is another "house of seduction," **Chantal Thomass** (211 rue St-Honoré), which is full of the kind of lingerie, hosiery, nightwear, and beachwear that will make a femme fatale of any woman. It's worth coming to this all-pink confection of a boutique just to gape at the changing rooms with their padded, baby-pink satin walls.

Those who, like Bill Clinton, appreciate the erotic potential of cigars shouldn't miss **A la Civette** (157 rue St-Honoré). Since it opened in 1716 it has been frequented by the famous womanizer Casanova (see pp. 52–54), British statesman Sir Winston Churchill, and novelist Colette (see p. 21), among others. Colette is said to have smoked cigars in bed, and even as early as 1903, a brand of cigar was among the merchandising spin-offs of her racy

TEA FOR TWO

Paris is famed the world over for the *grands crèmes* and other delicious coffees served at its many cafés. It's perhaps less well known as an equally good place to take tea, which is beloved just as much by Parisians. Often featuring extravagant decor, Paris's many *salons de thé* are civilized places for a date, and though they can be found in practically every district, they are especially prominent in the area around the Louvre. **Angelina** (226 rue de Rivoli) may be too well known for its own good, but if you taste its exotic hot chocolates you will understand why word has spread. A more off-the-beaten-path option is the adorable **Muscade** (36 rue de Monpensier), located within the Palais-Royal, with its views of the fountains and gardens.

Les Cafés Verlet (256 rue St-Honoré) has ambiance in spades, especially in its *salon à l'étage*, an intimate upstairs room reminiscent of an artist's garret, which, accessed via a creaky narrow staircase, is perfect for a romantic tête-a-tête over espresso, a fruit tart, and candied fruits. The coffees can be as exotic as you dare try. The Yemenese is perfect if you're in the mood for a little spice. Alternatively, head to **Toraya** (10 rue St-Florentin) to sample a variety of Japanese teas served alongside exquisite pastries concocted by the supplier to the Imperial Palace in Tokyo. In the fall and winter months, you can warm up with hot chocolate flavored with *matcha* green tea after an invigorating walk in the Jardin des Tuileries (see p. 16).

Claudine novels. And she wasn't the only Parisian woman to enjoy a cigar. Though the habit among females was frowned upon in nonartistic circles, writers such as George Sand (see p. 212) and Gertrude Stein liked to indulge. In fact, Sand once mused, "A cigar numbs sorrows and fills the solitary hours with a million gracious images."

France is, for better or for worse, a land of smokers. However, even if the French movie classics are littered with scenes in which heartthrobs, such as Alain Delon and Jean-Paul Belmondo, make cigarette smoking look sizzlingly sexy (often in a postcoital context), the new ban on smoking in public places has driven smokers, rather pathetically, to chilly doorsteps and drafty alleyways. Cigars and pipes, on the other hand, retain some class and erotic charm. For many, the sweet, dark, spicy smoke of a pipe is part of the seductive scent of Paris herself. Near A la Civette and open almost as long (well, since 1818), back in the arcades of the Palais-Royal, **A l'Oriental** (22 galerie de Chartres) stocks thousands of beautiful handmade pipes in an astonishing array of shapes and sizes, all tightly packed, somehow, into the tiny premises. These pipes are stunning objects in their own right, but in the unlikely event that you cannot find one to please, you may order a custom-made version to your liking.

Lastly, at Paris's best treasure trove of vintage haute couture, **Didier Ludot** (20–24 galerie de Montpensier), you and your beau or belle can have a ball playing dress-up in the chicest of Parisian styles dating from the 1920s to the 1980s, by such names as Dior,

Chanel, Givenchy, and Hermès. There's more designer luxe—or, depending upon your take, designer kitsch—back toward the Louvre, at Place Colette, in the form of a métro station entrance designed by Jean-Michel Othoniel in 2000. Made from hammered metal and outsize baubles of multicolored Murano glass by Salviati, the installation is entitled *Le kiosque des noctambules* (The Sleepwalkers' Hut) because it shelters a silver bench designed for chance encounters.

PASSAGES COUVERTS AND A DIP IN THE WELL OF LOVE

North of the Palais-Royal, in the 2nd arrondissement, are some of the finest examples of Paris's atmospheric *passages couverts*—early-nineteenth-century malls running between two buildings and covered by glass, a design intended to protect wealthy shoppers from the rain and horses passing on the streets. In fact, this arrondissement is home to half of the *passages couverts* that have survived in Paris. These galleries are fine places for a lazy stroll, especially the Galerie Vivienne, built in 1823 in a neoclassical style, complete with gilded moldings, mosaic floors, paintings, and sculptures. Don't miss the goddesses and nymphs found inside the rotunda, or, at number 13, the grand staircase of a mansion that was once home to Eugène François Vidocq, a criminal who, in a strange turn of fate, went on to become the chief of the city's undercover investigations unit (Gérard Depardieu played him in the movie *Vidocq*).

Paris owes one of its best pâtisseries, Stohrer (51 rue Montorgueil), to the marriage of Marie Leszczyńska, daughter of the Polish king Stanisław I, to Louis XV in 1725. The princess's personal *pâtissier*, Nicolas Stohrer, followed her to the court of Versailles, and five years later opened his shop. Stohrer's most famous contribution to the culinary world, the *baba au rhum* (rum baba), was based on a brioche that Stanisław brought home from a trip. The *pâtissier* tweaked the dish to perfection with the addition of Malaga wine, saffron, custard, raisins, and grapes. You can still sample a *baba*, a name coined by the king after reading *The Thousand and One Nights*, at the pâtisserie today. Be sure to take a moment to admire the facade and interior of the pâtisserie, including the historic murals created by the nineteenth-century painter Paul Baudry, who also decorated the Palais Garnier (see p. 76).

Lovers, however, might prefer to sample Stohrer's *puits d'amour* (well of love), named after an operetta written by the Irish-born nineteenth-century composer Michael William Balfe. This puff pastry, filled with vanilla custard and caramelized on top, is still prepared in Stohrer's original late-nineteenth-century molds. Be warned, however: vanilla was listed as an aphrodisiac in old medicinal literature (see p. 233).

Le Grand Véfour
17 rue de Beaujolais
+33 (0)1 42 96 56 27

Widely held to be Paris's most beautiful restaurant, Le Grand Véfour is a special-occasion treat, famed far and wide for its Michelin-starred classic French cooking largely inspired by the cuisine of Savoy, the region of the Alps from which the chef, Guy Martin, hails. Let's hope it sets your date afire, for it will certainly burn a hole in your wallet—think in excess of €100 for a main course alone, or more than €250 for the *menu plaisir* (pleasure menu). Brass plaques on the tables attest to a long parade of famous diners, from Napoléon Bonaparte and Josephine (see p. 128), said to have had their first date here, to Jean-Paul Sartre and Simone de Beauvoir (see p. 53). Please note that Le Véfour is closed for the month of August, and that you must book far ahead for reservations year-round.

Le Pinxo
Renaissance Paris Vendôme Hotel
4 rue du Mont Thabor
+33 (0)1 40 20 72 00

Pinxo is Basque for "pinch," and this brasserie dedicated to the art of sharing is made for lovers. Many dishes are served in three portions to encourage partners to nibble from each other's plates. Eating with fingers is not considered a transgression here; in fact, at Le Pinxo, it is believed to enhance intimacy. The cuisine has a southwestern French slant—you might enjoy squid *à la plancha* (griddle-cooked) with ginger and chili peppers. The desserts are masterpieces: try La Belle Rose et Le Marron Sage (three delectable mousses: rose and lychee, chestnut and mascarpone, and coffee and cream). Pre- or post-dinner, enjoy a drink in the hotel's colonial Bar Chinois.

Brasserie Gallopin
40 rue Notre Dame des Victoires
+33 (0)1 42 36 45 38

It's hard to eat an intimate meal in the 2nd, with all the expense accounters in their suits busily cutting deals. Gallopin is a great exception with its gracious eighteenth-century dining room with its stained-glass windows, its excellent service, and its superb-value menus. This is a real slice of old Paris, in which you can enjoy classic dishes from steak tartare to chitterling sausage. Ravenous lovers might be tempted to share a *plateau Gallopin*, a glistening mountain of lobster, oysters, prawns, clams, and whelks. Dessert portions are enormous, too, so ask for two spoons to share the *crêpes flambées Alexandre*, crepes lit aflame in front of your eyes and served with a zesty citrus reduction sauce. On Valentine's Day, Gallopin offers a set menu that may include extra goodies, such as vouchers for spa treatments.

Bar de l'Entracte
47 rue de Montpensier
+33 (0)1 42 97 57 76

This tiny bar and restaurant, with its even tinier terrace (heated in the cooler months) and casual bric-a-brac decor, has true Parisian character. Warm and welcoming, it will dispel any notions you may have about the natives being frosty. As the name suggests, it's a good place for a pre- or

post-theater meal of unpretentious fare, such as pasta washed down with a carafe of house red, which makes it a real find in this expensive area. Single friends have told me that it's a great place to meet people, too …

STAYING

Le Meurice
228 rue de Rivoli
+33 (0)1 44 58 10 10
www.lemeurice.com

Less well known, at least among overseas visitors, than rivals Hôtel de Crillon (see p. 72) and George V (see p. 67), this long-standing palace-hotel has reinvented itself for the twenty-first century. With a Philippe Starck take on Salvador Dali in its reception area, and renovations that include a new spa and restaurants, you might worry that Le Meurice has lost its very French character. Don't panic. The rooms and suites remain luxuriantly Louis XVI in style, with marble bathrooms outfitted with deep tubs in which to wallow. For a honeymoon night you won't forget, book the vast *suite royale belle étoile* with its private terrace and 360 degree view of the city. Or ask about a romantic package, including pink champagne and pink petits fours, plus a bouquet of roses, available in a variety of rooms and suites at a wide range of prices.

Hôtel Edouard VII
39 avenue de l'Opéra
+33 (0)1 42 61 56 90
www.edouard7hotel.com

This hotel is another great little spot for those looking for an old Paris feel with a twist. A notch or two easier on the wallet than Le Meurice, it has quirky but not outlandish decor that offers a mix of contemporary elements and Murano glass chandeliers, marble, parquet floors, and Napoléon III furniture. The elegant boutique-style rooms have balconies, some that overlook the ravishing Opéra (see p. 76). The hotel's name derives from the fact that Queen Victoria's son, Edward VII, often stayed here.

3RD AND 4TH:

The Marais and the Îles

Songe à la douceur
D'aller là-bas vivre ensemble!
Aimer à loisir,
Aimer et mourir,
Au pays qui te ressemble!

Think of the rapture
Of living together there!
Of loving at will,
Of loving till death,
In the land that is like you!

—CHARLES BAUDELAIRE,
"L'invitation au voyage"

Paris is one of the world's greatest cities for simply strolling—up and down its streets and through its squares and gardens. On any given Sunday, no matter what the weather, you'll see Parisians and visitors of all ages ambling along, perhaps holding hands, maybe chatting, as they drink in the intoxicating beauty of their surroundings. Sometimes they'll stop for coffee and pastries before continuing on their ways, with no real destinations in mind. Indeed, aimlessness is the point. The French even have a word for it: *flâner*, for which there is no real equivalent in English. A *flâneur* is someone who saunters, strolls, or even loafs or drifts about. The poet-dandy Charles Baudelaire made *flânerie* into a veritable art form, a means of grasping the streets by walking them, and from there, at

least in Baudelaire's case, translating his experience of the city into a work of art. For the best places to stroll in Paris, see page 39.

The Marais and the Îles, Paris's islands in the Seine, have a unique village-like atmosphere that makes them arguably the city's loveliest spots for strolling. Of course, as with the Louvre, you won't be alone; their particular ambiance and mood give reason to seek them out. But choose your time wisely—visit midweek or in the off-season (avoid the height of summer)—and you'll fall hopelessly in love with this part of the city.

The Marais, which lies to the east of the Louvre and Les Halles, has somehow managed to retain its character, despite its popularity among both Parisians and tourists. One of Paris's prettiest neighborhoods, its narrow streets are lined with idiosyncratic, one-off boutiques and cafés. This wasn't always so. *Marais* means "swamp," and that's exactly what comprised this district when Paris was confined to the Seine islands. But even after the land was reclaimed and some grand buildings were constructed, including those framing the gorgeous Place des Vosges, the fate of the Marais was far from secure. By the eighteenth century, it was a slum and a Jewish ghetto. In fact, when Baron Georges-Eugène Haussmann (see pp. 75–76) was called in to remodel the city, he refused to touch the Marais, deeming

it worthy only of demolition. This bit of history, ironically, was what ensured the survival of what now constitutes the area's main charms: the narrow streets and clandestine courtyards. Lucky for us that it wasn't demolished, although the Marais wouldn't truly come into its own until 1969, when the minister of cultural affairs at the time, André Malraux, made it the city's first "protected sector."

The largest of the islands in the Seine is the Île de la Cité, where Paris took seed. It was here that the Parisii tribe settled, until the Romans ousted them. Later, the island became the country's capital under Clovis I, the king of the Franks, and it remained Paris's busiest area through the Middle Ages. Today it's best known as home to the cathedral of Notre-Dame, although it houses many judicial buildings as well. The island is scenic enough: stroll to its leafy western tip, the Square du Vert-Galant, for a sight of the statue of the famously dashing and womanizing king Henri IV. The tree here is said to be the first to turn green when spring arrives in Paris, and it's a fine place for a picnic while watching the tour boats chug by and people meandering across the Pont Neuf, the oldest of the city's thirty-six bridges—the movie *Les amants du Pont Neuf* (see p. 57) was not filmed here but rather on a replica of the bridge constructed in the south of France.

What may be of more interest to couples is the unspeakably charming Île St-Louis, actually constructed from two islands: the Île aux Vaches (Island of the Cows), once pastureland, and the Île Notre-Dame, where judicial duels were held in medieval times. Today the Île St-Louis's main draws are its seventeenth-century mansions, built by lords and financiers after the islands were joined, and the cobbled streets and shaded quays lined with bakeries, cheese shops, boutiques, and cafés.

A PERFECT SQUARE, WORKS OF LOVE, AND A VINTAGE MARKET

Paris *is* its history, perhaps more than any other city in the world bar London. Few spots better demonstrate this statement than the magnificent **Place des Vosges**, the city's oldest square. The Place des Vosges is also a true square—460 feet at each length. Built by Henri IV in the early seventeenth century, it was originally known as the Place Royale and was inaugurated with a grand carousel celebrating the marriage of Louis XIII and Anne of Austria. Yet, however exemplary of European royal city planning the square is, and despite its aristocratic pedigree and demeanor, no royal has ever lived here. But this fact didn't stop the style of the Places des Vosges from being hugely influential—subsequent residential squares in cities around Europe were based upon it.

Any tour of the Marais must either begin or end with a stroll through the well-tended square itself, by its tidy lawns and mature linden trees, and through the arcades of the buildings surrounding it, home to many atmospheric cafés as well as, often, a variety of street musicians. It's easy to miss, but what may be most interesting about the Place des Vosges is the fact that the houses surrounding it are all of the same design, with red–brick and vaulted arcades on square pillars, and with steep roofs of blue slate punctuated by small-paned dormer windows. Unsurprisingly, plenty of famous faces chose to make the square their home: scriveners Victor Hugo (to whom a small museum is dedicated in the Hôtel de Rohan-Guéménée; 6 Place des Vosges), Théophile Gautier, and Alphonse Daudet, as well as the courtesan Marion Delorme, who was notorious for her affairs with important men of the seventeenth century.

Sneak through the arcade on the southeastern side of the Place to find the **Hôtel de Sully** (62 rue St-Antoine) a mansion once owned by Henri IV's minister, Maximilien de Béthune, the Duke of Sully. Now occupied by government offices and open only to the public for guided tours on weekends, it's worth seeking out for its enchanting seventeenth-century gardens, which are little known except to the most discerning locals. The gardens are surrounded by ivy-covered historic buildings, which make them fabulous spots for picnics *à deux*, especially when the occasional busking violinist is on hand to serenade you.

The Place des Vosges and Hôtel de Sully are on the eastern edge of the Marais, but the streets to the west are full of interesting finds, too. The rue des Rosiers remains a focal point for Paris's Jewish community, and the long rue des Francs-Bourgeois is lined with trendy and quirky boutiques and galleries (all of which are open on Sunday, a rarity in Paris). The northern Marais has a strong Chinese contingent, and there is a concentration of gay clubs, cabarets, and cafés along rue Sainte-Croix de la Bretonnerie and rue Vieille du Temple. All of this, together with the plentiful graffiti, prevents the Marais from descending into chocolate-box over-prettiness, despite its protected status.

There are also several museums and historic buildings in the Marais. The **Musée Cognacq-Jay** (8 rue Elzévir) bears witness to the passion shared by Ernest Cognacq, the founder of La Samaritaine department stores, and his wife, Louise Jay, for eighteenth-century art and furniture. Along with paintings and sculptures by famous artists, including Jean-Honoré Fragonard (see p. 200), there are entire rooms reconstructed in the eighteenth-century style, one with an extravagantly embroidered bedcover and bronze candelabra fashioned in the shape of a nymph. More evocations of Paris past lie inside the **Musée Carnavalet-Histoire de Paris** (23 rue de Sévigné), the city's history museum. This building is so vast that it houses an Art Deco jewelry boutique designed in 1901 for jeweler Georges Fouquet by Czech artist Alphonse Mucha, and dismantled and reconstructed within the museum in 1920. The glittering 1920s ballroom of the Hôtel de Wendel was also moved here and rebuilt piece by piece.

WHITE NIGHTS

While some Parisian museums have late hours on a weekly basis, an even more anticipated date among culture-loving night owls is the **Nuit des Musées** (www.nuitdesmusees.culture.fr), which occurs in mid-May. At this annual event, many of the city's (and the country's) museums remain open until 1 a.m. and offer free admission. Special exhibitions, talks, and workshops are also scheduled by many of the participating venues.

A bit more unbridled and chaotic, but perhaps even more fun, the **Nuit Blanche** (www.paris.fr) in October gives occasion for museums, as well as many of the city's monuments and historic buildings, movie theaters, parks, and even swimming pools, to remain open until 7 a.m. Venues change year to year, with art installations popping up in train stations, churches, and other unconventional spaces. Night transport is stepped up for the evening, restaurants offer special menus, and there's free breakfast offered to those who make it through the night.

One of the world's most passionate and libidinous artists was Pablo Picasso, many of whose works you can see at the **Musée National Picasso** (5 rue de Thorigny). The artist never actually lived in this building, the Hôtel Salé (Salt Mansion), the name of which is derived from the trade of its first owner who was a salt-tax collector. But Picasso was a French resident for four decades, and at the time he died, he was married to a French woman, Jacqueline Roque, the muse of his old age. Among the several thousand works exhibited here, which span Picasso's long career, are several portraits of the artist's many loves, including Jacqueline Roque (see p. 204), Marie-Thérèse Walter (see p. 182), Dora Maar, and Françoise Gilot (see p. 205). He also painted other women from his artistic milieu—seek out the portraits of Nusch Éluard, second wife of the Surrealist poet Paul Éluard, and American photographer Lee Miller (see p. 117).

Jacqueline, who was twenty-seven when she met the seventy-year-old Picasso, was the only woman the artist painted for the last seventeen years of his life. She must have kept the spark alive, for even into the late 1960s and early 1970s—not long before he died, in 1973, at the age of ninety-one—he seems to have been particularly preoccupied with love and sex: *Le baiser* (*The Kiss*) and *L'etreinte* (*The Embrace*), both of which are on display in the museum, date from that time.

Picasso also features prominently a few blocks away, on the western fringes of the Marais, at the **Centre Pompidou** (Place Georges Pompidou). One of Paris's most oft-visited buildings, as much for its notorious inside-out modern architecture as for its collections, the Centre is a paean to the passion of the former president of France Georges Pompidou and his wife, Claude, for collecting, celebrating, and promoting modern and contemporary art, which they believed would help society to develop and modernize. The fourth floor has an entire room dedicated to the favorite works of Madame Pompidou, who outlived her husband by more than three decades and continued to support the arts after his death.

The crowds and the scale of the building make the Centre Pompidou far from an intimate retreat, but a visit should be on the agenda of every art-lover. Themes that recur within its galleries are the alliances and fertile collaborations between artists, including Picasso and Georges Braque, Picasso and Julio González, Alexander Calder and Joan Miró, and Robert and Sonia Delaunay (see pp. 36–37). And there are plenty of explicitly erotic goings-on, too. For instance, room 13 of the upper floor, entitled Terre Erotique (Erotic Land), is focused on the prevalence of animal instincts in human beings, as revealed by Sigmund Freud's theory of the unconscious and by war. Brassaï, who is best known as a photographer (see pp. 106–107), is the artist most amply represented in this room, with several paintings and sculptures, including a siren and two Venuses, as well as a sculpture of the head of his friend Picasso.

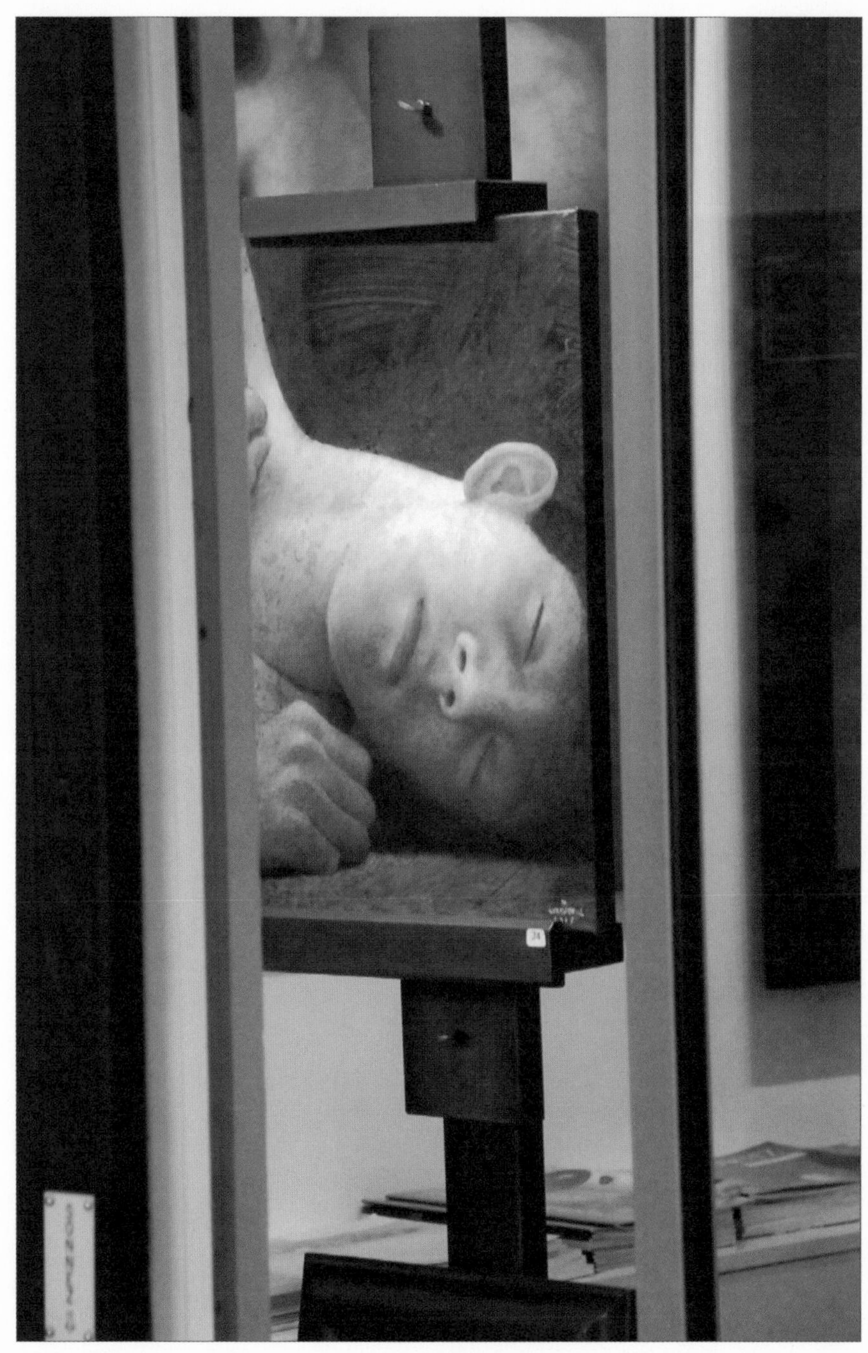

THE COLOR OF LOVE

One of the most fertile and harmonious of all artistic collaborations was the one between husband and wife Robert and Sonia Delaunay, to whom an entire room is devoted at the Centre Pompidou (see p. 34). The couple cofounded Orphism, an art movement characterized by the use of strong colors and abstract geometric shapes.

Born in the Ukraine, Sonia Terk came to Paris in 1905 to study at the Académie de la Palette in Montparnasse, where she lodged on the rue Campagne-Première, which was popular with many artists of the time. A marriage of mutual convenience with homosexual gallery owner Wilhelm Uhde provided her entry into the Paris art world but was quickly dissolved when Sonia met the young painter Robert Delaunay. In fact, Uhde assisted Sonia in divorce proceedings by fabricating adulterous letters to and from an invented mistress, privately commenting: "A friend of mine assumed he would be more skilled than I at making my wife happy, and it didn't occur to me to be an obstacle to their splendid future."

Sonia and Robert were drawn together by similar family histories but most of all by a shared love of modern art, and particularly of Expressionism and Fauvism. Sonia fell for Robert: "Immediately! He was so alive. He was searching. And he was full of new ideas."

Orphism's genesis was strange but fitting given Sonia's later success in the world of fashion and textile design. Concerning a fabric and fur quilt that she made for their son's crib, she explained: "About 1911 I had the idea of making for my son, who had just been born, a blanket composed of bits of fabric like those I had seen in the houses of Russian peasants. When it was finished, the arrangement of the pieces of material seemed to me to evoke Cubist conceptions and we then tried to apply the same process to other objects and paintings."

Inspired by this creation to move away from perspective and naturalism toward abstraction in her art, Sonia found herself in sync with her husband, who had also taken an interest in Cubism and in Michel-Eugène Chevreul's color theories. There wasn't a shred of rivalry to it at all: the couple exchanged ideas, worked side by side, and gave each other inspiration and constructive criticism, "breathing painting," Sonia said, "like others lived in alcohol or crime." Each night they would stroll together along the boulevard St-Michel in the 5th arrondissement, returning home to capture impressions of color that had struck them along the way. Sometimes they walked to the Eiffel Tower (see pp. 64–65), which became the subject of many of Robert's most famous works. The landmark tower, which to him was the ultimate symbol of modernity, became progressively fragmented and abstract in his paintings over time.

The pair's own term for their experiments with color and abstraction was *simultanéisme* (simultaneous design), which means that each of the elements in a work affects the elements beside it. This phenomenon is perhaps most clear in Sonia's large-scale *Bal Bullier* from 1912–13, which depicts dancers within the famous eponymous dance hall in the 5th, where the couple often met up with friends. Sonia was particularly inspired by the swirling movements of the fox-trot and tango, modern dance forms that lent themselves to her almost abstract sensibility.

Indeed, what she saw at the Bal Bullier inspired her throughout her career, and its influence can be seen in her applied arts—in her textile designs, stage sets, and fashion designs, for which she was an international success. At the time, Hollywood actresses couldn't get enough of her dresses. Sonia took up these commercial activities out of financial necessity, although she had always loved creating beautiful furniture, textiles, and other domestic objects for the family apartments on the rue des Grands Augustins (in the 6th) and the boulevard Malesherbes (in the 8th).

After Robert died in 1941, Sonia found herself incorporating black tones into her work, and she claimed to have found as many shades and textures of black as there are colors. Though she spent many years preserving her husband's memory, including making a sizeable donation of works to the Centre Pompidou, she continued to paint until she was ninety, living in an apartment filled with paintings by her husband. If you have the chance to visit the Centre Pompidou, you will be able to see their pieces side by side, leaving no doubt as to the richness of their collaboration.

In room 16 it's Man Ray's turn (see pp. 116–117), with a number of his "erotic experiments," including some distinctly S and M–themed photographs. Elsewhere, André Breton and his one-time wife Jacqueline Lamba (see p. 78) supply their individual versions of the *cadavre exquis* (exquisite corpse)—collagelike creations of figures from disparate body parts, a beloved Surrealist game elevated to an art form.

If all the art has worked up a hunger in you, you're not far from one of the best markets in all of Paris, not to mention the oldest and most romantic—which is really saying something. The **Marché des Enfants Rouges** is located in a pretty, covered hall hidden away behind an iron gate on the rue de Bretagne in the northern Marais. Sit shoulder to shoulder with Parisians at communal tables on the street to sample food from various stalls ranging from Japanese noodles to Moroccan dishes baked in tagines. Or, instead, head for the wonderfully authentic brasserie **L'Estaminet d'Arômes et Cépages** for hearty wedges of hot *boudin* (blood sausage) with apple sauce—a Parisian classic. The market, which was built in 1616 under Louis XIII and named after the children of a nearby orphanage who were dressed in red uniforms, is a fine place to stock up on the ingredients for a special dinner: rare wines, an amazing array of vegetables, fresh pasta, olive oils, seafood, and cheeses, plus the all-important bouquets of flowers.

AFLOAT IN PARIS

You're most likely to approach the Île St-Louis, which lies to the south of the Marais, from Notre-Dame, on the neighboring Ile de la Cité. If you do, you'll likely find the small bridge leading from the larger island populated by a jazz band or a mime giving a free performance, and setting the scene for the Île St-Louis's distinctive charms.

But halt for a moment, and take in this view of **Notre-Dame**, one of the world's most recognized landmarks. Napoléon I and Josephine (see p. 128) were crowned here by Pope Pius VII. It's also where Mary Queen of Scots married François, the dauphin of France, in 1558—an act that made her queen consort of France when he became François II, and where the womanizing Henri de Navarre, who became Henri IV, married Marguerite de Valois in 1572. As was the case then, only the crème de la crème of French society can hope to marry here today. From the vantage point of the back, without the crowds that throng the front,

MAKING LIKE BAUDELAIRE: PARIS'S BEST STROLLS

1ST: The Louvre by night; the Jardin des Tuileries by day; the arcades of the Palais-Royal. See pp. 14–20.
4TH: The Place des Vosges; the Île St-Louis. See pp. 31–43.
5TH: The Jardin des Plantes. See p. 47.
6TH: The Jardin du Luxembourg. See pp. 51–54.
8TH: The Axe Historique from the Arc de Triomphe to the Place de la Concorde (and on to the Louvre). See pp. 66–69.
9TH: Nouvelle Athènes. See pp. 79–80.
10TH: The Canal St-Martin. See pp. 82–83.
12TH: The Promenade Plantée. See p. 84.
15TH: By the Seine in the Parc André Citroën. See p. 121.
16TH: Art Nouveau relics in the 16th. See pp. 124–125.
18TH: The Cimetière de Montmartre. See p. 95.
19TH: The Parc des Buttes-Chaumont. See p. 89.

the cathedral on its island is like a magical ship ready to set sail, its flying buttresses all the more impressive. The gardens behind Notre-Dame are a little-known spot, resplendent with cherry blossoms in springtime and with roses in summer. If you love flowers, make a visit to the flower market at Place Louis-Lépine in the middle of the island.

Many people head to the **Île St-Louis** for the ice cream alone. The stuff confected by Berthillon is the city's favorite. Rue St-Louis en l'Île is home to Berthillon's main store as well as their divine *salon de thé,* which is the best place to sample the ice cream. There are approximately forty rich flavors from which to choose, from whisky-coffee to *marron glacé* (candied chestnut). They also offer late-morning breakfasts for those who have lingered in bed, pâtisseries, hot chocolates, and the like. You can get Berthillon ice cream at any restaurant or café on the island, but for atmosphere, this outpost can't be beat.

Other than sampling the ice cream, there's really very little to do on the Île St-Louis beyond investigating the art galleries and shops, among Paris's best spots for gift, souvenir, or gourmet food shopping. Here you'll find an array of items ranging from handcrafted puppets and up-market toys to posh chocolates and cheese. Although expensive, these souvenirs and treats are the perfect counterpoints to the oft-cloned offerings of the modern high street. Indeed, the island seems to belong to another time, and it's easy to summon up the ghosts of the great figures who once lived here: Voltaire, Honoré Daumier, Camille Claudel (see pp. 61–63), Paul Cézanne, and Charles Baudelaire. It is interesting to note that the latter wrote the poems constituting *Les fleurs du mal* (*The Flowers of Evil*) in his second-floor apartment of the Hôtel Lauzun (17 quai d'Anjou)—not a hotel, in fact, but a private mansion with famous fish-motif drainpipes and sumptuous gilded balconies.

Les fleurs du mal is partially an exploration of romantic and sexual love, with the narrator on a roller-coaster ride of *idéal* (intoxication) and *spleen* (anguish) as he seeks fulfillment through a variety of lovers. One, Jeanne Duval, described as the "mistress of mistresses" in the poem "Le balcon" ("The Balcony"), lived on the island, too, at rue le Regrattier, then known by the very wonderful name of rue de la Femme Sans Tête (Headless Woman Street) because of a broken street sign. Duval was the poet's on-again-off-again love for decades and his central muse. She is also the subject of *La maîtresse de Baudelaire allongée* (*Baudelaire's Mistress, Reclining*), by the painter Édouard Manet, who attended bohemian gatherings on the hotel's ground floor in the Club des Haschischins, where artists and writers partook of hashish in the form of green jelly.

The island, also home to duelists, runaways, and criminals—and once a swamp where cattle grazed—has long been a lovers' haunt. If you can't find the seclusion you seek here (which you certainly won't on any weekend), walk away from the main drag of cafés and shops in the direction of the southern quays.

EATING

Café Hugo
22 place des Vosges
+33 (0)1 42 72 64 04

The very best café within the charming café-laden arcades of the Marais's Place des Vosges, Café Hugo is open all day, making it great for breakfast, brunch, and afternoon tea, as well as for lunch and dinner, at good prices given the location and quality. You can order everything from a club sandwich to lamb chops with gratin potatoes—or perhaps just a Grand Marnier–flambéed crêpe and a glass of champagne. Despite the large terrace, which is heated in winter, there's a cozy, convivial feel to it all, with its charmingly crowded tables. The tuxedoed waiters lend a smart, romantic touch, as do the live jazz on Thursday evenings and the view over the endlessly awe-inspiring square.

Chez Julien
1 rue Pont-Louis-Philippe
+33 (0)1 42 78 31 64

The delicious decor is what brings folk to this wildly romantic Seine-side bistro on the edge of the Marais, with views over the Île St-Louis and Notre-Dame. Dating from 1780, the building is now a charming mishmash of styles, with a glass ceiling painted with chubby cherubs dating from 1900, trompe l'oeil murals, and a window through which you can play peekaboo between the dining room and bar area. Above one of the doors outside sit two brass pigeons dating from 1820, when the place was a hotel called Au Pigeon Blanc. Inside it's all tall mirrors and comfy velvet banquettes—the perfect place for a tryst over French classics, such as asparagus, foie gras, snail profiteroles, veal with mushrooms, crème brûlée, and cheese platters. The quality of the food can vary, but you won't go wrong with the Châteaubriand steak and fries washed down with a glass of a good red wine.

La Chaumière en l'Île
4 rue Jean Du Bellay
+33 (0)1 43 54 27 34

Utterly lacking in pretensions, the friendly "Island Cottage" at the end of the Île, with views over Notre-Dame that some of its rivals would kill for, has a terrace where you can kick back and watch the changing light of the Seine as the sun sets. It's an oasis of Paris as it must have been in days gone by, with closely ranged tables and a menu of rustic staples—hearty homemade cassoulet, onion soup, *croques* and crepes, main-course salads, snails, frogs' legs, steaks, and daily specials chalked on the blackboards. Prices are very fair given the location.

STAYING

Hôtel du Petit Moulin
29–31 rue du Poitou
+33 (0)1 42 74 10 10
www.paris-hotel-petitmoulin.com

The "Little Windmill" is the brainchild of fashion designer Christian Lacroix, who decorated the rooms with his trademark exuberance and wit and created a hotel that feels as if it could exist only in Paris. The effect is highlighted by the charm of the building itself, a registered historic monument that began as a bakery and retains its quaint original facade and *boulangerie* store sign. The seventeen rooms have been individually conceived with an eye to the different facets of the rich history of the surrounding area, and provide "seventeen ways to discover the Marais." This means that you will have your choice of rooms ranging in style from rustic (toile de Jouy fabrics) or historic (cornices, moldings, and wild trompe l'oeil frescoes), to Zen,

Scandinavian, or 1960s Pop. Some rooms have large roll-top baths that can easily fit two, and you can order room massages and meals from local restaurants after 8 p.m. This is a prime spot for adventurous couples who like to try unconventional lodgings, and the friendly but discreet staff has been known to slip honeymooners small gifts, such as Christian Lacroix key fobs.

Hôtel Caron de Beaumarchais
12 rue Vieille du Temple
+33 (0)1 42 72 34 12
www.carondebeaumarchais.com

This intimate nineteen-room hotel in the heart of the Marais is named for the eighteenth-century playwright who lived nearby, who uttered the immortal line: "Drinking when we are not thirsty and making love all year round, madam; that is all there is to distinguish us from other animals." Pierre-Augustin Caron de Beaumarchais's *Le mariage de Figaro* was adapted for the opera by Mozart, and the framed pages you see on the hotel's walls are from the work's first edition. Newlyweds celebrating their own marriage could do much worse than staying at this townhouse lit by candles and chandeliers, and, in winter, by the light of a flickering hearth. The antique decor, including a rare eighteenth-century pianoforte and a card table, creates a theatrical mood that is enhanced by the guestrooms with their sumptuous fabrics. An indulgent touch: breakfast can be brought up to your room until noon.

Murano Urban Resort
13 boulevard du Temple
+33 (0)1 42 71 20 00
www.muranoresort.com

Far from classic Paris, this fifty-two-room hotel—named after the Murano glass that sparkles in every corner by way of chandeliers, mirrors, and sculptures—is located on the fringes of the Marais and is resolutely twenty-first century in inspiration. If you're into mood lighting, vast beds, 1970s-style shag-pile carpets, and floor-to-ceiling mirrors, then the Murano is your place. The honeymoon suite with its gauzy drapery boasts a circular tub *and* a circular bed, while two other suites offer private swimming pools (otherwise, there's a pool and a hammam in the Anne Sémonin spa). The restaurant is unabashedly erotic, with its hot-pink chairs and banquettes, outsize white-leather sofa, and sensual Mediterranean food.

Hôtel du Jeu de Paume
54 rue St-Louis en l'Île
+33 (0)1 43 26 14 18
www.jeudepaumehotel.com

This four-star hotel is the most luxurious and warmly welcoming option on the Île St-Louis. A tranquil patio garden tempts you to linger over a drink amid palm trees, and there's also an internal courtyard from which a glass elevator runs up and down the seventeenth-century building. Originally an indoor venue for the French royal game of *jeu de paume*, a precursor of tennis, the hotel has been sympathetically restored to retain its old stone walls, vaulted ceilings, and wooden beams. Guest rooms—spacious for this cramped city—are less finished than the common areas but generally offer exposed beams too: for maximum romantic appeal, try to reserve a room in the attic or perhaps overlooking the inner garden.

5TH AND 6TH:

The Latin Quarter and St-Germain-des-Prés

Il n'y a plus d'après
A Saint-Germain-des-Prés
Plus d'après-demain
Plus d'après-midi
Il n'y a qu'aujourd'hui ...

There are no coming days
In Saint-Germain-des-Prés
No next week
No next day
There is only today ...

—From "Il n'y a plus d'après," by GUY BÉART

Paris's Left Bank is more synonymous with the life of the mind than that of the body—at least in the Latin Quarter, a part of both the 5th and 6th arrondissements, and so named because Latin was the language of learning in the Middle Ages both at the Sorbonne, which still dominates this section of Paris, and beyond.

Also in the 6th, St-Germain-des-Prés is similarly associated with the intellectual scene, particularly because of the hot duo of the Existentialist movement, Jean-Paul Sartre and Simone de Beauvoir (see p. 53), around whom its thrumming café society revolved. But the 6th arrondissement is also sodden with jazz, that sexiest of musical forms, which has

always had a stronghold here, thanks to the hip-cat writers and philosophers who made the area their stomping ground. Jazz was, in fact, the musical soundtrack to Existentialism. The best place to catch some of its wartime and postwar exuberance is the **Caveau de la Huchette** (5 rue de la Huchette), a stone-walled cellar famous for jazz shows that has been featured in several films: *Les tricheurs (The Cheaters)* by Marcel Carné, *La première fois (The First Time)* by Claude Berri, and *Rouge baiser (Red Kiss)* by Véra Belmont.

The Left Bank, like the adjoining Marais and Îles (see pp. 28–43), is a great area for strolling or—without any major sights to distract you—for idling away a few hours people-watching from the terrace of one of its world-renowned cafés, the most famous being Les Deux Magots and the Café de Flore. There are also some magnificent parks and obscure gardens in which to lose yourselves. That said, you might find yourself seduced by the shopping. Whether you appreciate an idiosyncratic boutique or a chic department store, within just a few blocks in St-Germain-des-Prés are some of the world's greatest retail outlets.

A GARDEN OF EARTHLY DELIGHTS

Begin well off the beaten track in the far eastern corner of the 5th arrondissement with one of Paris's most intriguing gardens, the **Jardin des Plantes**, and its strange mixture of attractions. On Sundays, it is a favorite spot among generations of Parisians for walking off lunch. It is well known for the botanical garden for which it is named, but it is also home to four galleries of the Muséum National d'Histoire Naturelle, a small zoo that once housed the royal menagerie, and a yew hedge maze, as well as one of the most delightfully quirky sights in all of Paris: a *manège* (merry-go-round) that features extinct species, such as the dodo, in lieu of the more commonplace horses.

Originally called the Jardin du Roi, the Jardin des Plantes began as a medicinal herb garden planted in the seventeenth century for Louis XIII by his physician. Now you can easily spend a morning just ambling, discovering its secret corners, its lovely statuary, and its decorative plants—don't miss the alpine garden, the beautiful Art Deco–style winter garden, the steamy Mexican hothouse, and the fragrant rose garden. You can also visit the botanical school on the premises. The museums are well worth a look, too. In particular, check out the Gallery of Mineralogy and Geology, where you'll be dazzled by some of the world's oldest and most precious minerals, crystals, and gemstones. Featuring extraordinary giant crystals from the mountains of Brazil, the collection ravishes the eyes.

If you're not inspired to head for the nearest jeweler to buy a glittering rock of your own, head to the **Grand Mosquée de Paris**, which is right by the Jardin des Plantes. Its complex includes a tea-room and restaurant where you can indulge in mint tea, tagines, and sticky North African pastries (see p. 58) and a 1920s hammam in which you can treat yourself to a sybaritic steam, *gommage* (scrub-down), and oily massage. You can also pick

DREAM SCREENS

There are few better ways to spend a rainy afternoon in Paris than by taking refuge in one of its movie theaters. A cinephile's heaven, this city has more art-house cinemas than any other, and it's claimed that there are more films being shown at any given moment in Paris than anywhere else in the world. Some venues are incredibly intimate, with auditoriums seating only thirty people, and many include a cozy bar to which you can retreat for a tête-à-tête after the showing.

A hotbed of intellectual activity, the Left Bank is a great place to catch a film classic in a romantic indie cinema—try the Action Christine (4 rue Christine) or Action Écoles (23 rue des Écoles) in the 5th, where you may see anything from Jean Cocteau's *Orphée* to Alfred Hitchcock's *Rebecca* or *Once Upon a Honeymoon*. Nearby is Le Champo (51 rue des Écoles), where you may catch classics by Marcel Carné set in Paris, such as *Les enfants du paradis* (see p. 56) or *Les portes de la nuit*, or current offerings from the likes of the Coen brothers. Night owls should look out for midnight screenings comprised of three movies followed by breakfast. Next to Le Champo is another beloved art house, Le Reflet Médicis (3 rue Champollion), which offers a wide range of films, from Jean Renoir to David Lynch, but is particularly known for film noir.

Or if you happen to be in the city in August, cool off from the heat of the day with a free open-air evening showing of a movie set in Paris, projected onto walls or temporary screens in various squares and parks around the city (see www.clairdelune.forumdes-images.net for details). Also in August, Parisians celebrate their return to the city from the summer holidays with the Trois Jours Trois Euros (Three Days Three Euros) event, during which you can see recent films for just three euros per ticket.

For movie schedules, buy a copy of *Figaroscope* at any newsstand. Note that *en VO*, or *version originale*, means a film is shown in its original language with French subtitles, as opposed to dubbed. Many movie theaters offer discounted showings before noon, as well as on Mondays and/or Wednesdays.

For my guide to the best films set in Paris, see pp. 56–57.

up Moroccan treats, such as copper cookware and striking fabrics, in the complex's souk, or join a guided tour of the handsome mosque itself.

If you're walking back toward St-Germain, a pleasant route is along the Seine, first via the open-air sculpture park of the Jardin Tino Rossi, then along the quai de Tournelles, where you'll find the first of the Left Bank's iconic *bouquinistes* (second-hand booksellers), who line the quays here, as well as those on the Îles and the Right Bank. Selling all manner of works, from scuffed paperbacks to hefty art tomes, bona fide antique books and engravings, and vintage posters (plus, in some cases, postcards and souvenirs), they have their origins in the sixteenth century, when some of the city's bridges had shops and stalls along their lengths. The booksellers were itinerant to begin with and operated from wheelbarrows until someone had the notion of using leather straps to attach trays to the bridge parapets. This practice continued until the late nineteenth century, when sellers were first allowed to fasten their boxes to the quaysides on a permanent basis. There's currently an eight-year wait to become a *bouquiniste* in Paris—no doubt because the rent is minimal.

As an alternative to walking along the river, leap aboard a **Batobus**, one of a fleet of glass-roofed riverboats that ply the Seine. There are stops at the Jardin des Plantes and St-Germain-des-Prés, as well as six other spots along the river, so you may hop on and off at whim.

MEDIEVAL DESIRES AND CRIMES OF PASSION

On your way to the Jardin du Luxembourg with its many alfresco pleasures (see below), allow yourselves to be pleasantly detained by the **Musée National du Moyen Âge** (formerly the Musée de Cluny), which is housed in a former abbots' mansion on Place Paul Painlevé that was built, in part, on the remains of Gallo-Roman baths. Historically, this building was used by François I to confine Mary Tudor, the widow of his predecessor Louis XII, in order to discover if she was pregnant. The remains of the thermal baths can still be seen in the *frigidarium* (cooling room), and there's a very fine display of medieval and Renaissance art and artifacts, including gold and ivory pieces, illuminated manuscripts, and sculptures.

The highlight, though, are the tapestries, most notably the wool and silk series entitled *La dame à la licorne (The Lady and the Unicorn)*, woven in Flanders in the late fifteenth century. Five of the cycle, which depicts a noble lady with a unicorn and a lion, are believed to represent the five senses; the sixth is harder to decipher, although its inscription, *À mon seul désir* ("To my only desire"), is thought to refer to love or understanding. The most remarkable thing about this museum is the way its collections have been used as inspiration for the succession of gardens surrounding it, which were created in 2000. They include the Forêt de la licorne (Unicorn Forest), complete with animal prints in the flagstones; a *ménagier* (kitchen garden) in which cabbages, onions, chives, and other vegetables are grown; a *jardin des simples médecines* (herbal medicine garden); a pathway bordered by wallflowers, valerian, and Christmas roses suggestive of ancient religious trails; and a courtyard with fragrant plants, such as honeysuckle and jasmine. To further tie in with the collection of the museum, there's a *tapis mille fleurs*, or "carpet" composed of a thousand flowers, referencing the backgrounds of the tapestries in the museum, which are in the *millefeuille* style—that is, made up of thousands of small flowers and plants.

If you're still in a historical frame of mind, right nearby is the **Panthéon**, where many of the great figures from French history—or at least parts of them—are laid to rest, if not in tombs proper then in urns bearing their ashes or their hearts. Some of the remains of the people interred have been removed for one reason or another, or, more disturbingly, are listed as having disappeared. However, it's worth a visit to the atmospheric crypt to pay your respects to the likes of Voltaire, Victor Hugo, Émile Zola, and Louis Braille. In 1995 physicist and chemist Marie Curie became the first woman to be accorded a place in the Panthéon, when her remains and those of her husband Pierre were transferred here. The only other remains of a female present are those of Sophie Berthelot, who was buried here with her husband, the chemist and politician Pierre-Eugène-Marcellin Berthelot. The pair

met when she was quite literally blown into his arms by a powerful gust of wind on the Pont Neuf. After a contented marriage lasting four decades, they died in 1907, within one hour of each other, and received the honor of a double state burial.

A few minutes' walk away, the **Jardin du Luxembourg** surrounds the Luxembourg Palace. Home to the serious-minded French Senate, this largest of Parisian parks, with its pond for miniature yachts, puppet theater and carousel, pony rides, chess tables, *pétanque* areas, and gazebo (where free musical performances are held—and best appreciated over wine on the terrace of the nearby café) is nevertheless a preserve for children and the young at heart. Although it is yet another place to wander in as aimless a fashion as possible, the "Luco," as locals have nicknamed it, does have some treasures worth seeking out, including Jules Dalou's *Monument to Delacroix*, the painter described by Charles Baudelaire as "passionately in love with passion, but coldly determined to express passion as clearly as possible." Other curiosities include the first, small-scale model of the Statue of Liberty (the final version was a gift from France to the United States), and the statues of French queens and other significant women around the pond, including Paris's patron saint, Geneviève, and Clotilde, wife of Clovis I, the king of the Franks. Don't miss the apple and pear orchard, or the beehives, both of which are lovingly tended by the Carthusian order (who offer beekeeping courses here). Another delightful spot is the Orangerie, an exhibition space in summer and home to the garden's orange trees, palm and pomegranate trees, rose laurels, and oleanders in the cooler months.

The early Romantic poet Gérard de Nerval, infamous for walking his pet lobster on a pale blue ribbon through the gardens, wrote about a would-be romantic encounter here in his poem "Un allée du Luxembourg" ("An Alley in the Luxembourg Gardens"):

She passed, the girl
Swift and lively as a bird:
In her hand a shining flower,
In her mouth a new refrain.

Perhaps she's the only one in the world,
Whose heart would respond to mine,
Who, entering my deep night,
Would illuminate it with a single glance.

But no—my youth is finished ...
Farewell, soft beam that enlightened me,
Perfume, girl, harmony ...
Happiness passed—it has fled.

A big draw of the gardens for lovers, and a notorious spot for romantic assignations, is the Fontaine de Médicis, created for Marie de Médicis, queen consort and widow of Henri IV, but now home to a grotto of goldfish. It was for Marie, lonely after Henri's assassination, that the entire park and palace were constructed. While living in the Louvre, she had asked that her childhood home, Florence's Palazzo Pitti, be re-created here. The fountain's centerpiece, which was added in the nineteenth century, is *Polyphème surprend Acis et Galatée (Polyphemus Surprising Acis and Galatea)*, the best-known work of the sculptor Auguste Ottin. Polyphemus, the mythological Cyclops, jealous because the Sicilian Nereid Galatea returns the shepherd Acis's love instead of his, is shown crouching over his rival, whom he's about to kill with a boulder. According to Ovid's *Metamorphoses*, the grief-stricken Galatea turns her lover's blood into Sicily's Acis River.

There were, no doubt, other tempestuous scenes on rue de Tournon, the street that takes you back toward the boulevard St-Germain: a plaque at number 12 commemorates its role as the one-time residence of the Venetian arch seducer Giovanni Giacomo Casanova, who came to Paris after fleeing jail in Italy, where he had been convicted of interest in magic and witchcraft. He became very rich by becoming one of the trustees of the first state

THE PHILOSOPHY OF LOVE

The renaming, in 2000, of the area in front of the Église St-Germain-des-Prés (Paris's oldest church) Place Jean-Paul Sartre et Simone de Beauvoir is but the latest chapter in a love affair and meeting of minds that lasted for more than half a century and that had a profound impact on the history of Western thought.

"What we have," Sartre is reported to have said to his fellow philosopher and writer De Beauvoir in the early days of their relationship, "is an essential love. But it is a good idea for us also to experience contingent love affairs."

To his surprise, De Beauvoir agreed to an open relationship, and the pair remained together for the rest of their lives, both as a couple and as collaborators. Their emphasis on freedom within their relationship was entirely in keeping with their creed of Existentialism and its insistence on the absence of a priori values and absolutes. In fact, as well as never marrying, the pair never set up a home together. Sartre lived on the rue Bonaparte (which runs up from the boulevard St-Germain to the Jardin du Luxembourg) and then later in Montparnasse, near De Beauvoir and Montparnasse cemetery, where the couple is united by a shared gravestone (see pp. 112–113).

But their "arrangement" may not have been as harmonious as it appeared to be: Sartre engaged in more affairs than De Beauvoir, invoking her wrath, while De Beauvoir had several longer-lasting relationships with both women and men, including filmmaker Claude Lanzmann (see p. 112) and the American novelist Nelson Algren (see p. 120), the latter provoking a serious crisis in her life.

Whatever the emotional costs of their respective affairs, De Beauvoir, who was championed as the mother of the women's movement because of her groundbreaking work *The Second Sex*, claimed that her relationship with Sartre was her "greatest achievement." Her last work, *Adieux: A Farewell to Sartre*, is a multilayered memoir of the last ten years of Sartre's life (including, painfully, his final moments) and features transcriptions of her interviews with him. Perhaps most revealing of all about the truth of their relationship, however, is De Beauvoir's posthumously published *Letters to Sartre*.

lottery and founding a silk workshop. He also served as a spy for Louis XV. But he squandered much of his wealth on his many lovers, which according to his autobiography, *History of My Life*, numbered one hundred and twenty-two. Casanova defined "real love" as "... the love that sometimes arises after sensual pleasure: if it does, it is immortal; the other kind inevitably goes stale, for it lies in mere fantasy." However, he also characterized love as an "incurable illness and a divine monster" after his paramour Henriette abandoned him.

You'll need to walk back around the Jardin du Luxembourg to see the collection of work and home/studio of sculptor Ossip Zadkine that was bequeathed to the state in 1982 by his wife, the painter Valentine Prax. The **Musée Zadkine** (100 bis rue d'Assas) is another intimate, seldom-visited spot, with a highly poetic garden full of sculptures. Sometimes it provides the setting for artistic workshops. Given Zadkine's preoccupation with trees, and, in the latter part of his career, with the possibility of a fusion between the human and vegetable worlds, it's fitting that plants and artwork have been offered a space in which to coexist.

FROM CAFÉ SOCIETY TO RETAIL HEAVEN

Café de Flore, Les Deux Magots, and Brasserie Lipp—the triumvirate of world-famous cafés on the boulevard St-Germain (where it meets the rue de Rennes)—define St-Germain-des-Prés. Even if they're inundated with tourists these days, they still speak potently of a time when artists and writers, including Picasso (see p. 34), Sartre (see p. 53), and Albert Camus, gathered here to talk and listen to music, following in the footsteps of the poets Paul Verlaine, Arthur Rimbaud, and Stéphane Mallarmé, and of the Surrealist André Breton (see p. 78).

But perhaps even more representative of the area than these artists and writers—indeed, she was described as "*la muse de* St-Germain-des-Prés" and the "Left Bank diva"—was the singer Juliette Gréco, with her kohl-rimmed eyes and trademark black turtleneck and slacks. To Sartre she was the girl with "millions of poems in her throat," including the songs "Parlez-moi d'amour" ("Talk to Me of Love"), "Déshabillez-moi" ("Undress Me"), and "Il n'y a plus d'après" ("Only Today"), written by Guy Béart, while to jazz legend Miles Davis she was "my first love." Gréco, who was trained in voice at the Paris Opéra and imprisoned during the war because her mother worked for the Resistance, met Davis when he came to Paris at age twenty-two, to play in the city's international jazz festival. Despite the language barrier, they had a passionate relationship, though Davis refused to marry her, saying that he would only make her unhappy. Gréco later recalled that theirs "was a great love affair, the kind you'd want everybody to experience. Throughout our lives, we were never lost to each other. Whenever he could, he would leave messages for me in the places I traveled in Europe: 'I was here, you weren't.'"

It's possible to escape the café crowds in this busy quartier of bistros, coffeehouses, jazz clubs, art galleries, bookstores, and publishing houses. The **Musée National Eugène Delacroix** (6 rue de Furstenberg) is a quiet spot where many of Delacroix's works are showcased in the context of his former apartment and garden studio. The Romantic painter lived here from 1857 to 1863, partly to be in the vicinity of the baroque **Église St-Sulpice**, where he was working on frescoes that are still visible in its Chapelle des Anges. The church, dubbed "the cathedral of the Left Bank," was where writer Victor Hugo wed his childhood friend Adèle Foucher, a union that resulted in the institutionalization of his brother Eugène, who was also in love with Foucher. St-Sulpice was the setting for the christenings of libertine novelist the Marquis de Sade and poet-*flâneur* Baudelaire (see p. 28).

When you've overdosed on culture, you're close to the rue de Sèvres, home of **Le Bon Marché**, designed by none other than Gustav Eiffel in 1852. As well as being the city's oldest department store, it is also one of its chicest and most expensive and truly Parisian. On the same street is its superb food hall, La Grande Épicerie de Paris—simply *the* place to stock up if you're heading for a lovers' picnic in the Jardin du Luxembourg (don't leave without buying a few slices of the luscious Spanish ham). For bread to die for, hop over to rue du Cherche-Midi, where **Poilâne** sells an incredible fifteen thousand loaves of its famous chewy sourdough bread every day.

Or, if your minds are on something other than food, hurry along to the softly lit basement of **Sonia Rykiel** (175 boulevard St-Germain). Here you'll find a range of ultra-chic and very expensive *objets érotiques*, including luxury sex toys and risqué, tongue-in-cheek lingerie, all displayed beautifully in black and pink satin, rhinestone-studded

evening bags. Alternatively, make a pilgrimage to **Sabbia Rosa** (73 rue des Sts-Pères), purveyor of high-class undies to screen-goddess Catherine Deneuve. Still run by the little old lady who opened the shop, it's all soft lighting, shimmering silks, and slinky satins—and everything is exclusive.

PICTURE-PERFECT PARIS

Many people fall for Paris long before arriving here, smitten by the images of its streets and landmarks appearing in the countless films celebrating the city. Here are some of my favorites, from grand classics to lesser-known gems. Watch them before you arrive to whet your appetite, or seek them out at Paris's atmospheric art-house cinemas, many of which are clustered on the Left Bank.

- L'Atalante (1934). Life on a barge for newlyweds Jean and Juliette, who are headed to Paris. Once there, Juliette is seduced by the city and runs away, setting the scene for an erotic montage of the pair's respective nocturnal longings. Director Jean Vigo died at age twenty-nine, just after the movie's first (unsuccessful) Paris run.
- Hôtel du Nord (1938). One of Marcel Carné's self-described "fatalistic romantic melodramas," a haunting, beautifully shot tale of lovers Renée and Pierre, who come to the eponymous canal-side hotel (now a restaurant; see p. 98) to complete a suicide pact.
- Les enfants du paradis (*Children of Paradise*; 1945). Shot during the Nazi Occupation, Carné's masterpiece about Garance, a beautiful courtesan in the Parisian theater milieu, and the four men who love her in different ways but never on her own terms.
- An American in Paris (1951). Vincente Minnelli's musical (with songs by George Gershwin) about an aspiring American painter in Paris (Gene Kelly), the heiress who discovers and thinks she owns him, and the girl he falls for (Leslie Caron), who is herself already engaged.
- The Last Time I Saw Paris (1954). Richard Brooks's soap opera–like but enjoyable tale of an American expatriate couple unraveling in Paris post-Liberation, based on a short story by F. Scott Fitzgerald and starring a radiant Elizabeth Taylor.
- Funny Face (1957). Stanley Donen's lighthearted musical romp in which a model (Audrey Hepburn) falls for a photographer (Fred Astaire) during photo shoots set against the city's most famous landmarks. Together, they dance their way through couture workshops and beatnik cafés, to a Gershwin soundtrack.

- Love in the Afternoon (1957). Gamine Audrey Hepburn again, this time in Billy Wilder's bittersweet romantic comedy about a detective's daughter trying to entrap a middle-aged playboy (Gary Cooper) but instead falling for him. Much of the action takes place at the Hôtel Ritz.
- Gigi (1958). Belle-époque shenanigans based on a novel by Colette (see p. 21), with Leslie Caron once more under the helm of Vincente Minnelli, this time singing and dancing her way through the Cinderella story of an emerging courtesan and her relationship with a wealthy playboy.
- À bout de souffle (*Breathless*; 1960). A classic by New Wave–master Jean-Luc Godard about the ill-fated love affair between a French small-time crook (Jean-Paul Belmondo) and a young American student (Jean Seberg).
- Paris la belle (*Beautiful Paris*; 1960). Director Pierre Prévert's documentary based on black-and-white shots of Paris filmed in 1928, followed by their 1959 color counterparts, with a dreamy narration and song lyrics by his brother, poet Jacques Prévert.
- Le dernier métro (*The Last Metro*; 1980). The great François Truffaut's story of life under Nazi occupation, with a Jewish director hiding out in the basement of his theater as his wife (Catherine Deneuve) falls for her leading man (Gérard Depardieu) upstairs.
- Henry & June (1990). The story of Anaïs Nin's messy relationship with Henry Miller (see pp. 108–109) and his wife June (Uma Thurman), set against a backdrop of 1930s bohemian Paris. Directed by Philip Kaufman, the film is based loosely on Nin's book of the same name.
- Les amants du Pont-Neuf (*The Lovers on the Bridge*; 1991). Leos Carax's skewed, often painful story of love between young vagrants—Alex, a circus performer, and Michele (Juliette Binoche), a painter slowly going blind—is set against Paris's oldest bridge. It's visually sumptuous in spite of the sometimes grim subject matter.
- Le fabuleux destin d'Amélie Poulain (*The Fabulous Destiny of Amelie Poulain*, or *Amelie*; 2001). An eccentric romantic comedy by *Delicatessen* director Jean-Pierre Jeunet about a shy waitress (Audrey Tautou) in a Montmartre café. Prone to flights of fancy, she sets out to make those around her happy and to find her own true love.
- Before Sunset (2004). A French environmentalist (Julie Delpy) and an American writer (Ethan Hawke) walk the streets of Paris nine years after their fleeting encounter in Vienna (*Before Sunrise*, also directed by Richard Linklater). Older, wiser, and—in his case—married, will they fall in love all over again?
- 2 Days in Paris (2007). Julie Delpy again, this time in the self-directed tale of a French girl bringing her American boyfriend to her home city to rekindle their romance.

Coups de Coeur

EATING

Restaurant de la Grand Mosquée de Paris
39 rue Geoffroy-St-Hilaire
+33 (0)1 43 31 38 20

Paris's largest mosque is a delightful spot, and not only because of its twentieth-century Hispano-Moorish architecture and sultry hamman (see p. 48). The mosque complex is also home to an atmospheric North African restaurant where you can sit on large cushions around tables created from large copper trays, and to an enchanting courtyard tearoom replete with fig trees and mosaics. The former is the place for couscous, tagines, and the like; the latter for a snack of Maghreb pastries oozing with honey and studded with pistachios, or infused with orange-blossom water (make sure to try the "gazelle's horns"—a sweet pastry horn filled with honey and nuts). Accompany them with a reviving, fresh mint tea served in a glass, a heart-racingly strong Turkish coffee, or for the full-blown experience, a *shisha*, or water pipe.

Le Procope
13 rue de l'Ancienne Comédie
+33 (0)1 40 46 79 00

Paris's first coffeehouse dates back to 1686 and is now a listed monument as well as a refined restaurant, rife with atmosphere and with the ghosts of those who have frequented it through the centuries: Voltaire (who, it's claimed, consumed forty cups of its coffee mixed with chocolate every day), the young Napoléon I, the revolutionaries Georges-Jacques Danton, Maximilien Robespierre, and Jean-Paul Marat, Oscar Wilde, George Sand (see p. 79) ... the list goes on. In keeping with this rich history, the decor is solidly historical without any cheesiness—substantial old paintings, marble busts, and eighteenth-century furniture are set against ocher-red walls. The food is solidly bourgeois, too: "drunken" coq au vin, roast veal with sage, and, as a stunning dessert, bourbon vanilla *millefeuille*. The perfect spot for a special date, Le Procope is guaranteed to impress.

Aux Charpentiers
10 rue Mabillon
+33 (0)1 43 26 30 05

The Carpenters, named after the nearby master carpenters' guild, is a relaxed old-school bistro dating from the turn of the twentieth century. Wholly lacking in pretensions, it is the ideal locale for a low-key (and good-value) date. Amid original woodwork that reinforces the carpentry theme, and in the company of local students, journalists, and editors, you can feast on such hearty specialties as calf's head and pigs' trotters. If that is too much, then the Scottish smoked salmon marinated in wildflower honey and dill is a light and winning starter, and the *plats du jour*, starring the likes of pork with lentils, duck with olives, rabbit, or shoulder of lamb, always satisfy. The staff is discreet courtesy personified, a factor that must have counted in former French president Jacques Chirac's decision to celebrate his sixtieth birthday here.

Restaurant Lapérouse
51 quai des Grands Augustins
+33 (0)1 56 79 24 31

Another restaurant popular with the political elite, who in days gone by often brought their mistresses here (to the upstairs *salons privées*, which used to lock from the inside), is the artfully decadent riverside Lapérouse. From the faded murals to the deep purple and red sofas of its bar, Le Velours (The Velvet), everything here conspires to evoke abandonment to the senses. Traditional bistro staples are enlivened by refreshing modern touches—foie gras is accompanied by apple chutney with ginger and green peppercorns, as well as the more usual dessert wine, while fresh truffles are shaved in front of your eyes onto a bed of mâche and Parmesan, and the saddle of rabbit is permeated with the heady flavors of lavender and rosemary. Lapérouse is an inspired choice for Valentine's Day, when the special menu includes champagne, cocktails, and a dessert to share.

La Maison de Thé & Le Shanghai Café
76 rue Bonaparte
+33 (0)1 40 51 95 17

The House of Tea, located across the square from St-Sulpice (see p. 55), whisks you to Asia with its selection of green, blue, red, black, and white Chinese teas, and with its clocks telling you the time in Hong Kong, Peking, Hanoi, and Rangoon. The teas are personally selected by the owner on her regular trips to plantations in the Far East. It's all very Zen, with great attention paid to preparing and serving your chosen blend in a teapot lovingly handcrafted into a shape that enhances the tea's flavor. Leisurely minded lovers might choose to go a step further in the indulgence stakes by asking for the full-scale traditional tea ceremony, which melds intoxicating fragrances in a beguiling, time-slowing ritual. The food here ranges from full lunch dishes, such as prawns in coconut milk and fruit salad infused with Guihua Wulong tea, to afternoon teas featuring exquisite platters of Asian pastries chosen for their yin or yang properties, such as the macarons of various hues.

STAYING

L'Hôtel
13 rue des Beaux-Arts
+33 (0)1 44 41 99 00
www.l-hotel.com

Bathed in accolades both for its accommodation and its restaurant (Michelin-starred since 2008), "The Hotel" is one for lovers of exuberance and opulence—as befits an establishment in which the writer Oscar Wilde died (in 1900, when it was a simpler pension), and which, in the past, attracted the likes of Richard Burton and Elizabeth Taylor, and Frank Sinatra and Ava Gardner. It's highly intimate, with just twenty rooms, all singular in style, size, and view and characterized by rich colors and fabrics. They are accessible via a dramatic central stairwell spiraling upward through this building that began life as the palace of Marguerite de Valois (later queen to Henri IV's king; see p. 144) and was then made into a *pavilion d'amour* (love pavilion). The penthouse suite has a private balcony, where you can breakfast *à deux* with views over the ancient church of St-Germain. From the hip, low-lit bar perfect for illicit encounters over cocktails, such as Le Velvet (vodka with red fruits and lemon), to the restaurant serving such aphrodisiac delights as a marinated carpaccio of scallop with Baerri Impérila caviar accompanied by clear lemongrass soup, to the private hammam and plunge pool in the stone-walled cellars, you'll be tempted never to leave the premises.

Hôtel Lutetia
45 boulevard Raspail
+33 (0)1 49 54 46 46
www.lutetia-paris.com
See pp. 130-131.

Hôtel St-Jacques
35 rue des Écoles
+33 (0)1 44 07 45 45
www.paris-hotel-stjacques.com

If the facade of this modest two-star hotel looks familiar, it's because you're thinking of the Audrey Hepburn and Cary Grant movie *Charade*, part of which was filmed here in 1963. Though it may not be the most luxurious option in town, it offers several surprises—not the least of which is the whimsical murals of old Parisian scenes, including those in the Toulouse-Lautrec salon, where you are welcome to relax over a glass (or what the heck, a bottle) of vintage champagne or an absinthe while leafing through one of the beautiful eighteenth- and nineteenth-century books from the owners' collection. The breakfast room, with its antique gramophone and cabaret mural, houses a piano that guests may play. The thirty-eight guestrooms are cozy, with the same slightly crazy charm as the rest of the hotel. For more space, plus a tub, ask for room 26, a deluxe-double corner room.

7TH AND 8TH:

The Eiffel Tower and the Champs-Élysées

Divinité malfaisante,
et pourtant je t'aime avec fureur.

Malevolent goddess,
and yet I love you furiously.

—AUGUSTE RODIN,
from a letter to Camille Claudel

The 7th arrondissement, home to Paris's iconic Eiffel Tower, and the 8th, to the Champs-Élysées, its most famous avenue, may not seem of immediate appeal to lovers in search of privacy and secretive locations. But as with all tourist favorites, these are neighborhoods that are not to be missed by those who want to get under the skin of Paris.

Spanning the river, the two are quite different in flavor. The 7th may be thronged with visitors eager to climb the Eiffel Tower to savor its heart-stopping views of the city, but it also has plenty of museums (some world famous but others only really visited by those in the know) and other tourist draws, such as the Hôtel des Invalides, which is the final resting place of Napoléon I and a good many other military heroes.

Aside from the tourist-swamped shopping, eating, and entertainment haven of the Champs-Élysées, the 8th is now largely a business district, as well as home to the president (his official residence is at the Élysée Palace). However, it's also the setting for some of Paris's dreamiest hotels, where serious romance can be had for serious money.

THE LOVE OF ART, THE ART OF LOVE

The 7th arrondissement flows seamlessly westward from St-Germain (see pp. 54–56), and though the chic shops gradually peter out in favor of residential streets, the sense of wealth and privilege increases—a fact due, in part, to the presence of various national institutions and government ministries, including the National Assembly and the Hôtel Matignon, which serves as the official home to the Prime Minister of France. The first museum you'll encounter is the **Musée Maillol** (61 rue de Grenelle). One of Paris's most obscure, it is dedicated to the sculptor Aristide Maillol, many of whose works grace the Jardin du Carrousel in front of the Louvre (see p. 16). Maillol used the female body, most notably the figure of his lifelong muse Dina Vierny, as a means of exploring the themes of youth, fertility, and death. Works such as *La méditerranée (The Mediterranean)* are so simple and pared down that Maillol is now viewed as having played a role in the development of abstract art, which is ironic given his classical roots. As if to confirm this, a number of abstract sculptures by Emile Gilioli can also be seen at the museum, as well as abstract paintings by Wassily Kandinsky, Ivan Pouni, and Serge Poliakoff. Dina Vierny, who set up the museum in Maillol's memory, was an avid collector of twentieth-century art.

Maillol's classically inspired work has often been contrasted with the sculptures of Auguste Rodin, whose more rugged, willful figures take on dramatic, often ecstatic poses. You can compare them yourself by walking a few streets west to the **Musée Rodin** (9 rue de Varenne), an alluring but often overrun museum best visited on a weekday out of season, when you can wander its lovely sculpture-filled gardens and rooms in tranquility. It's here in Rodin's mansion that you'll find his two most famous works: *Le penseur (The Thinker)* and *Le baiser (The Kiss)*. The latter, believed to be one of the most widely recognized sculptures in the world, was first called *Francesca da Rimini*, as it depicts the eponymous thirteenth-century Italian noblewoman who, as recounted in Dante's *Inferno*, falls in love with Paolo Malatesta, the younger brother of her husband Giovanni, while reading the story of Lancelot and Guinevere with him. Those with eagle eyes will notice that the couple's lips are not touching in the sculpture, which suggests that they were interrupted and murdered by Giovanni before they actually consummated their love with a kiss.

But there's so much more to see here than *Le baiser*, including a number of works by Camille Claudel, Rodin's lover and an accomplished sculptor in her own right. Claudel became a pupil of Rodin in 1883, but her work began to influence his, even as she learned from him. This state of affairs would have been ideal but for the fact that Rodin was already spoken for. By the 1890s, when Claudel was at the height of her artistic powers,

their relationship was foundering, which resulted in some satirical drawings of Rodin by Claudel. *Système cellulaire (The Cellular System)*, for instance, shows Rodin in chains, and being watched hawkishly by his long-term partner (and eventual wife) Rose Beuret, who is depicted as wielding a broom.

Rodin and Claudel's relationship finally ruptured for good in 1892. Although Claudel, having largely broken free of Rodin's influence, continued to produce great and original artwork, she never recovered psychologically. She descended, gradually, into madness, destroyed many of her works, and spent her last thirty years in an asylum. Perhaps it was guilt that led Rodin to suggest—or at least to assent to—the inclusion of many works by Claudel in the museum devoted to *his* work.

Stroll to the nearby **Musée d'Orsay** (1 rue de la Légion d'honneur) to see Claudel's *L'âge mûr (The Age of Maturity)*, which was created in stages in 1895, 1898, and 1907. This piece depicts her lover leaving to return to his wife (but also simultaneously being pulled, ineluctably, toward old age), as she, on her knees, begs him to stay. The artist's brother, writer Paul Claudel, wrote movingly of the work: "My sister Camille, imploring, humiliated, on her knees, that superb, proud creature, and what is being wrenched from her, right there before your very eyes, is her soul." If you want to learn more about this fascinating yet doomed relationship, watch the Oscar-nominated film *Camille Claudel*, starring Isabelle Adjani and Gérard Depardieu.

Rising majestically from the Seine's Left bank, the Musée d'Orsay is housed within the magnificent building that was formerly the Orsay railway station. Now featuring mainly French art from the mid-nineteenth century on, the Orsay is best known for its wonderful Impressionist collection. It's impossible to list all the major works on display here, but lovers won't want to miss the erotic masterpieces, many of them controversial in their time, including Gustave Courbet's graphic *L'origine du monde (The Origin of the World)*; Alexandre Cabanel's *Naissance de Vénus (The Birth of Venus)* and, echoing Rodin's *Le baiser*, his *Mort de Francesca da Rimini et de Paolo Malatesta (The Death of Francesca da Rimini and Paolo Malatesta)*, and Édouard Manet's *Olympia* and *Le déjeuner sur l'herbe (Luncheon on the Grass)*. There's another piece entitled the *Birth of Venus* within the museum's collection, this one by William-Adolphe Bouguereau. Both pieces depict the Greek myth of Venus's birth from the waves of the sea, following the castration of Uranus by his son, and the fertilization of the water by his severed genitalia. Note that the museum is open until nearly 10 p.m. on Thursdays, if you would prefer to visit the collection at a quieter time, or after dinner.

You might head on to the arrondissement's third museum, the **Musée du Quai Branly** (37 quai Branly), also known as the "MQB," which is devoted to the indigenous art, cultures, and civilizations of Africa, Asia, Oceania, and the Americas. Opened in 2006, the

ASIAN DELIGHT

One of the world's most unusual and surely most extravagant wedding presents resulted in one of Paris's most offbeat and romantic nooks: La Pagode (57 bis, rue de Babylone) in the 7th. A gift from Aristide Boucicaut, founder of the Bon Marché department store (see p. 55) in neighboring St-Germain-des-Prés, the pagoda was created in 1895 within a tiny but ornate Japanese-style garden. To this day it retains its wonderful tiled and carved-wood facade, which has elevated its status to that of historic monument.

First used for parties and balls, the pagoda was turned into a movie theater in 1931 and that is what it remains today, retaining at least some of its original decor. Its most notable feature is perhaps the Salle Japonaise, which is a superb place for a movie date, especially if your tastes in film tend toward art house rather than Hollywood blockbuster. There's also a leafy terrace outside the pagoda, where you can enjoy tea amid the bamboos and stone lions, in the company of the cinema housecat, Licorice.

As for the bride, Madame Boucicaut, there's a statue of her in the Place Boucicaut off rue de Babylone, back in the 6th.

museum boasts a striking "living wall," a vertical garden with grass and plants growing on part of the facade. There's also a more traditional garden on-site, complete with hidden pathways and small pools by which to dream of the exotic climes inspired by the museum's collections. The garden offers a shady café, or there's also a glass-roofed restaurant, Les Ombres, on the top floor with to-die-for views of the nearby Eiffel Tower and the river.

PARIS'S PHALLUS

A trip to the Eiffel Tower is inevitable; it's a tourist trap for certain, but one that must be included on any itinerary. Now that it has become the icon of Paris, it's difficult to imagine that it was first conceived of as a temporary structure—the entrance arch for the Exposition Universelle de Paris of 1889—and moreover, that it had been designed for the previous Exposition, held in Barcelona, and rejected as too strange. This view was also echoed by many Parisians when the tower was finally completed in their city.

This being Paris, where aesthetics are everything, the tower is painted three different shades. It's darker at the base and slightly lighter toward the top, so that when one looks up from the ground, the structure appears uniformly colored. These days, one gets the sense that Parisians couldn't be more proud of their symbol. In fact, the tower becomes even more of a focal point for the city on special occasions: There are fireworks displays on Bastille Day and New Year's Eve, and an ice rink is installed on the first platform during the winter. French electro-acoustic music pioneer Jean-Michel Jarre has played twice on the structure, the city's millennium celebrations were hosted here, and in 2008 it was bathed in blue light and decorated with twelve golden stars to mark France's presidency of the European Union. But any night of the week, and any week of the year, Parisians and visitors are treated to a free light show, a permanent installation since 2000.

The lines are always lengthy but especially terrifying on weekends in the summer months. For preferential treatment, book a table at Le Jules Verne (see p. 71), the tower's own restaurant, which has a private lift. Its dining room on the second tier offers some of the most romantic views of the city. The tower also has one of the capital's most stunningly sited wedding reception venues (see p. 223).

In our post-Freudian world, it's of course impossible to escape references to the Eiffel Tower as resembling the male member. Even Dan Brown in *The Da Vinci Code* describes it as a "thousand-foot phallus," while in 2008 an American woman with an objects fetish actually married the structure in an intimate ceremony. So don't be surprised if you come away from the tower with other things on your mind ...

INTO THE 8TH: LUXE AND LIBERTINAGE

The Pont de l'Alma takes you over the Seine to the 8th arrondissement. The first thing you'll see on the other side of the river is the Flame of Liberty, a full-size replica of the flame held by New York's Statue of Liberty and now an unofficial shrine to Diana, princess of Wales, who died after a car crash in the bridge's tunnel with her lover Dodi Al Fayed in 1997.

Walking up the prestigious avenue George V will give you the immediate flavor of the neighborhood: Here are the showrooms for haute-couture giants Yves Saint Laurent and Givenchy, and some of Paris's swankiest hotels, including the Hôtel Fouquet's Barrière (see p. 73) and the Four Seasons Hôtel George V, which is a prime venue for wedding receptions (see box) and home to one of the city's most sybaritic spas (see box). Meanwhile, the world-renowned and much-imitated **Le Crazy Horse de Paris** (12 avenue George V) has been hosting erotic cabarets, complete with displays of magic, mime, and juggling, for more than half a century. These days, shows at the famous cabaret feature celebrities such as Pamela Anderson, Dita Von Teese, and Arielle Dombasle, wife of the eminent French philosopher Bernard-Henri Lévy.

And so on to the sound and fury that is the **Champs-Élysées**, one of the most famous streets in the world and Europe's most expensive section of real estate. The Champs-Élysées is named after the Elysian Fields of Greek mythology, the part of the underworld where the souls of the heroic and virtuous find their final resting places. The Parisian Champs-Élysées, in fact, was comprised of fields and market gardens until Marie de Médicis, wife of Henri IV, had the notion of extending the pathway through the gardens of her Tuileries Palace

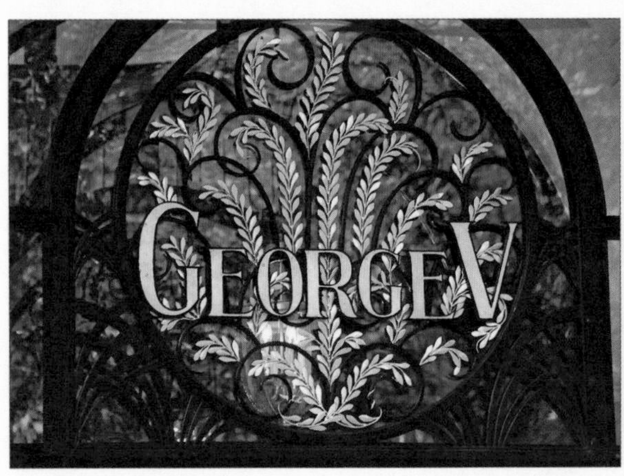

SPA-ING PARTNERS

If your wallet cannot take the strain of spending the night at a hotel in one of Paris's most chic and expensive neighborhoods, then you're free to book a treatment at one of their world-class spas. Some of these spas will even let you indulge *à deux*. The spa at the famous **Four Seasons Hôtel George V** (31 avenue George V), for instance, invites you to have a full-body Swedish massage with your partner in a private room staffed with two therapists. For women, they also offer the tempting "A stroll to Versailles" package. Inspired by Marie Antoinette's beauty secrets, it is comprised of a steamed orange-blossom body scrub, a massage with warm shea butter, and a milky facial.

Or head to the **Hôtel Plaza Athénée Paris** (25 avenue Montaigne) to stage your own reenactment of the final episode of *Sex and the City*, when Carrie finally gets her man. The Athenée's new Dior Institut spa also offers a double VIP *cabine* for couples' massages, with special offers available on treatments as part of the hotel's Valentine's Day package.

(now long gone) westward by creating an avenue of trees. Thus began the Axe Historique—a straight line of sight linking the Louvre (see pp. 14–20), the Place de la Concorde at the bottom of the Champs-Élysées, and the Arc de Triomphe at the top of it, and latterly the modern cube of the Grande Arche de la Défense in the business district in western Paris.

These days the Champs-Élysées is an odd one-and-a-quarter-mile strip of luxury shops, chain stores, touristy restaurants, burger joints, car showrooms, and movie theaters that is perpetually thronged with people strolling and chatting in that languorous Parisian way. It's certainly not, as the French have described it, *la plus belle avenue du monde* (the world's most beautiful avenue), although it does have an undeniable majesty that transcends its commercial nature. The best time for a stroll here is during the evening, as the light is dying over Paris and the trees and buildings of the avenue are illuminated. Get into the mood over a cocktail at **French Love** (37 bis, rue de Ponthieu), a glamorous but discreet bar off the Champs, with glass boudoir lamps and a *fumoir* (smoking booth) within an old red phone booth from London—you need to ring the doorbell to gain access.

Begin at the Arc de Triomphe and descend slowly, past the shops and cinemas, toward the awesome sight of the Louvre's Pyramide (see p. 14). After the traffic circle, the avenue is bordered by the Jardins des Champs-Élysées, embellished with fountains and punctuated by a few sights, including the Grand Palais, an exhibition hall that Chanel often uses for its fashion shows and that also houses a science museum, the Palais de la Découverte. The neighboring **Musée du Petit Palais** (avenue Winston-Churchill), the municipal fine arts museum, is not the most exciting gallery in Paris, but you might like to pay a visit to Pierre Bonnard's *Nu dans le bain* (*Nude in the Bath*). The model for this painting—as was almost always the case with Bonnard—was his wife Marthe. Bonnard often painted Marthe having a soak—she spent a lot of time in the bathroom, perhaps because she suffered from a skin condition, tuberculosis, or OCD. The artist rarely painted his wife's face in detail; indeed, he's so notorious for depicting her as young and blooming, even when she was in her fifties, that American writer Raymond Carver wrote a poem about the couple, entitled "Bonnard's Nudes":

His wife. Forty years he painted her.
Again and again. The nude in the last painting
the same young nude as the first. His wife.

As he remembered her young. As she was young.
His wife in her bath. At her dressing table
in front of the mirror. Undressed.

His wife with her hands under her breasts
looking out on the garden.
The sun bestowing warmth and color.

Every living thing in bloom there.
She young and tremulous and most desirable.
When she died, he painted a while longer.

A few landscapes. Then died.
And was put down next to her.
His young wife.

Also within the Jardins des Champs-Élysées is the historic **Théâtre Marigny**, where stars such as Roman Polanski, Jean-Paul Belmondo, Alain Delon, John Malkovich, and Anouk Aimée (in *Love Letters*) have directed or played. The theater offers backstage tours to give visitors a deeper insight into this fascinating venue.

Past the Élysée Palace, official home to the president, you come to the vast and thrillingly chaotic **Place de la Concorde**. The square's seventy-five-foot-tall Luxor Obelisk, which once stood at the entrance to the temple of Luxor, was given to the French by the viceroy of Egypt in the nineteenth century. Briefly covered by a giant pink condom during a commando-style operation by Act Up, a group aiming to politicize the AIDS debate, in 1992, the Obelisk marks the spot where a guillotine stood during the French Revolution. It's here that Louis XVI and Marie-Antoinette (see p. 126), Georges-Jacques Danton, Maximilien Robespierre, and Charlotte Corday, among others, met their grisly ends in front of cheering crowds.

As she stepped up to the guillotine, condemned for treason, Marie-Antoinette perhaps let her gaze linger, nostalgically or maybe bitterly, on one of the impressive stone buildings lining the north side of the square, initially built for government offices but soon after turned into the super-luxurious **Hôtel de Crillon** with its Jardin d'Hiver (see p. 72). Here the French queen, renowned for her extravagance, spent many leisurely afternoons taking music lessons or just hanging out with her friends.

Looking up the rue Royale, which runs beside the Crillon away from the Place, you will get a full-on view of **La Madeleine**, the church where most of Paris's society weddings take place. It's worth a peek inside for its lavish gilded decor and famous organ, which has been played over the years by many world-class organists, including Camille Saint-Saëns and Gabriel Fauré. On your way, slip into **Ladurée** (16 rue Royale) for its famous, melt-in-your-mouth mini-macarons. Created in flavors ranging from the classic (vanilla, coffee, and pistachio) to the more experimental (lime and basil), they make great gifts—especially for Valentine's Day, when they're available in a slightly tart blueberry incarnation, presented in a matching box with a "declaration" of your choice. You may also choose to deliver your sweets with a bottle of Ladurée house champagne in a purple box.

Linger for an hour or two in the tearoom of this main branch of Ladurée. Its exuberant frescoes, which depict angelic pastry chefs and voluptuous ladies, were inspired by the ceilings of the Palais Garnier (see p. 76) and the Sistine Chapel. The tearoom offers super-rich dishes, such as foie gras with mango-jasmine macarons, as well as *kugelhopf* (a sweet Bundt cake), and other kinds of fantastical and indulgent macaron-based desserts.

Another institution on the rue Royale is **Maxim's de Paris** (3 rue Royale), which has been featured or mentioned in many works of art, including the operetta and ballet *The Merry Widow*, Jean Renoir's *La Grande Illusion*, and *Gigi*, which stars Maurice Chevalier and tells the story of the training of a belle-époque courtesan (see p. 57). The restaurant, which has retained its striking Art Nouveau decor, is owned by fashion designer Pierre Cardin, and in recent years it has been outfitted with the **Musée Art Nouveau**, just upstairs. The museum's "1900 Collection" showcases Cardin's private collection of Art Nouveau objects and decoration within the somewhat kitschy fictional setting of the twelve-room "love chambers" of a turn-of-the-twentieth-century courtesan.

There are other small, and relatively unknown, museums to detain you in the 8th, mainly near the **Parc Monceau**, toward the northern end of the lengthy boulevard

Malesherbes. The park, informally English in inspiration, is of interest to those who love to wander idly. It boasts several architectural models of curiosities from around the world, including a pyramid, a Dutch windmill, and a Chinese fort, as well as statues of various famous French figures, among them Frédéric Chopin (see p. 212) and Guy de Maupassant. Claude Monet (see pp. 174–175) was known to come here often and painted the park three times; it was also a favorite of the Romantic composer Hector Berlioz.

The first museum in the vicinity and one of Paris's oldest is the **Musée Cernuschi** (7 avenue Vélasquez). Set in the charming mansion of nineteenth-century Italian politician, economist, and collector Henri Cernuschi, it's devoted to Chinese and other Far Eastern art. Courtesans (eternal objects of fascination, it seems) appear in many of the paintings here, and the museum often puts on special events, including concerts of ancient Persian music and demonstrations of ikebana, the Japanese art of flower arranging.

The last museum of interest in this neighborhood is the **Musée Jacquemart-André** (158 boulevard Haussmann) named after another banker, Édouard André, and his wife, society painter Nélie Jacquemart, whose stunning art collection was amassed during their annual perambulations in Italy and elsewhere. The first floor has a good deal of the eighteenth-century French art that was so admired by André, with many voluptuous goddesses floating on clouds within gilt frames. Another highlight is the glass-roofed winter garden, with its marble, lush plants, and formidable double staircase. Jacquemart continued to travel and acquire art after her husband's death, and when she passed away, her will expressed the desire to allow the public to see the place "where a pair of amateur lovers of art lived out a life of enjoyment and luxury." Also on view are the couple's private apartment and their splendid reception rooms, while within the museum's parlor, beneath an opulent ceiling painted by Giovanni Battista Tiepolo, is one of the city's most charming cafés.

Not far from the museum, at 102 boulevard Haussmann, is the building where the novelist Marcel Proust wrote part of his masterpiece *À la recherche du temps perdu* (*Remembrance of Things Past*). Proust had moved here after the apartment was vacated by his great-uncle Louis Weil, who served as the model for Uncle Adolphe, one of Odette de Crécy's lovers in the great novel. Odette in turn was partially based on actress and model Méry Laurent, one of whose patrons was Dr. Thomas Evans, an American dentist living in the same building. Although the furnishings are long gone, having been transferred to the Musée Carnavalet-Histoire de Paris in the Marais (see p. 33), you may still see Proust's old room—just ask at the bank that now occupies the building.

Otherwise, follow the boulevard Haussmann, one of Paris's most famous thoroughfares, into the 9th arrondissement… see pages 75–76.

EATING

Le Jules Verne
Eiffel Tower
+33 (0)1 45 55 61 44

Although this Michelin-starred restaurant is of the highest gastronomic caliber, and, since 2008, is presided over by superstar chef Alain Ducasse, nobody comes to Le Jules Verne for the food alone. Between the ironwork of one of the world's most famous structures, the Eiffel Tower (see pp. 64–65), the panoramic views from this restaurant on the second floor of the tower (more than four hundred feet off the ground) are such that you can dine with the city spread around and beneath you. The long-standing restaurant has been revamped in recent times, but it is really the views that take center stage. Beautiful in the changing light of day but utterly stunning by night, the whole city glitters at your feet like a basket of jewels. You may even end up proposing from the sheer romance of it all. *Prix fixe* menus at lunch and dinner bring this special-occasion venue into the price range of ordinary mortals; dishes are predominantly French with a contemporary slant and may include marinated salmon with lemon, caviar, and vodka with a mimosa garnish, or a bitter chocolate and passion-fruit dome.

Marius et Janette/Bistrot de Marius
4 and 6 avenue George V
+ 33 (0)1 47 23 41 88 and +33 (0)1 40 70 11 76

These sister restaurants famed for their seafood lie between the Eiffel Tower and the Champs-Élysées, a few steps from the right bank of the river. Marius et Janette oozes luxury and glamour, with an interior inspired by yachts and subtle maritime imagery. The menu is heavy on oysters and other shellfish from a variety of French regions, which provides lots of opportunities for lovers to share. Try the Grand Plateau de l'Écailler, a vast seafood platter for two, or splurge on a whole gilthead bream baked in a salt crust. If you're feeling less extravagant, the neighboring Bistrot de Marius is casual and typically Parisian in style, with red banquettes and old cabaret posters. It offers equally fresh fish, from crab gazpacho to roasted monkfish with thyme, at kinder prices. If it's on the menu, share a *gros baba au rhum*—a decadently moist sponge cake drenched in syrup and cream, served with a shot glass of rum to pour over it.

Rollet Pradier
6 rue de Bourgogne
+33 (0)1 45 51 78 36

A few steps from the Musée Rodin (see pp. 61–63), Rollet Pradier offers the best of several worlds. On the first floor you can buy luscious breads, pastries, chocolates, and Ladurée macarons (see p. 69), stock up on foie gras, or grab a hot *croque monsieur* to take to the secretive little garden in front of the very pretty Basilique Sainte-Clotilde, which is just around the corner on rue Las Cases. Meanwhile, on the second floor, a classically French, low-key but elegant restaurant offers good fish (including smoked salmon with warm lentil salad, tuna tournedos with pepper, and skate in black butter), simple steaks, fabulous chocolate desserts, and fine wines. Relatively unknown, Rollet Pradier attracts both locals and workers from the nearby ministries. Closed in the evenings, this is the perfect place for a lunch assignation away from the tourist hordes and close to the museums and Eiffel Tower, or to linger over a lovers' breakfast or afternoon tea.

Le Jardin d'Hiver
Hôtel de Crillon
10 Place de la Concorde
+33 (0)1 44 71 15 00

The Hôtel de Crillon (see p. 69) may not be within most visitors' budgets, but the romantic spot shouldn't be missed altogether. One of its most tempting (and affordable) nooks is its Jardin d'Hiver (Winter Garden), a cozy retreat for coffees and cakes, afternoon teas accompanied by live harp music, light daytime fare, and evening drinks. Install yourselves in a deep sofa or wing chairs amid a sybaritic decor of purples and gold to sample a Baccarat (pink champagne with cranberry juice and lime) and admire the famous Baccarat liquor cellar, its crystal and bronze glowing in the salon's silky-soft light. In the summer months, the Winter Garden unfolds into the hotel's stunning courtyard—a tranquil haven in the heart of the city.

STAYING

Hôtel Lancaster
7 rue de Berri
+33 (0)1 40 76 40 76
www.hotel-lancaster.fr

While many hotels in this area are ostentatious, the Lancaster knows that less is often more, and the luxury it offers is of a restrained, rather old-fashioned nature. This is the kind of place

where you might bump into a doddering old French aristocrat carrying a glass of champagne up to his room (although, naturally, room service is available). Despite being a part of a Spanish hotel chain, you would never guess as it is utterly Parisian in feel, crammed with seventeenth-century antiques and ornaments. The Lancaster's trump cards include its intimacy (it has fifty-seven rooms or suites within a nineteenth-century mansion) and its little oasis of a garden filled with sculptures, pools, fountains, and plants. Romance junkies should snag the Marlene Dietrich suite, where the actress lived for more than three years, or the Suite Rouge, with red-silk covered walls, a mansard ceiling, and two balconies with views of the Eiffel Tower and the Basilique du Sacré-Coeur (see p. 93) respectively. The restaurant is a fine place for a Valentine's Day feast, with its "His" and "Hers" menus featuring the likes of foie gras with blackcurrant and truffles, duckling with artichoke hearts, a dessert of chocolate and roasted mango, plus a surprise gift. Look for Valentine's Day packages, which are often comprised of a room upgrade, a bottle of pink Champagne, and pâtisseries, as well as thefeast to be shared.

Hôtel Fouquet's Barrière Paris
46 avenue George V
+33 (0)1 40 69 60 00,
www.fouquets-barriere.com

The city's first five-star hotel built since 1928 and relatively new to the Parisian scene, Fouquet's Barrière fits right in with its brave modern take on the grand classical decor of the palace-hotel. Head into Fouquet's, one of its eateries, and you will find yourself surrounded by history, as for more than a century this restaurant has been a focal point of French cultural life that has attracted such names as Charlie Chaplin, Marlene Dietrich, Theodore Roosevelt, and Jacqueline Kennedy Onassis. Located on the corner of the avenue George V and the Champs-Élysées, the restaurant is one of Paris's prime people-watching spots. Within the hotel's guest rooms, decadence and luxury meet high tech, with sumptuous fabrics, personal butlers, and wall mirrors that transform into TVs. Book

the Duplex Eiffel for access to a large terrace and views of the iconic tower as well as the suite's sumptuous gold decor. Make sure to ask about the occasional "Just Married!" honeymoon offers. The hotel also has a gorgeous spa.

Hôtel de la Trémoille
14 rue de la Trémoille
+33 (0)1 56 52 14 00
www.hotel-tremoille.com

Located in the heart of the ultra-chic Golden Triangle (formed by the Champs-Élysées, avenue George V, and avenue Montaigne), La Trémoille is second to none in the unique privacy it offers its guests—room service is provided through a system of hatches linking each room to the corridor, which allows your midnight snack to be delivered without anyone's needing to enter your room. The rooms are outfitted in silks, mohair, and synthetic furs—and if you're in a suite, boast classic Paris rooftop views. If you do venture outside your cocoon, the in-house Louis^2 restaurant, bar, and lounge may lure you with the promise of such rich delights as lobster brandade, Jerusalem artichoke salad scented with truffle, or roasted scallops. For the ultimate indulgence, book the Zen couple weekend package, which includes massages and treatments in the well-being center, complete with a sizzling sauna.

9TH–12TH, 17TH–20TH:

Northern and Eastern Paris

"Dans notre vie, il y a une seule couleur,
comme sur une palette d'artiste,
qui donne le sens de la vie et de l'art.
C'est la couleur de l'amour."

In our life there is a single color,
as on an artist's palette,
which provides the meaning of life and art.
It is the color of love.

—MARC CHAGALL

North and east of the central arrondissements, Paris is more culturally and ethnically diverse—and, in many ways, even more compelling than the most frequented and better-known parts of the city. The 9th arrondissement sets the scene. This schizophrenic neighborhood veers wildly from operatic elegance to edgy romance, as it is home to both the opulent Palais Garnier opera house and the former red-light district of Pigalle. Pigalle still retains many of its famous sex clubs and peep shows but is also gentrifying, in parts at least.

The 10th arrondissement can be sleazy too, as areas surrounding train stations tend to be, but the Gare du Nord and Gare de l'Est are—like almost all Parisian train stations—imbued with a sense of romanticism. The former welcomes visitors aboard Eurostar from across the English Channel or from Belgium, while the latter may tempt you to leap aboard an overnight train bound for Vienna or even Budapest. These sorts of unplanned escapes would have been even more romantic in the glory days of train travel, when the waiting train might have been the Orient Express. But resist the urge. Just beyond the stations is one of Paris's little-known gems, the Canal St-Martin, with its somnolent fishermen, uncrowded bars, and opportunities to take a subterranean boat ride through a Revolutionary crypt. And then there's also the vibrant 11th arrondissement, one of Paris's best bets for hip nightlife.

The 12th arrondissement is largely a residential neighborhood, bordered on the east side by the vast park of the Bois de Vincennes, which can be reached via the Promenade Plantée, an old railway line that has become a charming hidden walking route. While you're in the 12th, make sure to admire the Gare de Lyon, perhaps Paris's most romantic train station by virtue of its classic architecture and magnificent Art Deco restaurant and bar, Le Train Bleu (see p. 99), a place so alluring it might very well cause you to miss your train.

The 12th arrondissement segues, to the north, into the 20th arrondissement, a traditionally working-class but increasingly fashionable neighborhood. Tourists sometimes find themselves in this area of Paris, but usually, they stick around only to pay an obligatory visit to Jim Morrison in the Cimetière du Père-Lachaise, where the front man for the Doors lies in rest (one hopes) among some of the greatest names from France and farther afield. The 19th arrondissement, still north of the 20th, is favored by Parisians in the know for its somewhat wild Parc des Buttes-Chaumont.

And so into the 18th arrondissement, one of Paris's most touristy neighborhoods, which despite its popularity is one of its prettiest. Montmartre is chock-full of art history, and were it not for the crowds, the rip-off cafés, the beret-wearing self-proclaimed artists selling gaudy canvases, and the clichéd accordion music, this area would be an incredibly romantic place. But as in all of Paris, secrets reside in this well-trodden neighborhood, just waiting to be uncovered by resourceful lovers.

Mainly residential in nature, the 17th arrondissement offers a peaceful respite after you've braved the hordes in Montmartre. Place de Clichy, where the 17th meets Montmartre and two other arrondissements, is famously associated with the ribald. The sexually voracious American novelist Henry Miller is known to have walked through the Place de Clichy daily on his way to the office of the *Chicago Tribune*, and you can still visit some of his favorite haunts on the square today.

THE 9TH: FROM OPERA TO SING-ALONG CAFÉS

The main route from the 8th arrondissement into the 9th is the boulevard Haussmann, which extends more than a mile and a half. Named after Georges-Eugène Haussmann, the self-styled baron to whom Napoléon III dedicated the task of remodeling large parts of the city, this classic Parisian boulevard is wide and tree-lined, and edged with smart apartments and restaurants. For many visitors, it is the quintessential Paris, recognizable from many paintings of the city by the Impressionist Gustave Caillebotte (you can view several of them in the Musée d'Orsay; see p. 63).

Before continuing along the boulevard, take a detour just south of it, to Paris's original opera house, the **Palais Garnier**. With its baroque, chocolate-box facade and restored Rococo interior, complete with a double staircase and grand foyer, the Palais is a much better bet for an evening *à deux*—whether to see an opera, a concert, or a ballet—than the newer, brasher, and better-known Opéra Bastille. Reserve a box for maximum romantic impact (this is a vast auditorium with 2,200 seats), and don't forget to look up at the gorgeous (if controversial and perhaps incongruous) 1960s ceiling by Marc Chagall, featuring flying lovers, floating angels, and other scenes from famous operas and ballets.

The Palais Garnier was the building that inspired Gaston Leroux's skewed Gothic romance, *Phantom of the Opera*, partly because it's located above a subterranean lake, which in the novel leads the Opéra employees to believe that the building is haunted. If you can't make a performance, wander around the public areas, which include the library-museum, or join one of the guided tours. Don't miss a peek at Jean-Baptiste Carpeaux's *La Danse*, the wanton-looking sculpture on the facade (or rather a copy of it—the original was whisked off to the Musée d'Orsay). Commissioned in the 1860s, Carpeaux's depiction of Bacchanalian revelry was decried in its day as an offense to common decency.

Emerging from the theater, you'll find two of Paris's greatest *grands magasins* (department stores): **Galeries Lafayette** (40 boulevard Haussmann) and **Au Printemps** (64 boulevard Haussmann). The Galeries, which offer ten stories of luxury boutiques and jewelers, are worth visiting for their famous early-twentieth-century glass-and-steel dome and Art Deco staircases alone. They have something to suit all tastes, whether you are searching for killer Gucci heels, top-name lingerie, or a pair of gemstone-studded wrist manacles. There's also a dedicated bridal department and gift registry on the premises.

Au Printemps is a designated historic monument, with its own Art Nouveau cupola that rivals the architecture of the Galeries' dome. Beneath the cupola, you can dine at the **Brasserie Printemps** on traditional cuisine inflected with modern touches. There's also **Déli-Cieux,** a rooftop buffet restaurant with panoramic views, and an utterly romantic **Ladurée** tea-and-macaron salon (for the main branch, see p. 69). But Au Printemps' main draw is the shopping, which is phenomenal. Shoe addicts may choose from a staggering collection of ninety thousand pairs, while fashion mavens will find the finest labels from

MAD LOVE

Gustave Moreau was viewed by the Surrealist movement as one of their major influences, and the Musée Gustave-Moreau (see p. 80) was a favorite haunt of the spokesman for the group, André Breton. The 9th district was important to novelist and poet Breton in other ways, too: it was here, at the junction of rue Lafayette and rue du Faubourg Poissonière, that he first arranged to meet the elusive, nonconformist, and eventually mad heroine of his equally elusive 1928 romance *Nadja*, in which he explores the natures of identity, memory, time, space, and ultimately reality itself.

Over the course of this autobiographical novel, Breton and Nadja wander around Paris, experiencing all kinds of strange coincidences, odd events, and epiphanies, For a while, at least, Nadja is the recipient of the "mad love" (*l'amour fou*) in which the Surrealists, and particularly Breton, placed their faith. This love was characterized by an obsession that destabilizes and even deranges. In his strange, fragmented novel-meets-autobiography-meets-manifesto *L'amour fou*, Breton describes love as both a mystery and a revelation. In spite of the fact that much of the book deals with Breton's recently collapsed marriage to painter Jacqueline Lamba, the work challenges "the widespread opinion that love wears out, like the diamond, in its own dust." He concludes the book with the hope that their daughter, Aube, will herself be "madly loved."

Coincidentally, when Breton met Jacqueline in 1934, she was working as an aquatic dancer in the Coliseum, a cabaret on the rue de Rochechouart, just a few streets away from the street on which he had had his rendezvous with Nadja. Breton and Jacqueline married only two months after meeting; after the ceremony the wedding party headed off for a picnic, during which the bride posed nude for the photographer Man Ray (see pp. 116–117) in a reenactment of Manet's *Le déjeuner sur l'herbe (Luncheon on the Grass)*.

the Place Vendôme, avenue Montaigne, and Faubourg St-Honoré assembled under one roof. If you're into naughty underpinnings, there's an outpost of the British cult lingerie label Agent Provocateur. Au Printemps is also a fine place to set up your wedding registry and to choose rings, outfits, and even your honeymoon. The Web site (www.printemps.com) contains valuable advice on everything from invitations to creating your own wedding blog, should you feel the need to tell the whole world.

Due north is an obscure little neighborhood known as **La Nouvelle Athènes** (New Athens), after the neoclassical follies that were constructed by its population of wealthy artists, writers, composers, and actors. Later, prominent women, among them actresses from the Comédie-Française, painters' wives, and the novelist George Sand, built elegant houses here, some of them with curved facades.

Today, La Nouvelle Athènes is a quiet, little-visited spot in which to wander. Start at the **rue Fontaine**, where, at numbers 19, 19 bis, and 21, the Post-Impressionist painter Henri de Toulouse-Lautrec, best known for his paintings of the Montmartre demimonde (see pp. 91–93), first resided after arriving in Paris from the Pyrénées. At number 19, the famously diminutive artist is said to have fallen into a ménage à trois with his landlord and landlady, Albert and Lily Grenier, which he subsequently documented in a series of erotic drawings.

La Nouvelle Athènes is also home to some suitably romantic museums. The first is the charming **Musée de la Vie Romantique** (16 rue Chaptal). Contrary to what its name might suggest, this is not a museum of romantic life, yet, located in a nineteenth-century hotel accessed via a quaint cobblestoned and tree-lined drive, it is a good place to bring a lover. Come to wander through its pretty courtyard rose garden, to share a cake or tart in its conservatory tearoom, or to simply enjoy a concert or public reading in fair weather. Incongruously, for Pigalle, this is a tasteful shrine to the Romantic movement, which celebrated intense emotion and wild nature. Dutch painter Ary Scheffer and his nephew, the poet Ernest Renan, both part of the Romantic movement, lived in this very building. What may be of the most interest is the museum's exhibit on George Sand, the woman of letters infamous for dressing like a man, for smoking cigars (see p. 24), and for her high-profile affairs with the poet Alfred de Musset and the composer Frédéric Chopin, among others. Sand's jewelry, furniture, watercolors, and personal effects, including her cigarette box, occupy the first floor. Don't miss the mold of Chopin's hand, which was probably made shortly before his breakup with Sand.

La Nouvelle Athènes was also once famous for its *lorettes* (elegant courtesans), among them La Paiva, a celebrated courtesan from the time of Napoléon III, who gained a reputation for bleeding wealthy young men dry in order to fund her lavish lifestyle. She must have had something incandescent about her—even after her death, it's said that her husband of later life, Count Guido Henckel von Donnersmarck, would sob for hours on end beside her body, which he had stored in a large vessel of embalming fluid.

This area, fascinating for its many artistic and literary links, inspired La Nouvelle Athènes, a café on nearby **Place Pigalle**, where artists such as Henri Matisse (see pp. 194–195), Vincent van Gogh (see p. 213), Édouard Manet, and Edgar Degas used to paint. In fact,

Degas's famously maudlin *L'absinthe*, on view in the Musée d'Orsay (see p. 63), was painted inside. Place Pigalle is also where artists from Montmartre would come to find models. Toulouse-Lautrec first spotted the red-headed laundress Carmen Gaudin here.

In the 1940s, however, La Nouvelle Athènes café became Le Sphynx, a striptease club that attracted Nazis and, later, the liberation troops. This transformation would signal the decline of the area, and although the club is no more, the square is still ridden with sex shops. Despite its seedy history, Pigalle has inspired several classic French songs, including "Pigalle de mon coeur" by Bérengère and "Place Pigalle" by classic chansonnier Maurice Chevalier. Edith Piaf's "Elle fréquentait la rue Pigalle" is a depressing number about a prostitute rescued from the mire but then cast back into it by her fickle lover.

Around the corner from the Musée de la Vie Romantique is the **Musée Gustave-Moreau** (14 rue de La Rochefoucauld), the former home and studio of the Symbolist painter Gustave Moreau. Here you can wander at leisure through the artist's beautifully preserved apartment, which includes a boudoir containing the effects and furniture of his longtime muse and possible lover, Alexandrine Dureux, which Moreau had moved from her nearby apartment when she died at age fifty-four in 1890. Moreau painted *Orphée sur la tombe d'Eurydice (Orpheus at the Tomb of Eurydice)* in response to Dureux's death, and he described the work as thus: "The soul is alone. It has lost everything that was to it splendor, strength, and sweetness. It weeps, giving way to inconsolable solitude."

Moreau was probably drawn to the tale of Orpheus because of its theme of the potential for love and art to overcome death. According to the works of Virgil and Ovid, Orpheus followed his dead wife, Eurydice, into the underworld, where he sang so beautifully of the pain of his loss that the god Pluto let him reclaim his love on the condition that he lead her into the light without glancing back. Orpheus couldn't stop himself from looking back at her, and so lost her for good.

Another dramatic artwork on display in the museum is the biblical *Danse de Salomé (Dance of Salome)*, in which Moreau explored the common Symbolist (and Freudian) themes of Eros (love) and Thanatos (death), and their many ties. For more sexy artworks, both secular and profane, head for the **Musée de l'Erotisme** just around the corner in the 18th (see p. 96).

Close to rue Lafayette and the spot where Breton met Nadja (see p. 78), at rue Richer, is the legendary **Folies-Bergère**. Opened in 1870, the cabaret quickly became notorious for performances by Josephine Baker, nicknamed the "Bronze Venus" or "Black Pearl," or "La Baker"' by the French, who rose to fame after dancing on the streets of St. Louis, Missouri as a teenager. Famed at the Folies-Bergère for her *Danse sauvage* (Wild Dance), which she performed wearing little besides a skirt made of fake bananas, Baker became an icon, inspiring the writers, artists, and fashion designers of her time, including Ernest Hemingway, F. Scott Fitzgerald (see p. 205), Pablo Picasso (see p. 34), and Christian Dior.

The Folies-Bergère also served as subject matter for the last major work of the painter Édouard Manet. His painting *Le bar aux Folies-Bergère (The Bar at the Folies-Bergère)* is almost as famous for its optical contradictions as for its portrayal of a slice of music-hall life in the 1880s. Another star from the famous cabaret was Mistinguett, renowned for her long "ostrich" legs, her turbulent love life, and her song "Oui, je suis de Paris" ("Yes, I'm from Paris"). Other illustrious names to have graced the Folies-Bergère stage, with its grand, sweeping staircase, include Colette (see p. 21), and the unlikely trio of Charlie Chaplin, W. C. Fields, and Stan Laurel. Hungarian-born photographer Brassaï documented the backstage glamour of the cabaret in many of his images, among them "L'oiseau de feu aux Folies-Bergère" ("The Firebird at the Folies-Bergère"). Such images embody Brassaï's quest to "seize the Paris night" (see pp. 106–107).

The music hall is worth visiting for its historic, if circuslike, decor (think gaudy murals and lashings of gold paint). The theater still puts on shows, which run the gamut of poetry, dance, highbrow theater, and popular classics, such as *Cabaret*—all of them best watched over a glass or two of champagne.

South of here, the legendary **Max Linder Panorama** (24 boulevard Poissonnière) attempts to re-create the atmosphere of early movie projections with its orchestra stalls and excellent acoustics, and seats covered in black velvet and walls painted black to ensure there's no distraction from the panoramic screen. Burlesque actor Max Linder set up the venue in the early nineteenth century to show mainly Chaplin films. In the 1930s, it was transformed into an Art Deco picture palace; modernizations have been careful to retain the 1930s vibe, hence the elegant box office, vintage movie posters, marble floors, and stucco frescoes. Today's programming might include romantic classics such as *Gone with the Wind*, or a special showing of silent movies with piano accompaniment.

Alternatively, just north of here is the eccentric little **Le Limonaire** (18 cité Bergère), which bills itself as "*un peu un bistrot á vins ... mais surtout un bistrot á chansons*" (in part a wine bistro ... but above all a song bistro), with the emphasis on classic, lyric-driven French chansons of the kind associated with Edith Piaf, Georges Brassens, and Jacques Brel (see p. 92). All performances are free; a hat is passed around and people in the audience throw in money according to how highly they rate the show. On Mondays at 8 p.m., Le Limonaire offers its guests, if they so choose, the opportunity to pen and perform personalized lyrics to famous melodies. On the third Sunday of each month, the bar, just like the Max Linder, offers a silent film showcase, accompanied by live piano music.

10TH–12TH: WALKING THROUGH HISTORY

The 10th arrondissement, home to two mighty railway stations, provides many visitors with their first glimpse of Paris: a chaotic world of screeching taxis and neon signs vying for your attention. But in the mix of it all there are some nuggets of gold worth digging out. Near the Gare de l'Est is one of Paris's very few covered cast-iron markets that has survived from the nineteenth century, the **Marché Couvert St-Quentin** (85 bis, boulevard Magenta). This market is filled with friendly stallholders selling flowers, fish, meat, fruit, and vegetables, including Portuguese specialties such as chorizo and dried cod. Close by, there's an explosion of silk and frothy lace within the tiny, two-room **Musée de l'Éventail** (2 boulevard de Strasbourg), a private museum dedicated to fans and fan-making. Only open three afternoons a week, the museum is another spot that you are likely to have to yourself. The fans, which range in style from traditional Asian to modern and are made from wood, pearl, ivory, shell, and even bone, are displayed within a well-conserved period decor of blue tapestry walls embroidered with fleurs-de-lis in gold thread.

It's a short walk to the main draw of this district, but a walk that leads you, in many ways, back through time. The **Canal St-Martin** runs for more than two and a half miles from the Square Frédérick Lemaître to the Place de la Bataille de Stalingrad (in the 19th), and was dug in 1825 under Napoléon I, to supply Paris with food, water, and materials. The canal has seen little commercial traffic since 1960, when it was, unbelievably, almost paved over to make way for a highway.

A large stretch of the canal is hidden from view, from the Square Frédérick Lemaître to the Place de la Bastille to the south. If you decide to take one of Paris's most poetic trips aboard an open-topped boat, which depart from the Bassin de la Villette and its old flour mills in the 19th arrondissement (see p. 90), you'll soon descend into a series of linked underground vaults, the **Voûte du Temple, Voûte Richard Lenoir,** and **Voûte de la Bastille**. This long, otherworldly tunnel passes beneath a crypt that holds the remains of the victims of two Revolutions and a homesick mummy that Napoléon I brought back from Egypt.

If you decide to cruise the Canal St-Martin, and it seems at all familiar, you may be recalling it from a few memorable scenes in the movie *Amélie* or the beloved Marcel Carné classic of 1938, *Hôtel du Nord* (for both, see pp. 56–57). The Hôtel du Nord lives on in its new incarnation as a bar and restaurant by the same name (see p. 98).

The boat that is offered for the cruises in the canal is actually named after one of *Hôtel du Nord*'s stars, Arletty. When the boat passes the hotel on its scheduled cruise, the onboard commentary gives way to a broadcast of some of the film's immortal lines:

"*Atmosphère, atmosphère. Est-ce que j'ai une gueule d'atmosphère?*" ("Atmosphere, atmosphere. Do I have the mug for atmosphere?"). The ride ends after about three hours, passing through the modern Bassin de l'Arsenal, with its yachts and houseboats, and docking along the Seine. Otherwise, stroll along the canal and watch the barges navigate the locks and arched iron footbridges as you move along the boatmen's paths, lined with plane and chestnut trees, beside the still waters and the half-asleep fishermen.

Lovers of contemporary art in all its manifestations, and those in search of little-visited parts of Paris, should head for the **Place Ste-Marthe**, which is full of bohemian bistros and bars that tend towards the louche. Each May, young painters, sculptors, photographers, and installation artists from around the square fling open the doors of their ateliers for the Portes Ouvertes event (www.ateliers-artistes-belleville.org). This area is popular with students who have spilled over from the nearby **rue Oberkampf**, a long street leading up the Ménilmontant hill from the 11th arrondissement toward the 19th and 20th. Formerly seedy and still quite gritty, the rue Oberkampf is home to some of Paris's hippest bars and bistros, as well as the occasional couscous restaurant, ethnic boutique, and junk store thrown in for good measure. Just off the rue Oberkampf is a tiny museum dedicated to Edith Piaf, located inside the apartment of one of the singer's biographers. The private **Musée Edith Piaf** (5 rue Crespin-du-Gast) displays some of Piaf's personal effects to visitors by appointment only. Among the gold and platinum records and Piaf's trademark little black dresses is a life-size teddy bear given to her by her last husband, and some boxing gloves that belonged to Marcel Cerdan, the love of her life (see pp. 87–88).

In the 12th arrondissement, you will discover one of Paris's most enchanting lesser-known spots, one that seems a world away from the urban delights of the rue Oberkampf. A railway track that had fallen into disuse was converted into the **Promenade Plantée**, also called the Coulée Verte (Green Flow), a pathway bordered by roses, lavender, cherry trees, maples, limes, and other pretty plants. The walkway affords unusual views over various parts of the city, including voyeuristic glimpses into apartments. There are stone steps or little elevators to enter the pathway en route, but the trail officially begins at the avenue Daumesnil, just behind the modern opera house. Here, the old redbrick railway arches, or the Viaduc des Arts as they are called, house artisan workshops that are open to the public. Visitors will see master craftspeople, including violin-makers and tapestry restorers, at work.

The route eventually dips back to street level, along the shopping street of the allée Vivaldi and through the **Jardin de Reuilly**, a garden on the site of an old freight station with an open-air café and pretty lawns for picnicking. The trail ends at the gates of the **Bois de Vincennes**, a park that surrounds a château that served as the site for several royal marriages. The dungeons of the château are also well known for having held, from 1777 to 1784, the Marquis de Sade. Here, he made the acquaintance of another erotic writer and prisoner, Honoré-Gabriel Riqueti, the count of Mirabeau, although the two grew to detest one another.

If you follow the route from the east back toward the Bastille, make time to browse at the **Marché aux Puces d'Aligre** on Place d'Aligre near the Ledru-Rollin métro stop. Unlike Paris's more famous flea markets, this is a good place to find great secondhand items without the inflated prices. Fans of the romantic movie *Before Sunset* (see p. 57) will want to make the pilgrimage to the Pure Café at rue Jean Macé, a few minutes' walk to the northeast of the market. This quintessentially Parisian bar with its horseshoe-shaped zinc bar is the spot to which Celine brings Jesse in Paris nine years after their one-night stand in Vienna, and where he falls in love with her all over again.

THE 19TH AND 20TH: DANCING WITH THE DEAD

North of the 12th arrondissement is the 20th, and north of that is the 19th. These areas are off the radar of most tourists, except in the case of the **Cimetière du Père-Lachaise**, where music fans and hippies alike flock to pay homage (and, often, smoke dope) at the grave of Jim Morrison—much to the displeasure of those with relatives here, many of whose headstones have been defaced. Aside from paying homage to the front man for the Doors, there are countless reasons to visit the cemetery. Paris's biggest burial ground, the

TOGETHER FOREVER?

It's 1115 or thereabouts, and intellectually gifted and curious Héloïse, the niece of one of the clergy of the cathedral of Notre-Dame, Canon Fulbert, is sent to study under the eminent philosopher Pierre Abélard. The two fall madly in love, but the age gap, disapproval by the canon, and the repercussions on Abélard's theological career make for a tricky situation. After Héloïse becomes pregnant, the pair realizes that they are in danger and flee to Abélard's native Brittany. The canon organizes a secret marriage for the couple, ostensibly to preserve the dignity of his niece and to bring her back to Paris. The newlyweds, however, discover the canon's real intention is to ruin Abélard so that the canon can have Héloïse for himself. Giving up their child, Astrolabe, Abélard and Héloïse each take a vow of Holy Orders, and continue, as a monk and nun, and later as an abbott and abbess, to express their undying love for each other through a correspondence that lasts twenty years.

Among the many inspired things that Héloïse professes to her lover is that "God is my witness that if Augustus, emperor of the whole world, thought fit to honor me with marriage and conferred all the earth upon me to possess for ever, it would be dearer and more honorable to me to be called not his empress but your whore."

Six centuries later, Joséphine Bonaparte, moved by the story, ordered that the lovers be entombed together at Père-Lachaise. Some experts dispute that the remains actually made it there, while others assert that only Abélard is within the tomb. These particulars don't prevent lovers, and the lovelorn, from making pilgrimages to the monument to leave letters paying tribute to the pair, or asking for true love—under the canopy of the site created from fragments of a defunct abbey.

Père-Lachaise is also the resting place of a dizzying number of great names from France and abroad. Must-sees for lovers include Oscar Wilde's grave, an Art Deco extravaganza planted with lipstick kisses by some adoring visitors, and that of Edith Piaf (see p. 86), which is strewn with roses. But most romantic of all is the tomb claimed to contain the remains of Abélard and Héloïse, medieval stars of one of the most famous—and doomed—love stories of all time (see p. 85).

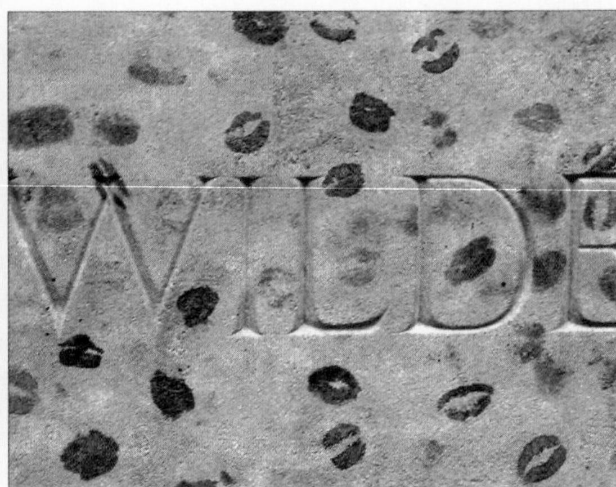

The theme of romance from beyond the grave continues at the tomb of American writer Gertrude Stein and her partner Alice B. Toklas, who were inseparable in life and remain so in death, a fact that is echoed by their double-sided, shared gravestone. Oddly enough, the tomb of Victor Noir, a journalist who was killed in a duel with Napoléon I's nephew, Pierre-Napoléon Bonaparte, is somewhat raunchy. This tomb has become notorious for the way the "member" of the deceased (who was said to have been a playboy in his day) is depicted as pushing open his partly unbuttoned fly. This grave has become a symbol of fertility, with couples coming to leave flowers in Noir's hat, kiss his lips, and even have a furtive rub of his manhood.

Everyone will find someone along Père-Lachaise's winding paths to whom they wish to pay their respects. If you prefer to explore the cemetery on a guided tour, look up Bertrand Beyern's offerings at www.afif.asso.fr. His tours, which are only offered in French, include "Amour au Père-Lachaise" or "Le Père-Lachaise Erotique."

You could spend an entire day at Père-Lachaise and you would not regret it. Don't, however, miss out on what else is offered in the 20th. The conjoined twin districts of Ménilmontant and Belleville are well known for the successive waves of immigrants that enliven the arrondissement and make it the vibrant cultural cocktail that it is. In Belleville, African communities coexist with Paris's second-largest Chinatown, but also with French West Indian, Polish, Armenian, and Turk populations, among others. To meet a real Belleville character, pop into the 1930s *fromagerie* at the northwest corner of the cemetery (5 place Auguste-Métivier). Here, Madame Jouanneau will be pleased to regale you with local history as you peruse her expansive stock of cheeses.

SONGS OF LOVE AND LOSS

It is in Belleville that the most beloved of French popular singers, Edith Piaf, was born in 1915. According to a wall plaque on the rue de Belleville, she entered the world under a lamppost in front of number 71 of that street, although her birth certificate states more prosaically, but no doubt more accurately, that she was born at the local hospital. Piaf, who is perhaps France's greatest ever *chansonnier* (see p. 92), specialized in ballads. Among her most famous are "La vie en rose" and "Non, je ne regrette rien" ("No, I regret nothing"). The stoicism expressed in the latter is perhaps a reference to the singer's path through life, which was never an easy one, especially when it came to her amorous dealings.

Abandoned in infancy by her café singer and street acrobat parents, Piaf lived with her maternal grandmother on the rue Rébeval, close to the rue de Belleville, before she was sent to live with her paternal grandmother, who ran a brothel in Normandy. One biography claims that as a child, blind from age three to seven, she was miraculously healed when the prostitutes in Normandy pooled their money and took her on a pilgrimage to a shrine of Saint Theresa. Her musical career began when, after having joined her father on a busking tour of France, she returned to Paris on her own and began singing on the streets of Pigalle and Ménilmontant, and in the suburbs.

At sixteen, Piaf fell for a delivery boy and gave birth to a child. Their daughter, however—the only child Piaf was ever to have—died at the age of two. Afterward, the singer took up with a pimp, who extorted a commission on her artistic earnings. Things also got violent, and when Piaf decided to separate from him, he attempted to shoot her.

In 1936 Piaf's burgeoning career was threatened when the nightclub owner Louis Leplée, who had discovered the singer in Pigalle, was murdered by gangsters. It was at this time that Piaf adopted her stage name, shook herself free of her dubious acquaintances, and took up, professionally and romantically, with lyricist Raymond Asso. This fertile collaboration ended during World War II, when Asso was drafted. At this time, Piaf discovered actor and singer Yves Montand, with whom she fell in love. She featured Montand in her act, but his fame grew quickly to rival her own, and they broke up shortly after. Piaf also helped to launch the career of singer Charles Aznavour. She was, in fact, with Aznavour in 1951, when she had the first of three car crashes that would result in her addiction to morphine.

Later in life, after having lost the love of her life, boxer Marcel Cerdan, in a plane crash in 1949, Piaf married the singer Jacques Pills in 1952, quickly divorcing him in 1956. From 1962 until her death at age forty-seven the following year, Piaf was married to hairdresser-turned-singer/actor Théo Sarapo, twenty years her junior and almost certainly bisexual. Together they had a hit with the duet "*A quoi ça sert l'amour?*" ("What Good is Love?").

Piaf is buried in Père-Lachaise beside her last husband and her daughter, Marcelle, beneath the motto "Love Conquers All." It's fitting that she came to rest in the neighborhood of her birth, since much of the charm of her songs resides in her working-class Belleville accent (comparable to the Cockney accent of an east Londoner). You can get an advance look at the neighborhood by watching the 2007 film of her life, *La môme (La vie en Rose)*, for which Marion Cotillard earned an Oscar (for best actress) the following year. For Piaf fans, there's also a museum dedicated to her (see p. 83), and a local square named after her. The square contains both a statue of Piaf and an unpretentious little watering hole called the Bar Edith Piaf, decorated with drawings, paintings, and photos of her.

When you stand in Belleville now, it's hard to believe that as recently as the eighteenth century this neighborhood was an area of windmills, taverns, fields, and vines. A small vineyard in the **Parc de Belleville** is a nod to the days when local grapes were used to produce a cheap wine called *piquette*. Today, the vineyard grows an upscale pinot meunier from Champagne and a chardonnay from Bourgogne. The Parc de Belleville, established in 1988, is one of Paris's newest parks, and, located on a tall hill, also its highest, making it a good place to come for panoramic views. Fittingly for a spot where you can sit and watch clouds and other atmospheric phenomena in the skies over the city, the park houses a Maison de l'Air (House of Air) which provides a space for informative and often ecologically themed exhibitions on the city's air and atmosphere, examining such themes as how plants germinate using the air. Otherwise, visit the park for its zigzagging walkways bordered by groves of trees, including lindens, Japanese pagoda trees, catalpas, dogwoods, mock oranges, and limes; or stroll along the rolling lawns and see Paris's tallest water fountain, a few shallow pools perfect for paddling in when summer fries the city, and an open-air theater.

The Parc de Belleville is located in the 20th arrondissement, not far from the larger and better-known **Parc des Buttes-Chaumont**, which occupies wild, hilly terrain in the 19th that once served as quarry land. The park is romantic and theatrical, veering on Gothic, with a lake; an abandoned railway track; a grotto with artificial stalactites and a waterfall; Chinese- and English-style gardens; and a cliff-top belvedere called the Temple de la Sibylle, modeled after an ancient Roman ruin. Some of the best views of the Basilique du Sacré-Coeur (see p. 93) can be enjoyed from this belvedere, which can be reached by stone steps or a suspension bridge dubbed, rather sinisterly, the Pont des Suicides, as it has been said to inspire some of those who cross it to leap to their deaths. The park was featured prominently in the novel *Le paysan de Paris (Paris Peasant* or *The Nightwalker)* by Louis Aragon, who, after wandering around it by night with his fellow Surrealist André Breton (see p. 79), described it as a "spellbinding mirage."

One of the main reasons that a visitor might venture into the 19th arrondissement is the **Parc de la Villette**, which is home to the **Cité des Sciences et de l'Industrie** exhibition center and to the **Cité de la Musique**. One of Europe's foremost music schools as well as a museum, the Cité de la Musique displays some real treasures for music-lovers, including a Stradivarius violin, a piano played by Franz Liszt, and Django Reinhardt's guitar. The

GREAT PARIS LOVERS

Some of the world's most passionate—and often ill-fated—love affairs have played out against a Parisian backdrop.

Abélard and Héloïse (see p. 85).
Napoléon and Joséphine Bonaparte (see p. 128)
Auguste Rodin and Camille Claudel (see pp. 61–63)
George Sand and Frédéric Chopin (see p. 79)
Amadeo Modigliani and Jeanne Hébuterne (see p. 114)
Jean-Paul Sartre and Simone de Beauvoir (see p. 53)
André Breton and Nadja (see p. 78)
Man Ray and Lee Miller (see pp. 116–117)
Henry Miller and Anaïs Nin (see pp. 107–109)
Serge Gainsbourg and Jane Birkin (see pp. 110–111)

museum also houses many fascinating instruments from around the globe, such as Indian sitars and African harps, and provides a range of guided tours and performances within its amphitheater, where musicians often play instruments from the collection (or facsimiles when the originals are too fragile). On some weekends, there are mini-concerts to accompany a stroll through the museum, plus the chance to talk with the performers.

Seek out the themed gardens in the Parc de la Villette. Some of these are strictly for children, while others are more thought provoking, such as the bamboo garden with electro-acoustic effects, the disorienting garden of mirrors, the garden of shadows with playful lighting, and the design garden commemorating victims of HIV and AIDS.

Before you make a foray into Montmartre, head down to the **Bassin de la Villette**, the starting point for boat trips along the Canal St-Martin (see pp. 82–83). Artists and craftspeople have colonized its old shipping wharves and warehouses. In August, the basin truly comes alive as one of Paris's three beaches (see p. 104), when you can relax on a chaise longue, have a picnic, or take a paddleboat, windsurfer, or canoe out on the water; and by night shimmy and strut at a traditional *bal musette*. Featuring *musette* (bagpipe) music, tango, salsa, country, and traditional dance, these *bals musettes* hark back to the famous *guinguettes* (dance-cafés) that occupied this neighborhood (as well as parts of the 5th, 11th, and 12th districts) in the 1880s. Though originally a working class pastime, *guinguettes* held a fascination for members of the upper class, who were especially titillated by staged police raids designed to heighten the thrill.

The Paris Plage at la Villette lets you relive the days when the basin was one of Paris's most popular meeting spots. But even if you venture to the basin outside of summer, the place is far from desolate. Among its year-round attractions are the ultra-hip **Péniche Cinéma** (Barge Cinema), a floating movie theater on the canal de l'Ourcq with an open-air deck overlooking the water—a congenial space for tapas and champagne.

THE 18TH: WHERE THE HEART RESIDES

Like the Louvre, Montmartre, which rises steeply up its *butte* (hill) toward the landmark Basilique du Sacré-Coeur, is saturated with tourists, cheesy restaurants, and mediocre street artists. Yet this is a neighborhood with many small-scale sights worth seeking out. From the mid 1800s on, Montmartre was a magnet for artists, beginning with Camille Pissarro and continuing with Vincent van Gogh (see pp. 213–214), Henri Matisse (see pp. 194–195), Henri de Toulouse-Lautrec (see p. 93), Pablo Picasso (see p. 34), and

Amadeo Modigliani (see p. 114) to name some of the most illustrious. Many of these artists lived and worked in **Le Bateau-Lavoir**, a ramshackle artists' commune in an old piano factory on rue Ravignan, in place Emile-Goudeau. Today a storefront bearing the name "Bateau Lavoir" displays black-and-white photos of the artists. The actual Bateau Lavoir, or Laundry Boat, named for its resemblance to one of the laundress's boats that used to float on the Seine, was destroyed by fire in the 1970s.

Working-class by origin, this district has long been synonymous with social decadence and more than a hint of sleaze; it used to be located outside the city limits and was hence exempt from city taxes, so it evolved into a popular drinking area, especially since the local nuns made wine. This liberal attitude toward drinking gave way to licentious entertainments around the turn of the nineteenth century, most notably in the popular cabarets of Le Moulin Rouge, Le Divan Japonais, and Le Chat Noir.

The worlds of nightlife and art were closely entwined and mutually sustaining, with artists inspired by local dancers and strippers, and by landmarks such as the **Moulin de la Galette** (83 rue Lépic), one of several windmills that used to punctuate the landscape of the former farmland. Now a touristy restaurant, the Moulin de la Galette used to be a *guinguette* notorious because its performers often "forgot" to put on their underwear. It was immortalized in paintings by Pierre-Auguste Renoir, Van Gogh, Toulouse-Lautrec, Kees van Dongen, Maurice Utrillo (the son of Suzanne Valadon; see p. 93), and Picasso. Meanwhile, artists both enjoyed and sometimes took an active role in the area's fabled nightlife. Composer Erik Satie (see p. 176), for instance, played the piano in Le Chat Noir.

You shouldn't leave Paris without a peek inside the famed **Moulin Rouge** (82 boulevard de Clichy), an 1889 cabaret that is easily spotted by the model of a red windmill on its roof. It's here that the cancan, a working-class party dance that was sexed up by semi-nude courtesans, was born. Over the years, the stage at the Moulin Rouge has been graced by greats such as Josephine Baker (see pp. 80–81), Ella Fitzgerald, Frank Sinatra, and Edith Piaf (see pp. 87–88). These days it still features slightly risqué adult entertainment: cancan, acrobatics, clowning, and magic acts. If that's not your thing, come for an eyeful of the turn-of-the-twentieth-century decor, which includes the originals of some of Henri de Toulouse-Lautrec's revolutionary posters.

Toulouse-Lautrec (see p. 93) made his name with poster designs and erotic works depicting Montmartre performers, including Louise Weber, nicknamed La Goulue (The Glutton), who is said to have popularized the cancan. Weber, who was also dubbed the "Queen of Montmartre," began her career at the Moulin de la Galette and gained her undignified nickname from her habit of downing the contents of clients' glasses when dancing past their tables. Her other calling cards included her panties adorned with an embroidered

GREAT PARIS SONGS

When the French talk of "chanson," they mean more than just any old song—they mean the "realist" songs that, having evolved gradually from medieval epic poems such as "Le chanson de Roland" ("The Song of Roland") and courtly love songs, were performed in the café-concerts and cabarets of Montmartre from the 1880s to World War II. Lyric-driven and frequently sentimental, the *chanson* borrowed themes from the harsh realities of working-class life and were usually sung in a working-class accent, as was the case with Edith Piaf (see pp. 87–88). Such songs were often accompanied by accordion music. In time, Left Bank cabarets developed their own strand called the *chanson Rive Gauche*.

You can hear traditional chansons at **Au Lapin Agile** (21 rue de Saules) in Montmartre, first known as the Cabaret des Assassins and popular with Picasso and Utrillo. Less touristy is **Le Limonaire** in nearby Pigalle (see p. 81), or try **Le Vieux Belleville** (12 rue des Envierges) in the 20th, where you can listen to Edith Piaf and Maurice Chevalier songs over platters of sausage and cheese.

The tradition of chanson has continued but has also evolved, via the vocal styling of Serge Gainsbourg (see pp. 110–111), to the boundary-breaking work by artists as diverse as the vocal experimentalist known simply as Camille and rappers MC Solaar and Diam's. Having taken seed in Paris, the tradition naturally embraces songs that use the city itself as subject matter or setting, and listening to a Paris-inspired chanson is guaranteed to transport you to Paris in a heartbeat, wherever you are in the world.

"Sous les ponts de Paris" (1913), **Georgel**
"J'ai deux amours, mon pays et Paris" (1931), **Josephine Baker**
"Les amants de Paris" (1948), "Sous le ciel de Paris" (1954), and "Le Métro de Paris" (1960), **Edith Piaf**
"Ménilmontant" (1939) and "Revoir Paris" (1947), **Charles Trénet**
"J'aime Paris au mois de mai" (1965), "J'aime flâner sur les grands boulevards" (1951), and "La Bohème" (1966), **Charles Aznavour**
"A Saint-Germain-des-Prés" (1969), **Léo Ferré**
"Les prénoms de Paris" (1972), **Jacques Brel**
"Bouge de là" (1990), **MC Solaar**
"Paris" (2002), **Camille**

heart, which she would flash at the audience by swirling the hem of her dress, and the way she could flip off men's hats with her toes while performing high kicks. Among the artist's other models were Yvette Guilbert, singer of licentious songs about her poor background and lost love, and dancer Jane Avril, who replaced Weber when she left the Moulin Rouge.

Le Moulin Rouge has inspired several movies. The most recent, from 2001, stars Nicole Kidman and Ewan McGregor and features fully invented characters. The 1952 film, directed by John Huston, is a partly fictionalized account of Toulouse-Lautrec's life in Paris, featuring Jane Avril (played by Zsa Zsa Gabor), Louise Weber, and Marie Charlet. Marie Charlet was the seventeen-year-old model with whom the artist had his first relationship, a situation that caused strife within his aristocratic family. Despite Toulouse-Lautrec's physical shortcomings—congenital defects left his legs stunted—he also had a relationship with the legendary beauty Suzanne Valadon, another of his models and also the subject of various nude photographic portraits now in the Musée de Montmartre (see p. 94). Valadon was a great artist in her own right, famous for her female nudes and for her painting *Adam et Ève*, the first work by a female artist to show a nude man and woman together—she used herself and her boy-toy André Utter as models.

Valadon lived next door to Toulouse-Lautrec when he had his studio on the fifth floor of 7 rue Tourlaque by the Cimetière de Montmartre (see pp. 95–96). It's here that he created his famous posters and paintings of the cancan dancers, circus performers, and prostitutes in local brothels—and also where he held his infamous orgies on Friday nights. The works of this time—his major artistic legacy—were heavily influenced by his fascination with Japanese art, especially the colored erotic prints by Kitagawa Utamaro. His lesser-known works include more domestic scenes, such as *Dans le lit (In Bed),* a painting of a couple in bed beneath the sheets, which you can see at the Musée d'Orsay (see p. 63).

Toulouse-Lautrec, who defined love as "when the desire to be desired takes you so badly that you feel you could die of it," had affairs with many of his models, including Jane Avril, but never married: his abiding love affair seems to have been the artistic one that he had with Montmartre and its inhabitants. His other passion, one that played a large part in his early death at the age of thirty-six, was for drinking absinthe or "the green fairy," especially in the *tremblement de terre* (earthquake) cocktail, a potent mixture of the anise-flavored spirit and cognac, said to have been invented by Toulouse-Lautrec himself.

At the top of the neighborhood of Montmartre and worlds away from the Moulin Rouge in spirit is the **Basilique du Sacré-Coeur**, which despite the name has no romantic connotations. (It is dedicated to the Sacred Heart of Jesus, representing divine love for humanity.) Perched on the *butte* (hill) like a sugar-frosted wedding cake, the church with its Romano-Byzantine design, and pollution- and weather-proof white travertine stone, sits

uneasily with the rest of the city's architecture but is a fine place to visit for the spectacular panoramic views from the top of its dome and for its pretty garden.

You can take a road train, which is often overrun with tourists, a special bus, or a funicular train up to the Basilica, or you can ascend slowly via Montmartre's steep winding streets, narrow passageways, and tottering, vertiginous staircases. The dwindling of Montmartre's bohemian spirit was lamented as early as 1965, in the Charles Aznavour song "La bohème," which ends with the phrase, "Et les lilas sont morts" ("And the lilacs are dead"). Certainly, the touristy **Place du Tertre**, part of the old village to the west of the Sacré-Coeur, won't convince you otherwise. This is a real shame: the Place du Tertre is where, at the restaurant La Mère Catherine (which still exists), the word *bistro* is said to have originated. Apparently, the invading Cossacks used to shout: "Bistro! Bistro!" ("Quick! Quick!") as they entered a café or bar, and the term came to connote any modest eating establishment.

The nearby **Musée de Montmartre** (12 rue Cortot) will either console you or make you nostalgic for the neighborhood's lost past with its vintage movie posters—some by Jean Cocteau—paintings, photographs, and historical documents. The building itself has a rich history: originally a seventeenth-century abbey, it was home to many artists and musicians, including Valadon, Utrillo, Van Gogh, Raoul Dufy, Renoir, and Satie, and it even has a working vineyard. In fact, in September, the handful of tiny vineyards in this area host a Fête des Vendanges, a harvest festival featuring wine-related and cultural events.

Near the Place du Tertre is the **Espace Dalí** (11 rue Poulbot), France's only permanent exhibition of the work of Salvador Dalí, superstar of the Surrealist movement. Dalí moved to Paris in 1928 and befriended René Magritte, Max Ernst, André Breton (see p. 78), and Paul Éluard. Dalí proceeded to steal Éluard's Russian-born wife Gala, and she became his lifelong, if unfaithful, muse. Gala seems to have been a femme fatale of the highest order: she and Éluard had previously formed a love triangle with Ernst, beginning in 1923, when the German artist used her as a model for his painting *La belle jardinière* (*The Beautiful Gardener*). This work was later burned by the Nazis for its subject matter—a dissected naked body. But even before the exhibition, the painting caused ructions. Éluard, who perceived the work as Ernst's way of outing their ménage à trois, stormed off to Singapore. Ernst and Gala took off in hot pursuit, and the amorous trio made a madcap course through the Far East and New Zealand—sometimes on different ships. Finally, in Vietnam, the reunited couple abandoned Ernst, and the triangle was ruptured for good.

Like the artists who painted the Moulin de la Galette (see p. 91), Dalí was a fan of the district's windmills, and this interest was nicely complemented by his passion for Miguel de Cervantes's novel *Don Quixote*, the story that inspired some of his engravings, which were partly carried out using sharp rhino horns and bread dipped in ink. You can see a 1956 lithograph of one of Dalí's Don Quixote series at the Espace Dalí, as well as some of the Surrealist's lesser-known sculptures, including *Adam et Ève* and *Femme en flamme* (*The Woman Aflame*), which are dramatically set against black walls.

Like Paris's other great cemeteries, the **Cimetière de Montmartre** a few minutes walk to the west, is an atmospheric and even whimsical place for a lovers' stroll. The cemetery is crisscrossed by deep ravines and is filled with Gothic tombs and mausoleums holding the remains of artistic greats, including Gustave Moreau (see p. 78). In Montmartre high culture jostles with low culture, and in this cemetery, it's no different—Louise Weber, aka La Goulue (see pp. 91–93), is buried here, as is the cancan composer himself, Jacques Offenbach. You'll also find the resting place of courtesan Marie Duplessis, the mistress of Alexandre Dumas, fils (Dumas is also buried here). The inspiration for the character of Marguerite Gautier in Dumas's romantic novel *La dame aux camélias* (*The Lady of the Camellias*), Duplessis was also composer Franz Liszt's lover, as well as a salon hostess popular among artists, writers, and politicians. In fact, she was so popular that her flamboyant funeral was attended by hundreds.

Perhaps the most touching memorial is the tomb of Marie Taglioni, which is located behind that of her fellow ballet dancer Vaslav Nijinsky. You'll know her tomb by the pile of ballet shoes on top of it, left in homage by the city's ballerinas. Taglioni was the first person to dance *en pointe*, and in her day, she inspired such a cult that a pair of her pointe shoes was sold for a vast sum, allegedly to be cooked in a sauce for some ballet fans to tuck into.

Come back to the land of the living with a walk down the rue des Abbesses. The street is well known by locals for its village-like ambiance, authentic Parisian bars serving pastis, and scattering of designer shops. In the Square des Jehan-Rictus off the Place des Abbesses, don't miss **Le mur des je t'aime** (I Love You Wall), a secret meeting place for lovers, inscribed a thousand times by a calligrapher with the words "I love you" in more than three hundred languages.

With your romantic appetite whetted, backtrack up the rue des Abbesses, to **Studio 28** (10 rue Tholozé), a 1920s venue designed by Jean Cocteau and described as "a cinema of masterpieces and a masterpiece of a cinema." Studio 28 is itself part of movie history, having hosted the first riot-provoking screening of Luis Buñuel's Surrealist masterpiece *L'âge d'or* (*The Golden Age*). In 2000 the cinema was immortalized on the big screen when part of *Amélie* (see p. 57) was filmed here. Even if you aren't catching a movie, the bar and its garden, which is heated in winter, is a wonderful place to linger over a glass of wine, a savory tart, or a homemade cake.

Alternatively, head down to the **Musée de l'Erotisme de Paris** (72 boulevard de Clichy), which rounds off this sexy neighborhood with surprisingly tasteful displays on all matters erotic. Fittingly for Montmartre, the emphasis is on artworks, many of which are from the Far East, amassed by its founders. Give your erotic imagination a spark by studying Chinese snug bottles painted with amorous scenes, Japanese figurines with mirrors at the base reflecting their private parts, Indonesian drums in the form of male figures with huge phalluses, and a wooden automata from India of a couple in flagrante delicto. For amateur historians of the city of love, an entire floor of the museum is dedicated to the story of Paris's brothels, many of which were clustered in this neighborhood. Temporary shows expand on the permanent collection and ensure that there's always a reason to return. There's even a gift shop packed with naughty treats to take back to your hotel room.

17TH: QUIET DAYS

After walking through the forest of tourists that occupy much of Montmartre, you'll experience the 17th arrondissement as a ragbag of disparate but intriguing and non-touristy elements: the Place de Clichy, which continues the grit and sleaze of Pigalle, the old village-turned-trendy residential area of the Batignolles, and the upscale neighborhood around the avenue des Ternes and Poncelet market to the southeast.

Though mostly without charm, the **Place de Clichy** will be of interest to admirers of Henry Miller, the American novelist whose somewhat autobiographical works were filled with graphic accounts of his amorous encounters (perhaps inevitably for someone whose middle name was Valentine). Miller came to Paris in the late 1920s, first with his wife June as part of a trip around Europe, and later on his own, to live. Grindingly poor, he often had to rely on his friends—including the writer Anaïs Nin (see pp. 108–109), with whom he had an intense affair that may or may not have involved his wife—for lodgings and sustenance. At one time Miller lived in Clichy itself, to the west of Paris, and he often passed through or spent time in the Place de Clichy, which he mentions in his works. A couple of his favorite cafés have remained, little changed since the 1930s. The unassuming **Au Petit Poucet** (1 rue de Biot) with its red awning, for instance, is where Miller used to write letters to Nin on the café's "Tom Thumb" letterhead. The very traditional **Brasserie Wepler** (14 Place de Clichy) was praised by Miller in his *Quiet Days in Clichy*, in which he describes how the "rosy glow which suffused the place emanated from the cluster of whores who usually congregated near the entrance." In fact, this café and brasserie positively reeks of its artistic associations, having been popular with poet Guillaume Apollinaire, the artists Picasso (see p. 34), Modigliani (see p. 114), Toulouse-Lautrec (see pp. 91–93), and Valadon (see p. 93), the movie director Claude Chabrol, and many other creative types. The brasserie also served as the inspiration for the description of the café terrace in the opening scene of Louis-Ferdinand Céline's novel *Voyage au bout de la nuit* (*Journey to the End of the Night*), and was the setting for some of the action in Truffaut's *Les quatre cent coups* (*The 400 Blows*). The establishment extends its impressive heritage by awarding its own literary prize, the Prix Wepler, to a contemporary author each year. The Brasserie Wepler, however, is most famous for its seafood menu, which features some of the finest of French oysters and best seafood platters in Paris, including the enticing Plateau Wepler, meant for sharing.

The sole museum in this arrondissement, the **Musée National Jean-Jacques Henner** (43 avenue de Villiers), is in a charming old mansion in the Batignolles district south of the Place de Clichy. You probably haven't heard of the Alsace painter whose self-portraits and other works on mythical themes or featuring dreamy landscapes that prefigure Symbolism fill all four floors of the museum. Yet this museum, aside from its status as another one of those little Parisian museums that you might have all to yourselves on a quiet weekday, is worth a visit for its historical ambiance alone. You'll have to go to the Musée d'Orsay (see p. 63) to see works by the Batignolles group of painters—Édouard Manet, Camille Pissarro, Edgar Degas, and Alfred Sisley—who would meet in the Café Guerbois on rue des Batignolles.

COUPS DE COEUR

EATING

Horus
25 rue de Douai
+33 (0)1 48 78 68 00

This is a cozy, intimate spot in Pigalle for inexpensive and delicious North African cuisine, with a soothing Middle Eastern soundtrack. Enjoy couscous, a tagine, and some pastries while decadently splayed on fat leather poufs on the floor. You will find a list of interesting teas ranging from strong, sweet Egyptian to fresh mint, as well as Egyptian *narguiles* (pipes) in a variety of seductive flavors, including honey, almond, and apricot.

Tea Folies
6 place Gustave Toudouze
+33 (0)1 42 80 08 44

A great spot for brunch, with an exceptional list of teas and especially good jams, this cute Pigalle bistro and tearoom continues to lure locals. With its shady terrace opening onto a charming square, Tea Folies is the perfect spot to spend a leisurely Sunday morning with your beau or belle. The salads and savory tarts are excellent, but be sure to save room for one of the delectable desserts, which include an almond and caramel-filled meringue, a refreshing lemon tart, and a chocolate cake drenched with custard.

Hôtel du Nord
102 quai des Jemmapes
+33 (0)1 40 40 78 78

Once nicknamed the Hôtel des Poux Volants (Hotel of the Flying Lice) for its lack of hygiene, this restaurant and bar on the banks of the Canal St-Martin (see pp. 82–83) was saved from demolition in 1984 by the actress Arletty. Arletty was the star of the atmospheric movie *Hôtel du Nord* (see p. 56), which took the real-life Hôtel du Nord as its setting. Arletty adored the building so much that when she died, her funeral cortege made a stop directly in front of it. Today, the Hôtel du Nord is no longer a hotel but an intimate eaterie that was decorated (fittingly) by a movie set designer, with tiled walls, a flagstone floor, and velvet curtains. The restaurant serves up simple fare such as fresh soup, pasta, and a special of the day, but you are free to just relax with a cocktail or glass of wine while you play a game of backgammon, chess, or dice, or browse the books in the library. The hotel is a great place to gaze out over the canal as you ponder the words of British novelist Graham Greene: "In [the film] *Hôtel du Nord* we believe in the desperate lovers and the suicide pact on the brass bed in the shabby room, just because of the bicyclists on the quay, the pimp quarrelling with his woman in another room, and the First-Communion party."

Sans Gêne Oberkampf
122 rue Oberkampf
+33 (0)1 47 00 70 11

Low lighting, a sultry soundtrack, all-day tapas and *planchas* (Spanish grills), and traditional French main dishes perked up with fresh herbs and often big enough to share between two are what this fashionable restaurant and lounge in the 11th excels in. Lovers should head straight downstairs to the vaulted cellar, where the ambiance is better suited to intimate conversation. Throughout the week, except on Sundays, the Sans Gêne offers a special menu that includes unlimited glasses

of wine. A shot of strawberry vodka on the house helps it all go down nicely. You can also visit their second branch in Batignolles in the 17th (see p. 97), on rue Legendre.

Restaurant Chez Paul
13 rue de Charonne
+33 (0)1 47 00 34 57

Ridiculously Parisian in the best sense of the word, this bistro in the 11th still looks as it did fifty years ago—when Monsieur Paul and his wife were at the helm—with its zinc bar, tiled floor, handwritten menu, and red-and-white checked tablecloths. It's no longer an insider secret, but locals who come for the authentically hearty cuisine continue to outnumber the tourists. Garlicky snails, steak tartare, peppered steak in brandy with *dauphinois* potatoes, and crème brûlée with violet flowers are among the delights you might lubricate with a pitcher of house red. Chez Paul is always packed and noisy, but that's just part of its intensely Gallic charm.

Le Train Bleu
2nd floor, Gare de Lyon
Place Louis-Armand
+33 (0)1 43 43 09 06

There can be few more beautiful or glamorous restaurants in the world than Le Train Bleu (The Blue Train), built within the impressive Gare de Lyon in the 12th for the Exposition Universelle de Paris of 1900. Now designated an historical monument, the restaurant has included among its many fans Coco Chanel, Brigitte Bardot, Jean Cocteau, and Marcel Pagnol. Classic dishes such as pigs' trotters with morel mushrooms, grilled sea bass with fennel confit, and breast of guinea fowl with sautéed foie gras are served within a gilded, belle-époque interior of cherubs, leather seating, sculptures, and paintings of the landscapes that were seen by travelers on the Paris-Lyon-Méditerranée train route. The dimly lit bar with its club-like atmosphere is an inspired choice for a lovers' rendezvous.

La Mère Lachaise
78 boulevard de Ménilmontant
+33 (0)1 47 97 61 60

This restaurant's interesting name is actually a pun on the Cimetière du Père-Lachaise, which is just two steps away (see pp. 84–86). La Mère Lachaise stands out from the other restaurants on boulevard de Ménilmontant in the 20th because of its fine terrace, warm welcome, and simple interior full of character: gleaming wood, bare light bulbs, and photograph-studded walls. This is a good spot for a lazy brunch before or after a Sunday stroll in the cemetery, but be sure to book ahead. And don't leave without sampling the Ti'punch (rum, sugarcane syrup, and lime), one of the best versions of the cocktail in the city.

Restaurant Guy Savoy
18 rue Troyon
+33 (0)1 43 80 40 61

A *grand restaurant* just off the top of the Champs-Élysées, Restaurant Guy Savoy in the 17th is the right place for a gastronomic treat in the safe hands of a celebrity chef. The setting is warmly modern, with African painting and sculptures. The cuisine is decadently rich and deeply sensual, and yet somehow light: think artichoke soup with black truffles and parmesan shavings served with a brioche with mushrooms and truffle butter; oysters set over an oyster purée and served with seawater jelly; and a dessert of blood oranges scented with saffron. As you enter, you will likely be greeted by Savoy himself, and his staff is charm personified.

STAYING

Hôtel Amour
8 rue Navarin
+33 (0)1 48 78 31 80
www.hotelamourparis.fr

A gaudy pink neon sign signals the existence of this arty Pigalle hotel devoted, as the name suggests, to love, with rooms available by the half day (at a 20 percent discount) should you be short of time—quite fittingly so, as the Hôtel Amour is a former brothel. The decor is flea market–meets–retro designer, with many of the twenty rooms decorated by artists, including Sophie Calle, a conceptual artist whose work has involved spying on hotel guests (don't worry—she doesn't do it at the Amour). All of the rooms are free of the distractions of telephones and TVs. Stipulate when booking if you'd like a room with a bathtub at the foot of your bed, for bath times

with a twist. For guests and non-guests alike, the restaurant is a great place for a tryst, with its 1970s ambiance, uncomplicated dishes, and summertime courtyard.

Hôtel Royal Fromentin
1 rue Fromentin
+33 (0)1 48 74 85 93
www.paris-hotel-royalfromentin.com

Not at all sleazy, despite its Pigalle location, this classic 1930s hotel retains its genuine Parisian character, with an antique cage-style elevator, complete with wood paneling and glass windows, and Art Deco glass in the windows running up beside its staircase. The fairy-tale views of the Basilique du Sacré-Coeur (see p. 93) from some of the guest rooms enhance the Parisian charm. But don't be led astray, for this hotel has maintained a frisson of naughtiness that makes it well suited for the neighborhood—its theatrical lobby and bar, plastered with vintage advertising posters and bedecked with caryatids, used to be a cabaret called Le Don Juan. The bar staff has been known to tempt guests with a ritualistic tasting of absinthe. This belle-époque drink par excellence, dubbed "the Muse," was the tipple of choice (and ultimate ruin) for many artists, writers, and performers who lived in this area.

Mama Shelter
109 rue de Bagnolet
+33 (0)1 43 48 48 48
www.mamashelter.com

A contender for the hippest place to stay in Paris, yet one without the aloofness that ordinarily accompanies many designer hotels, Mama Shelter offers a friendly staff, cozy common spaces, and guest rooms with five-star bedding and amenities—satinesque cotton sheets, Kiehl's toiletries, raindance showers, flat-screen iMacs, TVs, and DVD players—at three- or even two-star prices. Created by Philippe Starck, the Mama Shelter aims to be, like Paris herself, a sensual refuge, hence the maternal name. Although there isn't any room service, the guest rooms are equipped with microwaves and refrigerators, and the on-site shop stocks chocolates and other treats. This boho locale in the 20th—just a 10-minute walk east of Père-Lachaise cemetery (see pp. 84–86)—makes Mama Shelter a perfect choice for those who want a buzz but don't need to be in the heart of Paris. The hotel's restaurant serves simple and hearty fare, and the vast bar comes complete with intimate enclaves, inside which creative folk and lovers from around the globe huddle to conspire. Sink into a deep sofa and post playful announcements on the chalkboards and the TV screens built into columns between the tables, whether you want to meet someone, learn something new, or simply dream. Graffiti artfully scribbled on walls everywhere from the lifts to the guest rooms reminds you that "Human beings and dolphins are the only species who actively enjoy sex," and that "All you need is love," while a scrawl in the reception area playfully asks, "Can we hire a room by the hour?"

Hôtel de Banville
166 boulevard Berthier
+33 (0)1 42 67 70 16
www.hotelbanville.fr

Eschew Montmartre and its overpriced tourist-trap hotels for this genuine find in the 17th: a quiet spot and the perfect hotel in which to propose, or be proposed to (in which case, the staff will arrange champagne, flowers, chocolates, and anything else you may need). Sympathetically carved out of a 1930s building, the Hôtel de Banville, which is named after a poet, blends modern, boutique touches with old-fashioned detailing and mood. Some of the rooms have been marked as especially romantic: the sloping-roofed "Appartement de Marie" has Eiffel Tower views; the "Théodore de Banville" suite has a country-cottage feel, with embroidered organdy and toile de Jouy, furniture made from old shutters, a sunken bath, and antique mirrors; and finally the "Amélie" features a private balcony for breakfast on sunny mornings. In fact, breakfast can be served in your room at any time of the day, and the hotel also offers in-room massages. For a cozy evening, visit the piano bar, where, on Tuesday evenings, you can listen to the proprietress Madame Moreau sing jazz and French classics.

13TH–16TH:

Southern and Western Paris

> There is no progress in art,
> any more than there is progress
> in making love. There are simply
> different ways of doing it.
>
> —MAN RAY

The 13th through the 16th arrondissements may be short on the big-hitting attractions that characterize the central arrondissements, but their rich history and ethnic diversity make them compelling spots to explore—and you can often do so in the footsteps of some of the most famous Parisian artists and lovers. With its 1970s tower blocks and brutal modern architecture, the 13th can be worlds away from the Paris you know from tourist brochures and postcards. But what the arrondissement lacks in picturesque qualities, it makes up for in character, especially in Paris's main Chinatown, La Petite Asie (Little Asia).

From Little Asia, head into Montparnasse, which, like Montmartre in the north of the city (see p. 90), has an exceptional artistic heritage. Montparnasse, which comprises much of the 14th arrondissement and spills into the 15th, is less scenic than its northern counterpart, but for that very reason it's also less touristy, and every street, it seems, is awash with anecdotes about great liaisons that have changed the course of artistic history.

The 16th takes you off the tourist radar and into an area of quiet, respectable streets full of mansions and embassies; this arrondissement is Paris's wealthiest. A surprising number of small museums are hidden in its nooks and crannies, just waiting for you to discover their rich collections of art, fashion, design, and literary history. Some of the streets bear an architectural legacy that will transport you to a Paris of the history books. The *seizième*, as the 16th is known in French, is thus a prime destination for lovers seeking a world away from the crush of central Paris. It culminates in the vast Bois de Boulogne, where small lakes, ponds, and streams will convince you that you've left the city far behind.

13TH: THE SPICE OF LIFE

We start, unexpectedly, with a hospital, the vast **Pitié-Salpêtrière** (47–83 boulevard de l'Hôpital) just to the south of the Jardin des Plantes in the 5th arrondissement (see p. 47). Now a well-respected teaching center, the building has been, over time, a gunpowder factory, a prison for prostitutes, and then a center for the treatment of the mentally ill. The most famous reforms were those of Jean-Martin Charcot, who was a major influence on the young Sigmund Freud. Breton's "Nadja" (see p. 78)—real name Léona-Camille-Ghislaine D (her surname was kept confidential)—may have been among the "hysterics" Charcot sometimes used in his now-infamous public demonstrations at the hospital, for the interest—and perhaps titillation—of prominent men.

Take a stroll through the vast hospital grounds, where modern buildings are clustered around an ancient heart of classical courtyards and fountains. These days the Salpêtrière is a place for the heart as well as the nerves: Europe's first heart transplant was carried out at the hospital in 1968, and forty years later the former French president Jacques Chirac had his pacemaker fitted here. La Salpêtrière is also where Josephine Baker (see pp. 80–81) and Diana, princess of Wales, took their last breaths. The hospital's seventeenth-century chapel (47 boulevard de l'Hôpital) is a quiet, atmospheric place in which to wander.

Near here, the **Bibliothèque Nationale de France** (quai François-Mauriac) is the country's super-library, where everything that is published in France is stored. You may read within its walls only after applying for a ticket and attending an interview. However, there are also events open to the public, such as exhibitions of photography, as well as displays of some of the library's "exceptional treasures," which include Surrealist collages, a handwritten draft of a book by Marcel Proust (see p. 70), letters signed by famous artists, autographed manuscripts, rare publications by the likes of Charles Baudelaire (see p. 40), Paul Verlaine, and André Gide, and daguerreotypes of various subjects. Many such works were payments in-kind, given to the state by artists or collectors as a way of avoiding taxes while helping to preserve their national artistic heritage.

For more culture of a very living and vibrant kind, head down to the river by the library, where you'll find the deep-red former *bateau-feu* (lighthouse boat) known as

LIFE'S A BEACH: PARIS PLAGES

Paris hosted its first "summer beach" in 2002, on the Right Bank of the Seine, from the Louvre to the Pont de Sully at the end of the Île St-Louis. It was such a success that two more *plages* (beach areas) have sprung up in the intervening years: one on the Left Bank around Port de la Gare, beside the Bibliothèque Nationale, and the other at the Bassin de la Villette in northeast Paris (see p. 90). Depending on your choice of location, you can swim in a floating pool (the river itself is off-limits); play boules or beach volleyball; practice tai chi; scale a climbing wall; take a dance lesson; hop aboard a canoe, boat, or paddleboat; rollerblade, or—surely the real point of it all—flop onto a chaise lounge or into a hammock by a café, in the shade of a palm tree or beside a cooling fountain, with an ice cream in hand. Concerts stretch the summer daytime activities into the sultry, sweaty Paris night.

The *plages* are set up around July 20th and run for about four weeks. While the Right Bank beach offers the most activities, the Left Bank beach is fittingly more cultural, with drawing, painting, and writing workshops, free newspapers, book loans, and Wi-Fi access. Should you not be able to choose, there is a shuttle that plies the river between them.

Le Batofar (opposite 11 quai François-Mauriac). As well as hosting live music—ranging in tastes from electro to dancehall—and DJ parties, the boat has several bars, a café, and an exhibition space onboard. You don't need to dance till dawn to enjoy the ambience (although many do); you can just while away an afternoon sitting on one of the decks and watching the scene unfold over a glass or two of wine. Le Batofar is a particularly good place to hang out in the heat of summer, when the venue becomes one of the hubs of the Paris Plage (see box). Beside the boat is the **Piscine Josephine-Baker** (quai François-Mauriac), a specially constructed barge complete with a pool with a retractable roof for open-air swimming in warm weather, a sunbathing deck, solaria, and a café.

Walk several blocks west from the Bibliothèque Nationale by the river and you'll venture into **La Petite Asie**, recognizable for its high-rise apartment blocks, the prominence of Asian supermarkets, such as Paristore and Tang Frères, and the lilt of Cantonese, Vietnamese, and Khmer spoken on the streets. Paris's main Chinatown, or *quartier chinois,* took seed in the 1980s, when Chinese refugees poured into Paris from the former colony of French Indochina (now Vietnam, Laos, and Cambodia). Although there are no traditional tourist sights here, this neighborhood is a lively place in which to walk, to stop for authentic Asian food (see p. 129), or to treat yourself to a swathe of sumptuous Vietnamese fabric.

West of the northern section of the avenue d'Italie is the increasingly fashionable but relatively unknown **Butte-aux-Cailles** (Quails' Hill), which retains a village-like atmosphere (until 1860 it was actually fenced off from the city). Full of one-off cafés, restaurants, and stores on quaint cobblestoned streets lined with Art Nouveau houses, the Butte was a hotbed of working-class rebellion during the Paris Commune of 1871, for which there is a memorial at the Place de la Commune.

The Butte is largely colonized by artists, some of whom inhabit the timbered, steep-roofed former workers' villas of Petit Alsace, while others have made their homes in the little villas with hidden gardens of Petite Russie, which were built for Russian immigrants fleeing the Revolution. The standout architecture of the Butte also includes the 1920s **Piscine Butte-aux-Cailles** (5 place Paul-Verlaine), built on the site of a bathhouse that profited from a natural hot spring nearby. Today, the building retains its Art Nouveau exterior and has two outdoor pools that are heated year-round by the same hot spring.

Post-swim, choose from several charming spots to replenish your energy levels: **L'Oisive Thé** (1 rue Jean-Marie-Jego), a tea salon whose name translates as "idleness"; **Hansel and Gretel** (43 rue des Cinq Diamants), a tea salon and restaurant specializing in Alsace pastries, hot chocolates, and bouquets of lollipops; or, the sweetest of all, **Les Abeilles** (21 rue de la Butte-aux-Cailles), a "bee boutique" that sells more than fifty kinds of honey (including some from a local apiary), honey soaps, and house specialities such as

Leckerlis de Bâle, a spicy gingerbread with almonds, orange, and lemon peel. Les Abeilles also publishes its own newspaper, *Le petit journal des abeilles*, with articles for beekeepers, local parents and kids, and "any stray bees who happen to be passing through the Butte."

Due north in the 13th arrondissement, step back in time at the **Manufacture des Gobelins** (42 avenue des Gobelins), a fifteenth-century dye works that was transformed into a workshop to supply tapestry and furniture to the royal court. The factory, which is still charged with making tapestries for the state, invites visitors to admire the seventeenth-century looms and antique tapestries, to learn about weaving techniques, and to watch modern weavers at work during afternoon guided tours.

THE EYE OF PARIS

The modest rue de la Glacière to the far west of the 13th arrondissement was once home to a man who produced some of the most iconic views of Paris: the Hungarian-born photographer Brassaï. In the former Hôtel des Terrasses (64 rue de la Glacière), Brassaï set up a darkroom in the corner of his room and "for hour after hour," as his novelist friend Henry Miller (see pp. 108–109) related, "pored over [the] nightly harvest of photographs" that culminated in his 1933 book *Paris de nuit (Paris by Night)*. Although the subject matter was ordinary, these pictures—often taken in fog—possess an eerie, almost supernatural quality.

Rising at dusk, Brassaï would prowl the gaslit streets, photographing cafés, brothels such as the Chez Suzy, dance halls such as the Folies-Bergère (see pp. 80–81), and opium dens, along with the barflies, small-time crooks, cabaret performers, and "fallen" women who frequented them. Recognizable by the camera, tripod, and cumbersome bag of glass photographic plates that he carried around, Brassaï was often accompanied by Miller or other literary friends, such as Ernest Hemingway and the poet Léon-Paul Fargue.

These were images in which Miller saw "my own sacred body exposed, the body that I have written into every stone, every tree, every monument, park, fountain, statue, bridge, and dwelling of Paris." His reaction to Brassaï's photographs may not be as excessive as it first appears: these were aspects of French life that had not been photographed before and, especially, had not been documented by someone with such a perceptive—and provocative—vision as Brassaï, as anyone who looks at a work such as "Grosse poule, quartier d'Italie" ("Fat Whore, Italian Quarter")—taken in the 13th arrondissement—would attest.

But Brassäi did not spend all his time scrutinizing Paris's 1930s underbelly and recording it for posterity. As he wrote to his parents in the early 1930s: "It did happen that having spent the night among workers [...] and vagabonds, roughnecks and streetwalkers, I would be invited the next day to a soirée or masked ball of the aristocracy..." He also made portraits of many of his artist friends in the intimacy of their studios, among them Henri Matisse (see pp. 194–195), Pablo Picasso (see p. 34), and Alberto Giacometti.

After settling in Paris, Brassäi never returned to his homeland. In 1947 he became stateless, then he married his French girlfriend, Gilberte Mercedes Boyer—twenty years his junior—the following year. Boyer would take an active role in furthering her husband's career, helping to develop prints, writing descriptions of his subjects, and driving him around Paris on hunts for graffiti to photograph. She is also featured wearing a traditional Breton *coiffe* in a few of his images.

In addition to his photography, Brassaï was a talented artist. According to Picasso, Brassaï's drawings were even better than his photographs. His favorite subject, it seems, was women's buttocks—as Boyer once confided: "He agreed with the sculptor Aristide Maillol (see p. 16), who liked to say that they are the most beautiful form that nature has created."

Brassaï died in 1984 and was laid to rest in the Cimetière du Montparnasse (see pp. 112–113), in the company of many of his artist friends.

14TH AND 15TH: ART COLONIES AND OLD BONES

From the rue de la Glacière, it's a long, straight road up to Montparnasse. Take a detour off the boulevard St-Jacques if you're hooked on the story of Henry Miller and his sojourn in Paris. The writer lived for a while in the far south of the 14th at the Villa Seurat, a short street that was built as an artists' colony in the 1920s and named after the Pointillist painter Georges Seurat. It's here, in 1931, that Miller began writing *Tropic of Cancer* while staying with his poet and critic friend Michael Fraenkel. It's also where, encouraged by Fraenkel, he began writing in the manner in which he spoke, leading Miller to conclude: "The process of losing myself began at the Villa Seurat."

In 1934 (on the very day that *Tropic of Cancer* was published), Miller moved back to the Villa Seurat, though into a different apartment (no. 18), which, for a time, he shared with his lover Anaïs Nin, who had negotiated a good rent for him. Although Miller spent some passionate and productive hours at Nin's home in the suburbs at Louveciennes (see pp. 108–109), he was blissfully creative in his apartment in the 14th. It was here that he

FERTILE GROUND

The influential and free-spirited diarist Anaïs Nin found Henry Miller the much-loved apartment she occasionally shared with him at Villa Seurat, and also spent some time living on a Seine houseboat with another lover, Gonzalo More. Yet her heart was in the western suburbs of Paris, in the village of Louveciennes. It was in the house she rented at 2 bis, rue Montbuisson in Louveciennes that her writing really took off, leading her to describe the place as the "laboratory of her soul" in her journals.

Louveciennes was an inspired choice: it's home to a château that Louis XV gave the courtesan Madame du Barry as a love nest. It was also a favorite among Impressionist painters—Claude Monet (see pp. 174–175), Pierre-August Renoir, Camille Pissarro, Alfred Sisley, and others—who are estimated to have represented it in a combined total of more than 120 canvases. Louveciennes was also home to composer Camille Saint-Saëns in the 1860s. In addition, in 1959 Brigitte Bardot married Jacques Charrier in the village. Nin described it as resembling, in her mind, the village where Gustave Flaubert's famous adulteress Madame Bovary (see p. 177) lived and died.

It was at her Louveciennes house, in 1931, that Nin first met Henry Miller. After hearing about him through a mutual friend, at whose apartment Miller was crashing, the twenty-eight-year-old Nin read an article that he had written on the movie director Luis Buñuel. She fell in love with his words, which she felt were "slung like hatchets [...] like [...] wild drums in the midst of the Tuileries gardens," and invited him to dinner. Afterward she told her diary: "I have met Henry Miller ... When he first stepped out of the car and walked towards the door where I stood waiting, I saw a man I liked. In his writing he is flamboyant, virile, animal, magnificent. He is a man whom life makes drunk, I thought. He is like me."

Miller, for his part, described Nin's house as "an astrologic den, with violet blue lights and zodiacs on the wall, apricot-colored dining room and peach blossom bedrooms, black painted bookcases, bowls filled with strange stones."

It was a year later, after several flirty rendezvous at the Scandinavian-themed café Le Viking (29–31 rue Vavin), just off the boulevard du Montparnasse, that things went further between Nin and Miller. On March 4, 1932, the pair had a dispute at their favorite haunt, criticizing each other's approaches to writing. Nin left the table to dance the rumba alone. When she returned, Miller told her that he had seen the extent of her passionate nature in the way in which she moved. Nin responded with a note in violet ink, stating:

"I will be the one woman you will never have." After she left, Miller wrote her a letter of his own: "Three minutes after you have gone. No I can't restrain it. I tell you what you already know—I love you [...] Without you realizing it I have been living with you constantly. But I have been afraid to admit it—I thought it would terrify you."

Four days later they met again at Le Viking, where, faced by Nin's resistance, Miller took matters into his own hands. Wrote Nin: "Suddenly he leans over and engulfs me in a tremendous kiss. I do not want the kiss to end. He says, 'Come back to my room'." You can actually stay in the room in question—number 40 at the Hôtel Central (1 bis, rue du Maine, www.central-hotel-paris.com)—to re-enact the encounter.

From Louveciennes, Nin would send Miller notes when her spouse, Hugh, went away on business, commanding him: "Come and be my husband for a few days." But even when Hugh was home, Miller would be squirreled away in a guest room, and once Nin even set up an office for him in the old billiards room in Madame du Barry's former estate. In her diary, she confessed: "When he is here, Louveciennes is rich for me, alive. My body and mind vibrate continuously. I am not only more woman, but more writer, more thinker, more reader, more everything." Miller, meanwhile, described the period that began in Louveciennes as "the most important epoch of my life."

Louveciennes is thirty minutes by train from central Paris. A mecca for Nin fans over the years, the house on the rue Montbuisson bears a plaque commemorating Nin's residency here. Her home at Louveciennes fell into disrepair for a long time but is now home to Jean-Hugues Anglade, star of the film *Betty Blue*.

---

wrote *Tropic of Capricorn*, *Black Spring*, and *Max and the White Phagocytes*, as well as being the place where he entertained fellow writers, friends, and a whole range of Montparnasse characters. As his Austrian writer-friend Alfred Perlès said: "Henry Miller radiated from No. 18. Radiated is the correct word. There was a quixotic mood of coercion hanging about the place, like an atmosphere. On approaching, the least sensitive visitor must have become aware of an exceptional presence."

Head back up to boulevard St-Jacques and follow it as far as the Place Denfert-Rochereau. The previous name of this square was the Place d'Enfer (Hell Square), which seems fitting when you come upon the entrance to the gloomily romantic subterranean world of **Les Catacombes de Paris**—a repository for the bones of millions of Parisians brought here in the 1780s from the city's overcrowded, disease-infested cemeteries. Les Catacombes occupy part of a vast network of Roman quarries and tunnels that connect to form a

LOVE ON THE BEAT

When singer-songwriter Serge Gainsbourg died in 1991, then-president François Mitterrand described him as "our Baudelaire, our Apollinaire... [who] elevated the song to the level of art." His acclaim came in spite of the provocative nature of much of Gainsbourg's work, which included "Les sucettes," a song that, unbeknownst to the eighteen-year-old singer for whom he wrote it, was about licking more than *sucettes* (lollipops), and "Je t'aime moi non plus," which was publicly condemned by the Vatican for its erotic grunting and groaning. Perhaps most shocking of all was a song from the 1984 album *Love on the Beat*: a duet set to Frédéric Chopin's Etude No. 3 and called "Lemon Incest," which Gainbourg sang with his daughter Charlotte.

Gainsbourg never ran shy of excess, describing drinking, cigarettes, and beautiful women, as his "trilogy [...] an equilateral triangle, shall we say, of Gitanes, alcoholism, and girls." His lovers and co-singers included starlet Brigitte Bardot and the British actress and singer Jane Birkin, whom he may have wed in secret, which would have made her his third wife. The pair met while filming the movie *Slogan*. After shooting ended, Gainsbourg wooed Birkin by taking her on a nightlong tour of Paris clubs.

It was with Birkin that Gainbourg released his infamous "Je t'aime moi non plus." Modestly described by Gainsbourg as "the ultimate love song," it came out in 1969, as part of the album *69 Année érotique* (*69 Erotic Year*). The couple also collaborated on the 1971 concept album *Histoire de Melody Nelson*, about a middle-aged man who crashes his Rolls Royce into the bicycle of the eponymous nymphet in order to seduce her. The LP is widely regarded as Gainsbourg's masterpiece.

Birkin left Gainsbourg after thirteen years but they remained friends, and he continued to write songs for her, as well as for his third (or maybe fourth) wife, Bambou. After their breakup, Gainsbourg went on a downward spiral, and as one of his friends put it, "spent ten years committing suicide." He was buried among other great artists in the Cimetière du Montparnasse (see pp. 112–113). His apartment at 5 bis, rue de Verneuil in the 7th, which is adorned with poems and graffiti, is a pilgrimage site for fans, who still bring gifts, including packets of Gitanes.

---

honeycomb of nearly two hundred miles of galleries and caverns beneath the city, although not all of them are linked to this particular section. Charles X used to throw parties below ground before the Revolution, and the Resistance used the underground tunnels as their headquarters during World War II. Even today, the city's police find evidence of modern-day troglodytes: in 2004 a restaurant and a movie theater that had been used to screen film noir and modern thrillers were discovered in a cavern below the 16th arrondissement. There is often talk of other "cataphile" goings-on, ranging from subterranean picnics to orgies. There's even a special police force, dubbed *les cataflics*, which patrols Paris's subterranean world.

As you wander through the twilight world of the Catacombes, you will be glad of a lover's company—and a hand to hold—as you uncover row after row of skulls and other osseous relics of the remains of five or six million people, accompanied by the occasional quote on the inescapability of death. Creepily, the remains were brought across the city by handcart, under cover of night.

Get into the right frame of mind for artistic Montparnasse by heading to the **Fondation Cartier pour l'Art Contemporain** (261 boulevard Raspail). This museum of contemporary art surrounded by landscaped garden showcases up-and-coming artists, but also features work by stellar names such as Juergen Teller, Robert Adams, and David Lynch. It's so hip that the Velvet Underground and Patti Smith have performed here, as part of the ongoing series of "Nomadic Nights" nocturnal rendezvous, which feature performance art, fashion, and literature.

It's a short distance to Montparnasse proper, with its monolithic 1970s skyscraper. This section of Paris, like most of the neighboring 13th arrondissement, isn't very scenic. Oozing artistic history, however, Montparnasse will reward every scrap of shoe leather expended padding the sidewalks of its wide boulevards. You may want to begin at the **Tour Montparnasse** (15 avenue du Maine) itself. Although it is much reviled for the brutality of its architecture, the tower offers incredible, panoramic views of the city—as far as Orly Airport—from its 56th-floor outdoor viewing deck, restaurant, and café-bar. Come in the evening to witness a heart-stopping sunset, or catch one of the best views of the illuminated Eiffel Tower (see pp. 64–65), over a glass of champagne.

Like its sister cemeteries, Père-Lachaise (see pp. 84–86) and Montmartre (see pp. 113–121), the nearby **Cimetière du Montparnasse** bears the remains of a huge number of artistic greats from the Parisian scene. Wandering its pathways will bring you into contact with the poet Charles Baudelaire (see p. 40), Hungarian-born photographer Brassaï (see pp. 106–107), opera-house designer Charles Garnier, crooner Serge Gainsbourg (see pp. 110–111), and actress Jean Seberg, the American star of *À bout de souffle* (see p. 57), among others. Here, as elsewhere, lovers remain united in death—most notably, Jean-Paul Sartre and Simone de Beauvoir, who lived in separate rooms on separate floors of the **Hôtel Mistral** (24 rue Cels), just south of the cemetery, during the 1930s and, intermittently, during World War I. The hotel still exists, bearing a large white plaque with quotes from each on the subject of their relationship. Sartre's reads: "But there is one thing that never changes, which cannot change: which is that whatever happens, and whatever I become, I shall become it with you." Perhaps more telling, given the realities of their relationship (see p. 53), and certainly in a spirit more befitting the creed of Existentialism, is De Beauvoir's remark: "I was lying when I said that we are one. Between two individuals, harmony is never given, but must be won over and over again."

Sartre and De Beauvoir are more commonly associated with the St-Germain district just north of here (see p. 44), but De Beauvoir was born on the boulevard Raspail, spent part of her childhood on the boulevard du Montparnasse, and as a young woman lived on the rue de la Gaîté and at the Hôtel des Bains on rue Delambre. From 1955 until her death in 1986, she had a large studio apartment on rue Victor Schoelcher, the street running up the eastern side of the cemetery. For a few years she shared this studio with the young journalist and filmmaker Claude Lanzmann, while she was still in a relationship with Sartre. Meanwhile, Sartre took up with Lanzmann's sister, the actress Evelyne Rey, who went on to kill herself when he ended their long affair.

The Cimetière du Montparnasse is also home to the photographer Man Ray (see pp. 116–117) and his last wife, the dancer Juliet Browner. Browner died fifteen years after

Man Ray, but she was interred in the same tomb, which bears the epitaph: "Together again." Not too far away is the burial site of Man Ray's first wife, Kiki de Montparnasse. Pick up a map at the cemetery entrance to find these and other romantic spots; with a total of 34,000 graves, there's lots to discover. Don't miss *La séparation du couple*, a marble sculpture that depicts a naked man weeping bitterly as his paramour sinks into her grave. Once deemed too "obscene" for the Jardin du Luxembourg (see p. 51), the sculpture was brought here in 1965. There's also *Le baiser (The Kiss)* by Romanian sculptor Constantin Brancusi, a monument for his friend, the Russian medical student Tanya Rachewskaia, who killed herself out of love in 1910. Brancusi himself lies in another part of the cemetery.

A bit more lighthearted is the nearby tomb of inventor Charles Pigeon, which takes the form of a bed on which he lies with his wife, while an angel on top of their headboard watches over them. Don't worry if all these romantic associations make you linger too long. The tinkle of the guard's handbell as he makes his closing-time rounds of the cemetery will ensure that you don't get locked in for the night.

A few steps from the Cimetière du Montparnasse is the modern clamor of the vast **boulevard du Montparnasse**. Not as visually charming as many other streets in Paris, the boulevard is worth visiting for its historic cafés and restaurants, where artistic ghosts flit among modern-day diners. Montparnasse took over from Montmartre (see p. 90) as the city's creative hub in the *années folles* (crazy years) of the early twentieth century. Gritty and even sordid, it attracted poor and immigrant painters, sculptors, novelists, poets, and composers, many of whom were based in the rat-infested studios of La Ruche in the 15th arrondissement (see p. 119).

THE LOVERS OF MONTPARNASSE

One of the most tragic Parisian love affairs played itself out in the 6th arrondissement, just off the boulevard du Montparnasse, on rue de la Grande Chaumière. It was here in 1917 that the charismatic Italian painter Amadeo Modigliani met the striking nineteen-year-old art student and model Jeanne Hébuterne at the Académie Colarossi. The school was a hothouse for modern artists: Auguste Rodin (see pp. 61–62) taught here, and Camille Claudel and Paul Gauguin were among the students.

Hébuterne was disowned by her conservative and religious family when she took up with the wild and dissolute Modigliani, whose first one-man exhibition was closed down by the police because of the number of nudes it featured. After a spell in Nice, the couple rented an apartment on the same Paris street where they had met. Here, they painted portraits of one another and brought up their daughter, who was also named Jeanne. But Modigliani had long suffered from tuberculous meningitis, and this, combined with his heavy drinking, resulted in his death at just thirty-five years of age. A neighbor discovered his body with his distraught wife wrapped around him, unable to leave his side. Pregnant but inconsolable, Jeanne killed herself two days later by backing out of a fifth-floor window.

The two share a suitably artistic grave—often strewn with roses, and bearing the epitaphs "Struck down by Death at the moment of glory" and "Devoted companion to the extreme sacrifice"—in the Cimetière du Père-Lachaise (see pp. 84–86). It was not always so: Hébuterne was first buried outside Paris, and it took ten years for her family to relent and allow her to be brought to her common-law husband's side. It took even longer—more than thirty years—for them to consent to public access to Hébuterne's paintings, which are now often shown at Modigliani exhibitions around the world.

Two movies recount the romance: *Les amants de Montparnasse (The Lovers of Montparnasse*; 1958) with Gérard Philipe as Modigliani and Anouk Aimée as Hébuterne, and the English-language *Modigliani* (2004), starring Andy Garcia and Elsa Zylberstein.

The boulevard du Montparnasse is where artists met, exchanged news and ideas, and just plain partied. Some cafés let poverty-stricken artists rent tables by the hour for a few centimes, or accepted drawings as securities on debts, holding them and often displaying them on their walls until the artist was in a position to pay. Brasseries that have survived include **La Closerie des Lilas** (No. 171), where you'll find tables with brass nameplates for the likes of James Joyce and F. Scott Fitzgerald, and **Le Dôme** (No. 108), which Ernest Hemingway mentions in his Paris memoir *A Moveable Feast* (see pp. 120–121). Then there's **La Rotonde** (No. 105) and **Le Select** (No. 99), which was the first café to stay open all night.

The most famous, arguably, is **La Coupole** (102 boulevard Montparnasse; see also p. 129), the opening of which was attended by Jean Cocteau in 1927. A favorite of Picasso (see p. 34), sculptor Alberto Giacometti, painter Yves Klein, and others, La Coupole was also where Surrealist poet and novelist Louis Aragon (see p. 89) met his future wife and muse, the Russian-born writer Elsa Triolet. Henry Miller, Anaïs Nin (see pp. 108–109), and Lawrence Durrell spent so much time drinking and playing chess together here during the late 1930s that Durrell dubbed them "the three musketeers of La Coupole."

The poet Max Jacob said he came to Montparnasse to "sin disgracefully," and indeed, many of Montparnasse's famous faces also frequented Le Sphinx, which stood on boulevard Edgar-Quinet back toward the cemetery. An upscale brothel, Le Sphinx was mentioned by the photographer Brassaï (see pp. 106–107) in his book *The Secret Paris of the '30s*, in which he describes how: "the men could bring their wives and children. Going to the Sphinx was like a family outing. The little boys would stare wide-eyed at the Sylphs offering their charms, weaving stark naked in and out among the tables [...] For these children, the mystery had gone out of the huge numerals, the closed shutters." Giacometti said it was "a place more marvellous than any other," and he created a bronze entitled *Quatre figurines sur base (Four Figures on a Base)* depicting the naked women that he had seen there. The same street was also home to the lesbian nightclub Le Monocle (60 boulevard Edgar-Quinet).

MAN AND WOMEN

Buried in the Cimetière du Montparnasse with his last love, Juliet Browner, the American photographer Man Ray (born Emmanuel Radnitzky) was involved with several key women of the bohemian Montparnasse scene. Indeed, Alice Prin, his first companion during much of the decade that followed his arrival in Paris, was such a force in the 14th that she became known as Kiki de Montparnasse (*kiki* is lewd Spanish slang).

Man Ray—who at the time was still married to but separated from the Belgian poet Adon Lacroix—met Kiki in a café after seeing her have a slanging match with a waiter who wouldn't serve her because she wasn't wearing a hat. Street-savvy since being sent by her grandmother to the city to live with her mother at the age of twelve, Kiki was already working as a model for some of the foremost artists of the time, including Jean Cocteau, Maurice Utrillo, and Max Ernst (see p. 95). She moved in with Man Ray and posed for some of his most famous images, including *Le violon d'Ingres*, in which her body appears to have been partially transformed into a musical instrument, a Surrealist twist on the classic nude photograph. Man Ray achieved this by painting onto a photographic print and then re-photographing it. The title of the work references the painter Jean-Auguste-Dominique Ingres, from whom Man Ray drew his inspiration for the photograph. It also refers to the French idiom for a hobby, suggesting that the turbanned Kiki was Man Ray's favorite "pastime," just as the violin was Ingres's. Kiki was more than a toy, however. An artist in her own right, she sold out her exhibition at the Galerie au Sacre du Printemps in 1927, and was also a successful cabaret singer, performing clad in black hose and garters with her mouth painted into a Cupid's bow.

Kiki also starred in some of Man Ray's experimental short films, including *L'etoile de mer (The Starfish)*, which, adapted from a Surrealist poem by Man Ray's friend Robert Desnos, depicts the unraveling of a relationship. Partially shot through a sheet of glass to emphasize the distance between the couple and the fragility of their bond, the film bespeaks Man Ray's insecurities about his real-life relationship with Kiki: the pair separated not long after the film opened in 1928.

Man Ray was not alone for long. In 1929 he was quite literally accosted in Le Bâteau Ivre café by Lee Miller, an American *Vogue* model who had made up her mind to live in Paris and study with the man she regarded as the city's best photographer. Miller had just been to Man Ray's studio and been told by the concierge that he had gone away for the summer. Chancing upon her idol in the café, she walked up and introduced herself as his "new assistant." When Man Ray replied, "I don't take assistants, and anyway I am leaving now for my vacation," she countered, "Fine, I am coming with you."

May Ray fell hard for the beautiful yet coolly androgynous Miller, but their collaboration went beyond the physical. Together they perfected the technique of solarization: the exposure of partly developed prints to a flash of light to create an image that is both negative and positive, a process that Miller had discovered during an accident in the darkroom. The couple also worked on commercial projects such as brochures and society portraiture together, although Miller is said to have urged Man Ray to leave the money-earning work to her so that he could concentrate on his art.

Despite this spirit of self-sacrifice, Miller became a famous photographer in her own right, sometimes using Man Ray as a model just as he did her—most famously in her affectionate and playful "Man Ray Shaving." She also took some memorable shots of Pablo Picasso (see p. 34) and of Paris during photographic excursions with Man Ray, including her image entitled "Walkway, Paris." But the relationship itself was not to last. Unusually for a woman, Miller insisted on an open relationship, something Man Ray found difficult to accept. During Miller's affair with interior designer Zizzi Svirsky, Man Ray wrote to his partner, "I have loved you terrifically, jealously: it has reduced every other passion in me ..."

The couple split in 1931, after Miller fell in love with Aziz Eloui Bey, a wealthy Egyptian whose ravishing wife, Nimet Eloui Bey, had posed for both her and Man Ray. Nimet drank herself to death in a hotel room as a result, while Man Ray's dramatic reaction was ultimately bluster: he photographed himself with a rope round his neck, holding a gun, and then stalked the streets with his gun in his raincoat pocket, muttering about murder and suicide.

World War II forced Man Ray's return to the States, where he met Juliet Browner. The pair had a double wedding with their friends Max Ernst and Dorothea Tanning in 1946 and later returned to Paris. After Man Ray's death, Juliet gave many of his works to museums and set up a trust for his estate.

Meanwhile, rue de la Gaîté off boulevard Edgar-Quinet was home to several great music halls, including the **Bobino**, which, after a history of changing hands, is again a cabaret. This is where Josephine Baker (see pp. 80–81) gave her last performance in 1975 at the age of sixty-eight. Other greats to have graced its stage are Georges Brassens (see p. 119), Jacques Brel, Juliette Gréco (see p. 54), and Edith Piaf (see pp. 87–88). The Bobino was also featured in Joris-Karl Huysmans's first published novel *Marthe, histoire d'une fille (Martha, Story of a Girl)*—with "fille" connoting a prostitute. In the novel the heroine works in the club while carrying on a doomed love affair with a journalist.

If a raunchy cabaret is not your scene, just around the corner is the legendary **Rosebud** (11 bis, rue Delambre). This North American–style bar serves up U.S. favorites such as chili con carne amidst original 1930s décor and an intellectual vibe dating from its 1950s heyday, when it was a popular hangout for Jean-Paul Sartre (see p. 53), playwright Eugène Ionesco, novelist Marguerite Duras, and other stars of the literary firmament. It's still a good place to come and knock back an excellent Bloody Mary or whisky sour in the company of writers, journalists, painters, and the occasional huddle of students. Drinks are served up by bartenders in white tuxedoes to a soundtrack of old jazz records.

Further east you might like to pay homage to the two-star **Hôtel Istria** (29 rue Campagne Première), home to an incredible number of creative geniuses during the glory days of the 14th arrondissement, including Marcel Duchamp, Rainer Maria Rilke, Erik Satie (see p. 176), Tristan Tzara, Josephine Baker (see pp. 80–81), and Louis Aragon and his wife Elsa Triolet. Man Ray and Kiki de Montparnasse (see pp. 116–117) lived here for a while, too, before moving to the neighboring building. Kiki used to dance in Montparnasse's first nightclub, Le Jockey Club, which stood on the corner of rue Campagne Première and the boulevard du Montparnasse.

Beyond the Montparnasse Tower, in the 15th arrondissement, you will come upon the delightful ivy- and rose-swathed **Musée du Montparnasse** (21 avenue du Maine). Relatively new, this museum is housed in the former studio of Russian painter Marie Vassilieff, who provided drawing lessons, lectures, and conversation to many of the avant-garde artists of the early twentieth century, including her teacher Henri Matisse (see pp. 194–195) and Amadeo Modigliani (see p. 114). During World War I she turned the space into a canteen for struggling artists, serving up a glass of wine and a meal for a few centimes. These gatherings turned into raucous night-long parties at a time when Paris's restaurants and cafés were subject to a curfew; one such night saw a famous spat between a drunken Modigliani and the tiny Vassilieff, who pushed her fellow artist down the stairs when he arrived to pick a fight after not having been invited to a gathering attended by the writer Beatrice Hastings, with whom he had recently split up, and her new beau.

The museum is hidden away in a little cobblestoned alley with a flower store and a small artistic community of painters, architects, movie directors, producers, and actors. Inside the museum you can see temporary exhibitions based on the lives and work of "Les Montparnos," as the artists were known.

Nearby, the **Musée Bourdelle** (16–18 rue Antoine-Bourdelle) is another off-the-beaten-track museum, dedicated to the painter Antoine Bourdelle, whose work provides a bridge between the naturalism of Auguste Rodin (see pp. 62–63), his teacher, and the attenuated "shadow" figures of Alberto Giacometti, his pupil (see p. 116). Among the exhibition spaces of the museum and its inviting sculpture courtyard are plenty of intimate nooks, including the sculptor's musty old studio, which—filled with unfinished pieces, his threadbare bed, and his stove—looks just as it was when he died in 1929.

It's a fair walk southwest of here to the circular building known as **La Ruche** (the Beehive; 2 passage Dantzig). Designed by Gustav Eiffel as a temporary wine rotunda for the Exposition Universelle de Paris of 1900, the building was relocated to the 15th arrondissement to provide cheap studio spaces for young artists. Guillaume Apollinaire, Marc Chagall (see pp. 193-196), Robert Delaunay (see pp. 36–37), Amadeo Modigliani (see p. 114), Diego Rivera, and many others washed up here in the early twentieth century, making it the Montparnasse equivalent of Montmartre's Bateau-Lavoir (see p. 91).

La Ruche contains working studios to this day, having been saved from demolition a few decades back by its supporters, who included Jean-Paul Sartre (see p. 93), Alexander Calder, and Jean Renoir. You may write the Fondation La Ruche-Seydoux (2 passage Dantzig, Paris 75015) ahead of time to request a tour, or you can peruse old photographs and films of its residents at the Musée du Montparnasse (see opposite page).

There's still more to see in this little-visited quarter, most notably the **Parc Georges Brassens**, which occupies land that was a horse-market and abattoirs until the 1970s, and before that, the grounds for a market, gardens, and vineyards. The park is named for the singer Georges Brassens, who lived nearby at 9 impasse Florimont and later at 42 rue Santos-Dumont. Look out for Brassens's bust inside the park and for the pathways named after his songs. At the park entrance you'll note some magnificent bronze statues of hot-blooded bulls by animal sculptor Auguste-Nicolas Cain, which were brought here from the Trocadéro (see p. 122). Within the confines of the park are some of the impressive remnants from the market and abattoirs themselves, including gates topped by horse statues and an old belfry. There's also a belvedere perched on a wooded hill, a tiny vineyard, a rose garden, an herb garden, a scented garden that includes jasmine and honeysuckle, and a handful of beehives. Come on the weekend and browse through the antique and second-hand book market held in the old horse-trading hall.

BOOK LOVERS' PARIS

Paris has been the setting for many great works of literature. The following are guaranteed to whet your appetite in advance of your trip, or bring them along for the ride. Alternatively, look out for copies at book markets such as the one in the Parc Georges Brassens (see p. 119), at the stalls of the *bouquinistes* who line the Seine, or in the vast array of Parisian bookstores.

The city's best-known English-language bookseller is **Shakespeare & Co** (5 rue de la Bûcherie) in the 5th arrondissement, which has served as a hangout for many of the city's great writers, both expats and native, as well as the setting for the opening scene of the romantic movie *Before Sunset* (see p. 57).

- NANA (1880), Émile Zola. The masterpiece of the great chronicler of nineteenth-century society. The story follows a slum-born girl who becomes a high-class prostitute exploiting the decadent morals of her time. See also page 16.
- LÀ-BAS OR DOWN THERE/THE DAMNED (1891), Joris-Karl Huysmans. In nocturnal fin-de-siècle Paris, writer Durtal becomes obsessed with demonology while pursing an affair with the seductive Madame Chantelouve, who introduces him to the city's underbelly.
- THE PHANTOM OF THE OPERA (1911), Gaston Leroux. A classic novel—and originally a serialization—about a deformed man who lives in the catacombs of the Palais Garnier opera house (see p. 76) and secretly loves one of its stars.
- NADJA (1928), André Breton. Love goes mad in this elusive autobiographical novel by the leader of the Surrealist movement (see p. 78).
- THE DIARY OF ANAÏS NIN, VOLUME I (1931–34), Anaïs Nin. The first volume of the famous journals dealing with Nin's life in Louveciennes (see pp. 108–109), including the publication of her study on D. H. Lawrence and her meeting with Henry Miller.
- TROPIC OF CANCER (1934), Henry Miller's groundbreaking autobiographical novel about a young writer's literary and sexual adventures in 1930s Paris.
- GOOD MORNING, MIDNIGHT (1939), Jean Rhys. The British novelist's tale about a woman who returns to Paris to confront her memories—good and bad—in its cafés and bars.
- MAIGRET AND THE MAN ON THE BOULEVARD (1953), Georges Simenon. A man found stabbed in an alley off the boulevard St-Martin is discovered to have been leading a double life—of which his wife knew nothing.
- THE MANDARINS (1954), Simone de Beauvoir. Paris's intellectual society at the end of World War II is given a fictional spin with the Existentialist's roman à clef. The story of the novelist's own affair with Nelson Algren (see p. 53) features prominently.

- Giovanni's Room (1956), James Baldwin. The American novelist's story of a young man caught between his gay lover and conventional morality in 1950s Paris.
- A Moveable Feast (1964), Ernest Hemingway. The American novelist's account, posthumously published, of his life in 1920s Paris, featuring his first wife, Hadley, and literary associates—including F. Scott Fitzgerald (see p. 205), James Joyce, and Gertrude Stein—in the milieu of the now-famous Montparnasse brasseries (see p. 115).
- Perfume: The Story of a Murderer (1985), Patrick Süskind. The German novelist's tale of a boy from the slums of eighteenth-century Paris. His obsession with creating the ultimate perfume leads him to commit terrible crimes of passion (see p. 200).

There's another park named for a famous Frenchman to the far west of the 15th arrondissement beside the Seine. Once the site of an old Citroën car factory, the space was transformed into the quirky postmodern gardens of the **Parc André Citröen** in 1992. Follow the pathways that meander between themed and wild gardens, punctuated by vast hothouses filled with exotic and Mediterranean plants, stepping stones, computerized dancing fountains, and lawns; or take the suspended walkway alongside the elevated canal, and gaze at the reflected Parisian skies. In the Jardin en Mouvement, various wild grasses have been chosen for the different ways that they respond to wind speed. There are also six color-inspired gardens, each associated with a metal, a planet, a day of the week, a form of water, and a sense. The Silver Garden, for example, is associated with the metal silver, the moon, Monday, rivers, and sight. Best of all is the moored gas balloon, which takes you to an altitude of five hundred feet for gorgeous views of the Basilique du Sacré-Cœur (see p. 93), the cathedral of Notre-Dame (see p. 39), and the Seine as it flows through the heart of the city. Look across the Seine for a sneak preview of Paris's largest arrondissement, the 16th.

16TH: ACROSS THE WATER AND INTO THE TREES

Crossing the river north of the Parc André Citroën brings you to the Bois de Boulogne, a vast area of parkland two-and-a-half times larger than New York's Central Park. Before you allow yourself to claim its delights, consider another cultural interlude: north along the river, opposite the Eiffel Tower (see pp. 64–65), sprawls the impressive Palais de Chaillot, a two-part structure that was designed and built for the Exposition Internationale

of 1937 and now houses a strange mix of attractions: the Musée National de la Marine (National Maritime Museum); the Musée de l'Homme (Museum of Man); the new Cité de l'Architecture et du Patrimoine (City of Architecture & National Heritage), which includes the Musée National des Monuments Français (Museum of French Monuments), reopened after a period of dormancy; the Théâtre National de Chaillot; and a state-of-the-art aquarium. Each of these museums is of interest to those with a passion for its respective field, but the most objectively romantic is surely the **Musée National des Monuments Français**, with its three tranquil galleries filled with plaster models of historical buildings—both scale models and full-size reproductions of architectural elements—and sculptures from across history, with a focus on the French Romanesque and Gothic periods. The museum also houses frescoes and stained glass rescued from crumbling chateaus and churches, as well as fascinating and beguiling photographs of France in days gone by. It all seems a little spooky when you realize that some of the models were made from the molds of statues or windows that no longer exist.

Museums aside, the Trocadéro gardens are a good place to linger, with lawns surrounding cascading basins, water jets, and fountains, and statues that include the nudes *L'homme (The Man)* and *La femme (The Woman)* by Pierre Traverse and Daniel Bacqué respectively, and two sculpted blocks with more nude figures: *Jeunesse (Youth)* by Pierre Poisson and *Joie de vivre (Joy of Life)* by Léon Drivier. There's also a charming carousel beside the grounds should you fancy a spin.

Back toward the Place d'Iéna is the former mansion of the Vicomtesse Marie-Laure de Noailles. This eccentric aristocrat and patron of the avant-garde was the great-great-great-granddaughter of the libertine novelist the Marquis de Sade, while her maternal grandmother Laure de Sade was the inspiration behind one or more of Marcel Proust's characters in *À la recherche du temps perdu* (see p. 179). Marie and her bisexual husband, Charles, financed various avant-garde films, including Jean Cocteau's *Le sang d'un poète (The Blood of a Poet)* and Man Ray's *Les mystères du château de Dé (The Mysteries of the Chateau de Dé)*. In fact, the viscount and viscountess both appeared in the last film.

The mansion was legendary for its sparkling artistic gatherings and is now, fittingly, the headquarters of crystal manufacturer Baccarat, which boasts interiors designed by Philippe Starck and its own **Galerie-Musée Baccarat** (11 Place des États-Unis), which glitters with glasswork produced for exhibitions and world fairs, or commissioned by the wealthy or the famous such as Josephine Baker (see pp. 80–81), the emperor of Japan, and the Prince of Wales. One room of the gallery contains crystal furniture that was produced for Indian maharajahs and delivered to them on the backs of elephants. The restaurant on the premises, the Cristal Room, is a simply stunning place for a dinner date (see p. 130).

Paris's role as a global fashion capital is explored in the nineteenth-century palace of Maria de Brignole-Sale, duchess of Galliera, home to the **Musée Galliera de la Mode de la Ville de Paris** (10 avenue Pierre 1er de Serbie). Its ninety-thousand-plus fabulous items of haute couture and other fashions date back more than three centuries and include figure-constricting corsets, full-blown crinolines, and, for men, dashing uniforms and wedding suits. It's a great place to come on the Nuit des Musées (see p. 33)—past installations for the occasion have included gauzy *robes de lune* ("moon dresses") suspended from the ceiling to resemble shooting stars.

The wealthy area south and west of the Trocadéro, Passy, was home to Benjamin Franklin during the American Revolution, to the statesman Georges Clemenceau, whose apartment and garden you can visit (8 rue Benjamin Franklin), and to the writer Honoré de Balzac. Little-visited, the **Maison de Balzac** (47 rue Raynouard) is a tranquil spot where you can imbibe the atmosphere that reigned as the novelist sat at the very writing desk that you can still see today and corrected proofs for part of his epic *La comédie humaine*. Balzac's *comédie* is comprised of interlinking stories, plays, and novels—many of them set in Paris. Among the selection is *Mémoires de deux jeunes mariées (Letters of Two Brides)*, in which two young women—one who married for love, and the other who was more shrewdly calculating—exchange letters for more than a decade, charting the course of their respective relationships.

The **Cimetière de Passy** is not on the same scale as some of Paris's other cemeteries, but wandering its grounds, studying gravestones with the Eiffel Tower looming large over the river, makes for an unforgettable experience. This is the most aristocratic of Parisian graveyards, a fact attested to by the presence of a heated waiting room. Some unexpected names will pop up as you explore, including Bào Đại, the last emperor of Vietnam, and American silent film star Pearl White. There are also several familiar ones from the artistic sphere, including composer Claude Debussy, painter Édouard Manet, and Manet's sister-in-law Berthe Morisot, a talented artist in her own right. In fact, the world's largest collection of Morisot's work can be viewed just a short walk to the west, at the **Musée Marmottan Monet** (2 rue Louis-Boilly). Though the museum's name is misleading, it does boast the largest single collection of works by Claude Monet (see pp. 174–175), spanning every major stage of his career. Still, don't miss the chance to study Morisot's oeuvre, which includes a portrait of her husband Eugène Manet and their daughter Julie, plus other works by prominent Impressionists.

If you've lingered at Passy cemetery, don't miss the most impressive tomb of Marie Bashkirtseff, a Russian artist and feminist best known for her book *I Am the Most Interesting Book of All: The Diary of Marie Bashkirtseff*. It was Bashkirtseff who famously said: "Let us love only dogs! Men and cats are unworthy creatures." When she died of tuberculosis in 1884 at just twenty-five years of age, her remains were placed within a mausoleum re-creating her entire painting studio. It's now a historical national monument.

South of here, the 16th arrondissement surprises many visitors with the extraordinary wealth of its architectural heritage. If you were impressed by the Le Corbusier apartment within the Cité de l'Architecture et du Patrimoine in the Trocadéro (see p. 122), visit his **Villa La Roche** (10 square du Docteur Blanche). Designed in the 1920s as a private house for a banker and art collector, it is now a calm, light-infused museum with the world's largest collection of drawings, plans, and studies by the modernist architect.

This area is perhaps most fascinating for architecture lovers for the way it highlights the contrast between Le Corbusier's International style and the celebrated slightly earlier Art Nouveau work of Hector Guimard. Guimard's elaborate station entrances for the Paris métro, designed around 1900, are almost as iconic as the Eiffel Tower; the only two that have survived are in the 16th, at Porte Delphine and Place Victor Hugo. But this entire neighborhood, in which Guimard lived and worked, is dotted with the architect's trademark motifs: drooping, swirling, asymmetrical details appear on lampposts, street signs, and wrought-iron gates, or form the aesthetic for entire buildings. Fertile hunting grounds for Guimard's curving, cigarette smoke–like lines are the rue Françoise Millet, rue Agar, and Square Agar. As you spot these enchanting facets of architectural history, it's hard to imagine that Guimard was so derided in his lifetime; one journalist of the time described a particular gate as "a web woven by an inebriated spider."

Don't miss the **Hôtel Guimard** (122 avenue Mozart), a tall, narrow Art Nouveau mansion that Guimard built for his new wife, American portrait painter Adeline Oppenheim, and now apartments. The top story, with the large north-facing windows, was conceived as Oppenheim's studio, while the first floor served as the base for Guimard's own architectural practice. Close collaborators, Hector and Adeline lived by the motto, "Let's make our life a work of art." And so they did; Hector designed every aspect of their living arrangements from doorknobs, locks, and radiators to curtains and bedspreads. He even created Adeline's wedding dress and shoes when they married.

If the tale leaves you feeling romantic, take a slight detour to **Frédéric Malle** (140 avenue Victor Hugo). This perfume store, a dainty little boutique, is outfitted with a "smelling machine" that lets visitors experience the essence of the seventeen aromas created by nine world-class *parfumiers* and stored in the shop's refrigerated cabinets. Among the most seductive are "Carnal Flower," "Dans tes bras" ("In Your Arms"), and "French Lover."

At last we come to the **Bois de Boulogne**, a vast wooded park that has become infamous in recent years for its nighttime activities, although the city authorities have been working to eradicate the red-light district that has formed here. This ancient oak forest has long had its dark side: after housing several monasteries, it became overrun by robbers during the Hundred Years' War, then even after it became a pleasure ground when François I built the Château de Madrid (now demolished) on-site, highwaymen preyed on visitors.

Within the Bois de Boulogne, lawns alternate with clusters of surviving woodland that are threaded with winding *allées*, horse trails, and cycling paths. The cycling paths are a good place to come with one of the gray municipal Vélib' bicycles (www.velib.paris.fr). Pockets of privacy are easily found beside the park's numerous small lakes, ponds, and streams, although there are a few spots to seek out: the small neoclassical Château de Bagatelle with its orangery, lush rose garden, and water lily pond; the Jardin d'Acclimation, an amusement park with a little menagerie and a puppet theater; and the Jardin des Serres d'Auteuil, a botanical garden with hothouses.

The park's 1920s Château de la Muette (now offices) is the third castle to have been built on this site awash with history. The first was a hunting lodge that was adapted into a château for Henri IV's first wife, Marguerite de Valois. It was Louis XV, king from the age of nine, who rebuilt the castle extensively. He was also inordinately busy there, fathering ten royal children between 1727 and 1737, as well as entertaining many of his mistresses, including three who were sisters (Louise-Julie, Comtesse de Mailly; Pauline-Félicité, Marquise de Vintimille; and Marie-Anne de Mailly-Nesle, Duchesse de Châteauroux), Madame de Pompadour (see p. 137), and Madame du Barry (see p. 126). Later, the newly wed Louis XVI and Marie-Antoinette (see pp. 126–127) lived here.

If an elegant day at the horse races tempts you, the Bois is home to the Seine-side **Hippodrome de Longchamp**, a racecourse with its very own windmill. In early October, the Hippodrome hosts the prestigious Prix de l'Arc de Triomphe, when chic hats for women and suits and ties for men are the order of the day—this is Paris after all.

ROMANTIC CASTLES WITHIN EASY REACH OF PARIS

The Île-de-France *région* surrounding Paris is studded with charming castles awash with amorous associations. The highlights are:

PALACE OF VERSAILLES: The most-visited French chateau, Versailles lies thirteen miles southwest of Paris. Originally a hunting lodge, it was transformed by Louis XIV into one of the world's largest and most extravagant palaces, as well as a place from which to establish absolute personal rule. His first building campaign was completed in 1664, an event marked with a fabulous party, the "Plaisirs de l'île enchantée" ("Pleasures of the Enchanted Island"), which Louis gave, covertly, in honor of his mistress Louise de la Vallière. The pavilion of the Grand Trianon on the château's grounds was also built by Louis, for his next mistress, Françoise-Athénais de Rochechouart de Mortemart, Madame de Montespan—infamous for her involvement in the Affaire des Poisons (see p. 165). However, the current structure, which you can tour, was a later replacement that was inaugurated by the king and his secret wife, Françoise d'Aubigné Scarron, the Marquise de Maintenon.

Louis XIV's successor, Louis XV, continued in the same decadent vein, much to the disapproval of his wife Marie Leszczyńska but not of his mistresses Madame de Pompadour (see p. 137) and Madame du Barry (see p. 108), who had the run of a sumptuous second-floor apartment. Louis also built a small chateau on the grounds, the Petit Trianon, for Madame de Pompadour, but she died four years before construction ended, and it was Madame du Barry, and later Marie Antoinette, who enjoyed the run of it.

Louis IV's grandson, Louis XIV, scandalized by his grandfather's behavior, removed the secret "stairway of indiscretion" leading from the mistresses' quarters to the king's chamber. However, Marie-Antoinette, whom Louis XVI had married at the castle when he was the dauphin, carried on the tradition of extravagance and frivolity—to such a degree that the palace was stormed by a Revolutionary mob from Paris. In the splendid Chambre de la Reine (Queen's Bedroom), one can just make out the hidden door through which she escaped her assailants. The story is told in Sofia Coppola's film *Marie Antoinette* (2006), some of which—mainly the wedding-ball scenes—were shot on location here.

Should you wish to stay nearby, the Trianon Palace (www.trianonpalace.com) has grandeur and sophistication in keeping with its setting on the edge of the royal domain, with facilities that include a newly opened Guerlain spa and a two-Michelin-starred restaurant presided over by British super-chef Gordon Ramsay—so intimate that it has just ten tables.

Château de Fontainebleau: François I's former hunting lodge–turned palace is on the outskirts of the town of Fontainebleau within the forest of the same name, just thirty-five miles south of Paris. Other monarchs to live here (and to add to the palace) include Henri II and Catherine de Médicis.

As at Chenonceau (see pp. 141–147), Henri's mistress Diane de Poitiers's signature is prominent: the ballroom has the initials "H" and "D" interlaced. The palace was neglected after Louis XIV became preoccupied with Versailles but was restored to its former glory by Napoléon I (see p. 128), whose offices, bedroom, and bathroom you can still see. Other rooms include his wife Joséphine's Empire-style Salon Jaune (Yellow Salon), and the Queen's Boudoir or "Room of the Six Maries"—which counts Marie-Antoinette and Napoléon's second wife, Marie-Louise, among the six to occupy it.

The grounds feature a carp-filled lake with rowboats for hire, elegant parterres, and horse-drawn carriage rides. In one quiet corner of the grounds, you will find the informal Jardin de Diane (Diana's Garden), which includes a fountain topped with a statue of the hunting goddess with whom Diane de Poitiers associated herself (see pp. 141–147).

Fontainebleau has a wonderful hotel to detain you in the town for a night or two. L'Aigle Noir (www.hotelaiglenoir.com) offers honeymoon night/wedding anniversary packages, as well as Weekends Romantiques including two bottles of champagne, rose petals, and a box of erotic goodies. Room service is available most evenings, and there's a cozy salon with an honesty bar. If you want to buy your love some blooms, there's no better place than the florist Au Nom de la Rose (14 rue Grande) a few steps away.

Château de Malmaison: This chateau, twelve miles west of Paris, was purchased by Joséphine Bonaparte as a love nest for her husband Napoléon I. Within it are displays of some of their opulent clothing as well as a sampling of Napoléon-era decor, furnishings, and works of art. Located within the lovely grounds are nearly two hundred exotic species of plants that Joséphine was the first person in France to cultivate. Many exotic species of animals roamed freely through these grounds as well, including kangaroos, zebras, and black swans.

Although their relationship began passionately, Napoléon and Joséphine, a white Creole from Martinique, divorced as the result of her affair with a hussar lieutenant. Another possible reason for their split may have been her infertility, likely a result of the stress she suffered after being imprisoned during the Terror, when her first husband was guillotined. Napoléon and Joséphine remained on good terms, however, and Napoléon is quoted as having said: "I truly loved my Joséphine, but I did not respect her." His last words were "France, the Army, the Head of the Army, Joséphine."

Note that La Malmaison is near Louveciennes, should you wish to combine a visit to the chateau with a pilgrimage to the erstwhile home of erotic novelist Anaïs Nin.

COUPS DE COEUR

EATING

Le Temps des Cerises
18 rue de la Butte-aux-Cailles
+33 (0)1 45 89 69 48

The real deal, this workers' cooperative in the village-like Butte-aux-Cailles in the 13th arrondissement (see p. 105) seems frozen in time, serving tried-and-true rustic favourites and excellent wine. Its old-time atmosphere may even have you whistling the refrain to the eponymous song, written for the workers' uprising of the Commune de Paris and covered by many of the great French chansonniers. Clients old and new are welcomed as friends by the ebullient staff, while the "no cell phone" rule is a welcome touch, even if the place is almost invariably packed and noisy. As no reservations are taken, if there is no space to be found when you arrive, the staff will give you a little ticket and expedite you to the neighboring bar for an aperitif, with the promise to call you when a table is ready. The menu harbors such tempting dishes as foie gras with brioche, goat cheese wrapped in seaweed, Normandy blood sausage, and duck confit with gooseberries, plus a few dishes from farther afield (Spain, Italy, and Asia). This is a place to come and laugh, enjoy banter with the staff, and join in on conversations at neighboring tables.

Thai-Vien
56 avenue de Choisy
+33 (0)1 53 61 18 58

None of the restaurants in the Chinatown area of the 13th arrondissement will win any awards for their beauty, but Thai-Vien is worth crossing town for. Serving fully authentic Thai, Vietnamese, and Laotian dishes, it's also a great place for a fun, cheap date when you don't mind noise and bustle, and maybe even sharing a table with fellow diners. The canteenlike space holds only thirty covers, and no reservations are taken. Few concessions are made for the general French dislike of highly spiced food, although the delightful staff will guide you through the menu if you wish to avoid the real palate-scorchers. Specialties worth checking out are the *tom yam* (spicy shrimp and tomato soup) and *lab-sinh* (rare beef with lemongrass), washed down with pure coconut juice and rounded off by a silky-smooth *sai mai lo* (tapioca dessert) to share.

La Coupole
102 boulevard du Montparnasse
+33 (0)1 43 20 14 20

A legend from the moment it opened in the 1920s (see p. 115), La Coupole has remained an icon of glamour on a boulevard that has changed drastically since its artistic heyday. The decor alone, which includes twenty-seven columns embellished with paintings by students of Henri Matisse and Fernand Léger, and ornamental panels created by Marie Vassilieff (see p. 118), makes La Coupole worth the trip. The seafood bar is one of Paris's best, however, so make sure to treat yourself to oysters and a glass of champagne as you soak in the ambiance, among the ghosts of Ernest Hemingway, Henry Miller, and others. Or come to dance, as did Josephine Baker, Simone de Beauvoir, and Jean-Paul Sartre. Where it once offered tango and jazz, the basement club now plays everything from salsa to electro-soul and deep house. For further fascinating insights into La Coupole, take the free guided tour given by a local historian every Tuesday at 11 a.m.

Les Fondus de la Raclette
209 boulevard Raspail
+33 (0)1 43 27 00 13

The perfect spot for a gray winter's evening or a rainy lunchtime, Les Fondus de la Raclette is cozy and convivial, and ideal for sharing dishes. The wooden dining tables have grills built into them, so that you can melt your own raclette—a semi-firm, salted cheese from the mountainous Savoy region—before adding it to your plate of cured meats, potatoes, gherkins, baby onions, and sliced vegetables. Alternatively, you could share a fondue (cheese or chocolate), a *brasserade* (barbecued meats), or a *tartiflette* (sliced potatoes baked with lardons, Reblochon cheese, and white wine). You probably won't have room for one of the equally heartwarming desserts, but if you do, the apple crumble really stands out.

Cristal Room Paris
11 place des États-Unis
+33 (0)1 40 22 11 10

Possibly the most visually extravagant place to eat in all Paris—if not the entire world—the Cristal Room is set inside the former mansion that is also home to the Galerie-Musée Baccarat (see p. 123). You will dine in the very room where the Vicomtesse Marie-Laure de Noailles played host to the crème de la crème of the avant-garde art world. The interior has been updated by Philippe Starck and blends daring modernity with the mansion's original features: exposed bricks and pink-leather banquettes are juxtaposed with wooden panels, gilded moldings, giant crystal chandeliers, and playful nods to the Surrealist artists who once haunted the place. The extraordinary menu has been devised by Guy Martin of the Michelin-starred Le Grand Véfour (see p. 26)—think oyster ravioli, risotto with Parmesan and white truffle, and pigeon in pastry. The tableware is by Baccarat. For a very special intimate dinner, book the Salon Rose, where the pink of the padded ceiling, satin-clad walls, leather seating, and thick carpet is played off against a dramatic chandelier of black crystal. The Salon also features its own terrace.

Café Antoine
17 rue Jean de la Fontaine
+33 (0)1 40 50 14 30

The polar opposite of the Cristal Room, but a place no less historically interesting, this "micro-bistro" is located at street level on one of the blocks that Hector Guimard designed in the 16th arrondissement. The original proprietor, Antoine himself, opened the café shortly after the building was completed in 1911. The wonderful belle-époque decor remains essentially unchanged, including the porcelain tiles and old mirrors. The atmosphere is also incredibly intimate, as the big zinc bar leaves space for only four or five tables, to which a few are added outside in warmer months. The food is comprised of a handful of French classics, chalked up on a blackboard, and the house wine comes in pitchers. This is a place to slip back in time.

STAYING

For the Hôtel Mistral and the Hôtel Central, two budget hotels linked with literary lovers, see p. 112 and p. 109 respectively.

Hôtel Lutetia
45 boulevard Raspail
+33 (0)1 49 54 46 46
www.lutetia-paris.com

This imposing hotel located just within the 6th arrondissement, on the boulevard Raspail near the boulevard du Montparnasse, stands out for its magnificently sculpted Art Deco facade. Given the hotel's artistic pedigree—Josephine Baker (see pp. 80–81), Pablo Picasso (see p. 34), and the writers André Gide and Antoine de Saint-Exupéry all lived or stayed here at one point—this is the best luxury option from which to soak up the artistic history of the 14th arrondissement. The walls are covered by photos of past residents, and the lobby is often graced with pieces by notable contemporary artists. Those seeking a romantic venue are in illustrious company—none other than Charles de Gaulle spent his honeymoon here. The atmosphere couldn't be more Parisian, with the hotel's 1930s styling and furniture, Eiffel Tower views, and mellow jazz wafting from the glamorous bar. Upon request, Romance packages are available, or go for broke with a Celebration package offering a bottle of pink champagne accompanied by Baccarat champagne glasses you can take home. Of the three themed suites, the most romantic is the Eiffel Suite, a duplex with a wooden spiral staircase that leads to a cozy bedroom in the eaves, Eiffel Tower views from its two balconies, and a circular tub in the white-and-gold mosaic bathroom. There's a lively brasserie on-site, as well as a plush restaurant with interiors by Sonia Rykiel and a baccarat table set with beautiful colored glass.

Hôtel Sezz
6 avenue Frémiet
+33 (0)1 56 75 26 26
www.hotelsezz.com

Beyond the classic facade on a street leading up from the river in the smart arrondissement for which it is named ("Sezz" is a play on *seize* or *seizième*), this twenty-seven-room hotel conceals many surprises, from the absence of a check-in desk—a personal assistant greets you with a drink instead—to the ultra-modern decor. Rooms mix angular, masculine pieces of furniture with softer, more feminine touches: big leather and chrome beds, strewn with cashmere throws, rest in the middle of the room on thick, fluffy rugs, while the two-person bathtubs are clad in stone and glass but offer dreamy rooftop and, in some cases, Eiffel Tower views from their positions by the windows. You might be lured out of your room to investigate the Jacuzzi, steam room, and massage room, or else the champagne bar with its rose petal–shaped alcove for tête-à-têtes. The "Honeymoon Retreat" package includes rose petals, macarons, and a bottle of bubbly; visits to a private champagne cellar can also be arranged.

Eleanor
10 allée du Bord de l'Eau
+33 (0)1 40 50 16 78
www.eleanor.fr

Make like Anaïs Nin (see pp. 108–109), who once stayed on a riverboat moored on the Seine. This particular boat is set within the tranquil environs of the Bois de Boulogne at the very western extreme of the 16th arrondissement (see p. 125). Mostly available in summer, the *Eleanor* is home to a bona fide Parisian couple and is well loved and maintained, with two bedrooms, a large living room, and a spacious and airy deck saloon. After you've left the heat of the city behind you, the sundeck of the *Eleanor* is a delightful spot for idle breakfasts or alfresco barbecues on balmy evenings. Alternatively, Le Galion, a restaurant located on a neighboring barge, serves the likes of scallops with red pesto, or duck with tandoori and ginger. A veritable escape from the city, the Eleanor is particularly convenient if you're planning to attend the horse races at Longchamp (see p. 126).

AROUND PARIS AND FURTHER AFIELD

The Loire Valley

Champagne

Normandy and Brittany

Southern France

The Loire Valley

L'amour est l'emblème de l'éternité:
il confond toute la notion de temps;
efface toute la mémoire d'un commencement,
toute la crainte d'une extrémité.

Love is the symbol of eternity:
it confounds all notions of time;
effaces all memories of a beginning,
all fear of an end.

—MADAME DE STAËL

Champagne-colored skies studded by flocks of birds; purple willows trailing their branches in the wide expanses of pale-green water; historic towns with cobble-stoned streets and half-timbered buildings; swathes of fertile vineyard; and then, around the corner, as if summoned from some magical realm, the fabulous fairy-tale castles for which this region is world renowned: welcome to the Valley of the Kings. A former seat of power and later a retreat for successive French monarchs and the nobility, this is honey-mooning territory par excellence—a place of escape, where even the most famous chateaux are surrounded by gorgeous, landscaped gardens and vast parklands.

It is possible to take a whirlwind tour of the highlights of the Loire on a one-day excursion from Paris, but to do so would be to cheat yourselves of the chance to get under the skin of this enchanting region. The Loire Valley was made to be appreciated slowly. Emulate its gentle pace of life by taking its castles one at a time, exploring their hidden corners and secret passageways, and savoring them in retrospect as you dine on wonderful local produce, drink famed regional wines, and sleep the comfortable, cosseted sleep of kings and queens in one of the many castles that have been transformed into regal hotels.

The Loire Valley is vaunted for its purity—from the ideal accent of the locals (the region is known as the cradle of the French language) and the unspoiled landscape to the classic French architecture, food, and wine. For all of these attributes, there has been much bloodshed and heated passion throughout the Loire's history. It seems as though every chateau and historic site has a story to tell: tales of duplicity, adultery, and family feuds that would change the course of history of France and beyond.

The whole of the Loire Valley from Chalonnes in the west to Sully-sur-Loire in the east is on UNESCO's World Heritage List by virtue of its immense architectural importance and "exceptional cultural landscape." The relatively short section between Orléans and Saumur contains those castles and other sites, from artistic retreats to troglodyte caves, that exude the greatest sense of romance in my eyes. But one of the great pleasures of visiting this region is discovering its clandestine and abandoned corners. More than three hundred castles dot the idyllic landscape, and many more were destroyed during the Revolution, when their proprietors lost their heads to the guillotine. The prospect of privacy is hence much more than wishful thinking.

Bear in mind, too, that the Loire is about much more than its architecture, however breathtaking that may be. The rivers, vineyards, and forests full of stags and boar make the region a wonderful place for boating, cycling, or hot-air ballooning. If you are interested in an aerial tour by *montgolfière* (hot-air balloon), ask the local tourist office to recommend a firm.

In terms of timing, high summer can be crowded, as the chateaus are among France's most popular attractions. On the other hand, many castles and their gardens are beautifully illuminated on summer evenings, by candles or by solar lighting. Some chateaus also host special nocturnal events that are perfect for lovers visiting in the warmer months. Another reason to visit the Loire during the high season is that the river truly comes into its own at this time: fishermen cast their rods from their punt-like *barques* and local firms hire out rowboats and canoes to those who want to explore the river in a more leisurely manner.

But the Loire is seductively mellow out of season, too. Autumn sees the grape harvest and the sprouting of yellow and orange asparagus on the sandy riverbanks, while the winter offers the prospect of seeing the chateaus bedecked in snow and the trees heavy with festive clusters of mistletoe.

Unlike Paris, where regional and ethnic diversity is part of the culinary landscape, the Loire is a place for sampling *le terroir*, the local produce and wine. Local specialties focus on fish from the Loire River, including shad, eel, and zander, which are caught in picturesque *carrelets*—square nets that are lowered into the water. The Loire also produces some of the greatest French wines, most notably, crisp white Vouvray, which is best sampled *mousseux* (sparkling) or *pétillant* (semi-sparkling). In November, don't miss an opportunity to taste *bernache*, the juice from the first pressing of the grapes.

COURTLY INTRIGUES: CHAMBORD AND AROUND

Two hours southwest of Paris and a couple of miles west of the Loire River, the **Château de Chambord** provides a truly awe-inspiring introduction to the architecture of the Valley of the Kings. The inherent drama of this fantastical building, which melds French medieval forms with features of the Italian Renaissance, is heightened by its location within an old hunting forest that covers a massive thirteen thousand acres, encircled by twenty miles of stone walls. Driving or cycling to the castle is an adventure in and of itself, with wild boar and stags blinking warily at you through the trees.

The castle was built by François I as a hunting lodge—one that allowed him to be close to Claude de Thoury de Rohan-Gié, comtesse de Thoury, one of the last of the many mistresses he kept throughout his lifetime. The countess lived in the neighboring Château de Muides, and although this castle has long since disappeared, you can spot her coat of arms carved into Chambord's walls, along with François I's symbol of the salamander.

THE LITTLE QUEEN: MADAME DE POMPADOUR

Between the late Middle Ages and the Revolution it was all the rage for French kings—whose marriages were usually made on political grounds—to openly keep a royal mistress, or mistresses. Several of these women wielded great influence at court. Among them was Louis XV's famous mistress, Madame de Pompadour, whose riverside **Château de Ménars**, just a few miles from Chambord, you may admire from the outside.

As early as the age of nine, Madame de Pompadour, born Jeanne-Antoinette Poisson, was called *reinette* (little queen) by her mother after a fortune-teller foretold that the girl would one day reign over a king's heart. An accomplished actress and singer as well as a great beauty, Jeanne-Antoinette was married off to her guardian's nephew at the age of nineteen, and the couple had two children. Adored by her husband and the toast of Parisian society, she founded a salon where she hosted intellectuals such as Voltaire. It was this public attention that inspired the king's interest while he was mourning the death of his second official mistress, Marie-Anne de Mailly-Nesle, Duchese de Châteauroux.

Louis summoned Jeanne-Antoinette to attend a royal masked ball at the Palace of Versailles (see p. 126) soon after. The king was costumed, rather improbably, as a yew hedge while Madame de Pompadour was dressed as a shepherdess. Revealing his identity, the king engaged her in courtly conversation, and before long she became his mistress. She was quickly enmeshed in court life with all its politically motivated alliances, conspiracies, and enmities, some of which directly targeted her. Many of the king's courtiers dismissed her as a commoner, while another of Louis's mistresses, Marie-Louise O'Murphy de Boisfaily, also known as La Belle Morphyse, made an attempt to usurp her as official royal mistress. Madame de Pompadour held her own against these advances, claiming the support of a number of eminent literary friends and advisors.

After suffering two miscarriages, the marquise is believed to have arranged for lesser mistresses to attend to the king's pleasure. Although they were no longer lovers, the two remained great friends, and the king was devoted to her until her death at forty-two years of age from tuberculosis. You can read all about her in Nancy Mitford's classic, candid biography, *Madame de Pompadour*.

Chambord wasn't the king's residence year-round—he had royal chateaus nearby, at both Blois and Amboise (see pp. 151–153)—but it is the largest of the Loire chateaus, and as such took two decades to construct. Experts still disagree about the identity of its architect: some claim that it was none other than Leonardo da Vinci, the Italian Renaissance genius to whom François I had accorded residency at the Clos Lucé (see pp. 152–153). This theory is given credence by the fact that Leonardo had an interest in double-helix staircases, an example of which forms the building's spectacular centerpiece. The two helixes

GARDENS OF EARTHLY DELIGHT

Fittingly for a region known as the Garden of France, the Loire is filled with magnificent gardens—many of them surrounding the chateaus and created by some of the most famous landscapists in history. True garden aficionados flock to the Loire en masse between April and October, when the castle of **Chaumont-sur-Loire,** west along the river from Chambord, hosts its renowned Festival International des Jardins.

Based on a different theme each year, the festival offers garden displays ranging from the simple to the whimsical to the downright fantastical. Showstoppers from the last few years include a garden with blue-painted trees and a spiral-shaped garden with tomatoes growing on scaffolding. Wander the festival at night to be truly dazzled: since 2009 the gardens have been lit up for atmospheric nocturnal strolls.

The castle itself was once home to Catherine de Médicis, who was known to practice sorcery in the bell tower and to entertain astrologers, including Nostradamus, while her husband, Henri II, spent the bulk of his time with his long-term mistress Diane de Poitiers at the nearby Château de Chenonceau (see pp. 141–147). After Diane left Chaumont, other residents of the castle included Thomas à Becket and the Swiss writer Madame de Staël, who wrote *De l'Allemagne (On Germany)* within its walls after being exiled here by Napoléon I. This piece of writing would help to launch the Romantic movement in France. Take a walk through the glorious cedars to see the palatial stone-and-brick stables where the Prince and Princess de Broglie, descendants of Madame de Staël, kept their horses and an elephant—a gift from a maharajah guest. The creatures lived like kings within the velvet-lined stalls of this very luxurious stable.

that comprise the staircase ascend three stories without ever meeting, so that while you can see others on the opposite staircase, you will never come upon them. Some say that this design allowed the king to go up and down the stairs without having to come into direct contact with his servants.

Chambord boasts eighty-five staircases in total, as well as 440 rooms and 365 fireplaces—one for every day of the year. But the sheer scale and magnificence of the chateau, constructed in the shape of a Greek cross, is only truly appreciated from outside. François I instructed his architect to design a castle resembling the skyline of Constantinople, and the rooftop of the chateau does, in fact, have something of the appearance of a cityscape, with eleven types of towers and three kinds of chimneys, together with a disregard for the symmetry that one would expect in a chateau of this kind. The Romantic author François-René de Chateaubriand said it reminded him of a woman's locks disheveled by the wind.

Because François I never lived here, Chambord remained unheated and unfurnished. This meant that whenever the king visited with a hunting party, he would have to bring both furniture and supplies for a group of up to two thousand people, including guests, retinue, and staff. After François I died in 1547, Chambord fell into disrepair, and although it was rescued and restored on several occasions, it was always abandoned anew. During the Franco-Prussian War of 1870–71, the chateau was used as a field hospital. In 1939, as war loomed, the art collection from the Louvre, including the Venus de Milo (see p. 15) and the *Mona Lisa*, was safeguarded here.

The state finally restored the castle and opened it to the public after World War II. You may tour the replicas of royal apartments, which feature informative displays about the castle's many illustrious owners, and there is also a museum of hunting on the premises. It's wise to try to time your visit with one of the many special events, which range from elegant balls to evening walks on the grounds to witness the autumnal deer rut—or, as the French much more romantically describe it, the *période des amours*. Other attractions include horse shows, open-air opera performances, and *son-et-lumière* (sound-and-light) shows—during which the castle is illuminated and historical events are re-enacted—as well as game fairs and farmers' markets. When the weather is fine, there are few greater earthly pleasures than exploring the glorious reserve and its magnificent forest by horseback, horse-and-carriage, or bicycle. Another option is to putter about on the Cosson River, which flows through the grounds, in a rowboat or an electric boat.

Venture a short distance outside the magical walled kingdom of Chambord to admire the modest and yet very handsome chateau that lies at the heart of the estate where Chambord black raspberry liqueur has been produced since the seventeenth century. This seductive blend of handpicked raspberries and blackberries, Madagascan vanilla,

Moroccan citrus peel, honey, and cognac—which are left to steep in barrels during a short "marriage" period—is believed to have been enjoyed by Louis XIV when he stayed at the Château de Chambord. Its velvety taste is best savored neat, mixed with champagne, or as a part of a French martini, alongside vodka and peach schnapps; the liqueur is also wonderful over ice cream. Sold in distinctive globed bottles modeled on a *globus cruciger* to emphasize the royal connection, Chambord makes an original Valentine Day's gift.

Hidden away in the trees at the edge of Chambord's forest is the **Château de Villesavin**, a discreet chateau that conceals an offbeat Musée du Mariage (Wedding Museum). On view are more than one thousand five hundred well-preserved objects and wax figures that provide insights into the act of marriage as well as its traditions and accoutrements since 1840. Should a visit inspire you to take the plunge, the chateau has a pretty *orangerie* where wedding receptions are often held.

Romance gives way to high drama just to the southwest at the refined **Château de Cheverny**, where one aristocratic owner, Henri Hurault, exacted a terrible revenge after being told by Henri IV that his wife was cheating on him. Rushing home after hearing the news, Henri killed the man he discovered in bed with his wife. Afterward, he promptly summoned the local priest and asked his wife if she preferred to die by poison or the sword;

she chose the deadly vial. Henri's only punishment for his action was a short exile within the castle itself, after which he was free to remarry. In keeping with the dramas of its past, the Château de Cheverny was once gifted to Diane de Poitiers by Henri II, but she rejected it in favor of Chenonceau (see pp. 141–147).

The Château de Cheverny's Salle des Gardes (Guards' Room) contains references to amorous doings in the form of caryatids bearing the figures of Mars and Venus, plus a painting by Jean Mosnier entitled *La mort d'Adonis* (*The Death of Adonis*). There is also a collection of Mosnier's paintings of legendary couples in the extravagant Chambre du Roi (where no king ever actually stayed). Couples depicted include Theagenes and Chariclea, heroes of an ancient Greek romance, as well as Perseus and Andromeda, who married, according to legend, after Perseus saved Andromeda from a sea monster.

CHENONCEAU: THE LADIES' CASTLE

Both straddling and mirrored by the Cher River, about thirty-five miles southwest of Chambord, Chenonceau is another iconic castle among the chateaus of the Loire Valley. The history of this estate has been dominated by so many powerful, assertive women over the course of the centuries that Chenonceau has been nicknamed the Château des Dames.

Built in the early sixteenth century as a blend of late Gothic and early Renaissance architecture, Chenonceau became a royal piece of property after François I seized it to recoup unpaid debts. François's son and heir Henri II gave it to his favorite mistress Diane de Poitiers. He disguised the act as a donation to show his appreciation for the services of her late husband, Louis de Brézé, seigneur d'Anet (see p. 142). Although she never really lived here, Diane lavished it with love and attention. She ordered the construction of the arched bridge over the river, and she oversaw the planting of orchards and the vegetable and flower gardens alongside the river. Her reign at Chenonceau would not last, however; when Henri died, his wife Catherine de Médicis forced Diane to exchange it for the Château de Chaumont (see p. 138).

Having moved into Chenonceau, Catherine may have avoided the memories evoked by the Salle des Gardes—its ceiling is embellished with an intertwining *H* for Henri and *C* for Catherine, but Henri surreptitiously had the ceiling itself shaped to look like an *H* and a *D*, for Diane. Similarly, within the room that Diane de Poitiers took as her bedroom, the fireplace and the ceiling bear interlaced *H*s and *C*s that could be construed as forming a *D*. Today this room harbors a nineteenth-century portrait of Catherine hung over the hearth.

DIANE AND CATHERINE: ROYAL LOVE RIVALS

In an event described by Pope Clement VII as "the greatest match in the world," Florence-born Catherine de Médicis married Henri II, son of François I, in Marseille when they were both just fourteen years old. The great-niece of the pope, Catherine had no idea that she was entering into a union in which she would forever play second fiddle to her distant relative, Henri's lifelong love Diane de Poitiers.

Born into a high-ranking family in the French Alps, Diane de Poitiers was herself married at the age of fifteen to Louis de Brézé, seigneur d'Anet, who was nearly forty years her senior. After having two daughters with Louis, Diane was appointed lady-in-waiting to Claude de France, the wife of François I. During this time, Diane was present at the birth of Henri, Claude's second son. When the queen died, Diane became a sort of surrogate mother to the royal princes.

When the princes were young boys—just seven and eight years old—their father cruelly allowed them to be taken to Spain to be kept hostage in a castle in exchange for his release (he had been captured by Charles V's troops during battle). As the boys were leaving for Spain, Diane gave Henri a farewell kiss that seems to have sparked lifelong adoration on his part: it is Diane's image that is thought to have sustained him during his imprisonment, which lasted until he was twelve.

Henri married Catherine de Médicis with Diane's approval—Catherine and Diane were descended from the same aristocratic family. Catherine was less thrilled with the arrangement, viewing Diane as a meddling presence even though the older woman nursed her when she contracted scarlet fever.

By the time Catherine finally conceived her first son in 1544, Henri had already taken Diane de Poitiers as his mistress. He was nineteen and Diane, who had been widowed a few years previously, was thirty-eight years old. A devoted companion and important influence on the king, Diane was so politically astute that Henri allowed her to write some of his official correspondence and even sign some letters "HenriDiane." Diane, who was secure in the knowledge that Henri had never really cared for Catherine, encouraged him to father more children with the queen. Catherine, on the other hand, was consumed by jealousy. Diane was attractive and vigorous, and Henri made no secret of his adoration for her. Even when guests were present, he sat on Diane's knee while he discussed politics or played the guitar.

Catherine's bitterness came to a head when Henri gave Diane the Crown Jewels and the Château de Chenonceau (see p. 141), a royal property that the queen coveted. Catherine was powerless to act while the king was alive, but when he was mortally wounded during a jousting tournament, she took advantage—first refusing to let Diane see Henri even though he was calling for her, later banning Diane from his funeral, and finally forcing her to exchange the lovely Château de Chenonceau (see p. 141) for Chaumont (see p. 138).

Catherine flaunted her grief for her husband, draping herself in a French hood (a widow's cap) and flowing black mantle, and having emblems of her love for him carved into the stonework of her residences. She also commissioned a lavish monument that has been described as "the last and most brilliant of the royal tombs of the Renaissance" as her husband's final resting place. She enclosed his heart in a carved marble sculpture engraved with a poem by Pierre de Ronsard that explains that the king's real heart resides in Catherine's breast. Such extravagant mourning explains why poets of the time likened Catherine to Artemisia II, the Queen of Caria, whose extraordinary grief at the death of her husband, King Mausolus of Caria, led her to build the legendary Mausoleum at Halicarnassus—one of the Seven Wonders of the Ancient World.

As the mother of François II, Charles IX, and Henri III, who ascended to the throne at the ages of fifteen, ten, and twenty-three respectively, the widowed Catherine went on to hold almost unbounded power. When she died in 1589, Catherine joined Henri within a tomb topped with their effigies, which can be seen in the St. Denis Basilica in the northern suburbs of Paris—the burial site of nearly every French monarch since Clovis I.

Catherine's great rival Diane died more than two decades before her. The story of Diane de Poitiers and Henri is told, with a typical Hollywood disdain for historical accuracy, in the 1956 MGM movie *Diane*. The casting is also somewhat incongruous, with the main characters interpreted by Lana Turner and Roger Moore. The love affair between Diane and Henri is also the subject of the novel *The Serpent and the Moon: Two Rivals for the Love of a Renaissance King*, by Princess Michael of Kent.

Duplicitous monograms aside, Chenonceau became Catherine's favorite residence and served as a setting for many of her fabulous, even outrageous parties. One such gala was held to celebrate the coronation of her son François II in 1560 and included France's first-ever fireworks display. Other events were enlivened by fountains gushing with claret, or took the form of *bals travestis* when women dressed as men and men as women. Perhaps these splendid gatherings, dubbed the *triomphes de Chenonceau*, were—at least in part—

Catherine's way of exorcising Diane's ghost and showing the world that she was now firmly installed in the castle. Despite the celebratory nature of the parties, Catherine was an inveterate schemer, however—some of her party guests were in fact beautiful aristocrats whom she had enlisted to seduce and spy on young noblemen.

The Five Queens' Bedroom on the first floor of the castle showcases five female monarchs other than Catherine with whom the castle is associated: Catherine's two daughters, Marguerite de Valois (wife of Henri IV) and Elisabeth de Valois (wife of Philip II of Spain), and her three daughters-in-law, Mary Stuart (wife of François II), Elizabeth of Austria (wife of Charles IX), and Louise de Vaudémont (wife of Henri III). Their various coats of arms can be seen on the sixteenth-century coffered ceiling.

It was Louise de Vaudémont to whom the castle was ceded after Catherine's death, and at this time the lavish parties gave way to gloom. Louise was at Chenonceau when she was told of the assassination of her husband by the monk Jacques Clément. She covered the walls of Chenonceau with black tapestries decorated with skulls and crossbones, and roamed the castle's corridors or pined for Henri in her chamber dressed in the white weeds of the time. It was this mourning garb that earned Louise the nickname the White Queen. Her reconstructed bedroom within the castle, which retains its original ceiling, still contains the mourning objects attesting to the depth of her loss: widow's cordons (silver cords that were worn around the arms, first donned by Anne of Brittany after Charles VIII died; see p. 157), crowns of thorns, silver tears, and the Greek letter lambda, approximating Louise's initial, entwined with an *H* for Henri.

In 1624 Henri IV's favorite mistress, Gabrielle d'Estrées, duchesse de Beaufort, moved into Chenonceau. Gabrielle was twenty when she caught the king's eye, and it was she who suggested that he convert to Catholicism in order to claim the throne. Henri rewarded Gabrielle by having her marriage annulled and by publicly acknowledging her as his official mistress. A great diplomat and adviser, Gabrielle was also a fiercely loyal companion: even when pregnant, she would share the king's tent when he was on the battlefield, writing letters for him as well as cooking and making sure he had clean clothes.

Having bore the king three children (one of whom, César, duc de Vendôme, went on to own this castle), Gabrielle died giving birth to his fourth in 1599, shortly after he had vowed to marry her—an act that required him to apply to the pope for an annulment of his first marriage. Devastated by Gabrielle's death, the king broke royal protocol by becoming the first monarch to wear black in mourning. He also accorded his late mistress a lavish funeral that was fit for a queen. You can still see Gabrielle's former bedroom within the castle.

Gabrielle is believed to have been one of the models for the famous but unaccredited painting entitled *Portrait présumé de Gabrielle d'Estrées et de sa soeur la duchesse de Villars*

(*Assumed Portrait of Gabrielle d'Estrées and Her Sister the Duchess of Villars*). In this work, the women are depicted sitting naked in a bath, and the duchess is pinching her sister's nipple—a gesture believed to symbolize the fact that Gabrielle was pregnant. The ring that Gabrielle is holding is thought to be the king's coronation ring, which he gave to her when he vowed to marry her. This work can be found in the Louvre (see pp. 14–15), but here in the castle, within the former bedroom of François I, you can see a sizeable portrait by Ambroise Dubois of Gabrielle d'Estrées as Diana (the huntress of Roman mythology). The same room houses a portrait of Diane de Poitiers, also in the guise of Diana—Diane liked being associated with her near-namesake because the Roman goddess was also a symbol of chastity. The work of Francesco Primaticcio, the portrait was painted at Chenonceau and bears Diane's coat of arms. If you haven't had your fill of royal mistresses, inspect the painting *Les trois grâces* (*The Three Graces*) by Jean-Baptiste Van Loo, showing the De Nesle girls—three sisters, all of whom were lovers of Louis XV (see p. 137).

Since 1913 Chenonceau has been owned by the Menier family, producers of luxury chocolates. After allowing the chateau to be used as a hospital during World War I and then as an escape route for members of the Resistance during World War II—its bridge provided a link between Nazi-occupied France on one side of the river and the free zone on the other—the family has restored Chenonceau to its former glory. It's now the second most-visited chateau in all of France, which means that there's no chance that you'll have it to yourself. However, if you come on a weekday, you will be able to appreciate its many charms

and points of interest with fewer distractions. These include the Gallery—a magnificent ballroom that Catherine had built atop the bridge that Diane de Poitiers had constructed across the river—and Catherine's own bedroom, which has pieces of sixteenth-century sculpted furniture, tapestries with animals, proverbs, and fables, and Correggio's *L'éducation de l'amour* (*The Teaching of Love*), which was painted on wood.

Wander through the luscious gardens of Chenonceau, which—like the castle itself—bear witness to the battle between Diana and Catherine for supremacy. Both of their gardens are delights, dotted with pools and fountains, filled with climbing and stemmed roses and other plants, and affording stirring views over the river and the chateau. But Catherine, determined to make her mark on the estate for which she had yearned so long, went beyond the royal gardening standards of the day in creating a veritable garden of curiosities. Though the aviary, menagerie, and artificial cave that she installed no longer exist, you can still see the moats, the Bâtiment des Dômes (Building of the Domes), in which she set up France's first silkworm farm, and a quaint old courtyard that was a sixteenth-century farm. The Bâtiment des Dômes is also home to the Galerie des Dames (Ladies' Gallery), where wax figures of Diane and Catherine, Mary Stuart, and Louise de Vaudémont are clad in historical costumes. There are also Catherine Briçonnet, the woman who oversaw much of the castle's initial construction while her husband, Thomas Bohier, was away on business, and Louise Dupin and Marguerite Pelouze, later owners who each breathed new life into the estate.

After your dose of history at Chenonceau, lose yourself in the enchanting maze created from two thousand yews, the design of which was taken from an Italian plan created during Catherine de Médicis' time. In the heart of the maze you'll find a charming gazebo, while dotted around it are the sculpted female figures of the caryatids that Catherine added to the castle's facade and that Marguerite Pelouze removed three centuries later. You're free to stroll through the parkland and in high summer, to take a rowboat out on the Cher. For the ultimate romantic effect, come for a *promenade nocturne*, offered on weekends in June, and every evening in July and August, when the castle and gardens are expertly lit by Pierre Bideau (who is also responsible for illuminating the Eiffel Tower, the Great Pyramid, and the Acropolis in Athens) and filled with Baroque music composed by Arcangelo Corelli.

SOUTH OF CHENONCEAU: MONTRÉSOR AND LOCHES

From Chenonceau, it's a short drive south to one of the Loire's most alluring and least-visited corners, **Montrésor**—a spot so charming that it is a member of the official association of Les Plus Beaux Villages de France (The Most Beautiful Villages in France). This, the site of a medieval castle that has been demolished, rebuilt, and reconstructed over the years, is perched on a rocky spur overlooking the Indrois River. Montrésor was the base for many of the *filles de joie* (courtesans) and servants associated with the royal court: a Renaissance mansion, of which one wing remains, was built for them on the castle grounds.

The biggest surprise in Montrésor is the Polish street names—the castle is owned by a family of Polish origin, descendants of Count Xavier Branicki. This financier and art collector—most famous for his 1766 duel in Warsaw with Giovanni Giacomo Casanova (see pp. 52–53) over the actress/dancer Anna Binetti—bought and restored the chateau in 1849. The castle had fallen into disrepair after the Revolution.

Branicki hosted extravagant feasts at the castle, which were attended by some of his eminent friends, among them Napoléon III. Much of the castle remains intact, and the Second Empire parkland that surrounds it is studded by some delightful ruins: neo-Gothic towers and gateways overgrown with roses and weeds. The park also harbors some highly romantic statues, including a fallen archangel and a bronze copy of a statue that reclines on the tomb of an unknown Polish soldier in the Cimetière de Montmartre (see p. 95).

A guided tour of the castle's interior showcases the original nineteenth-century decor and a collection of Polish mementos and objets d'art, including portraits, busts, and paintings. There's also some Italian Renaissance furniture, elegant tableware, hunting trophies, and a stuffed wolf. Lastly, you can see a piano upon which Frédéric Chopin (see p. 79) once played—if it's quiet, you may be allowed to play on it—as well as a locked room filled with the chateau's *trésor* (treasure). Such riches include gold and silver tableware, beer steins, and coins; much of the booty once belonged to kings of Poland.

Otherwise, there is the atmospheric Montrésor village itself, which warrants a wander through its narrow lanes and picturesque ancient houses. Take a trip along Les Balcons de l'Indrois, a mile-long walkway beside the river that affords glorious views of the village. During the high summer, come at nightfall on a Friday or Saturday for Les Nuits Solaires when the Balcons are illuminated to create a nocturnal wonderland, with music, a soundtrack of nature-inspired sounds, and images projected onto the buildings.

The area that surrounds Montrésor is bathed in rural tranquillity and has an almost otherworldly quality—in fact, the nineteenth-century geographer Onésime Reclus said of the town of **Loches**, which is ten miles from Montrésor: "It brings to life a thousand years in one day." This village with its winding streets bordered by fifteenth- and sixteenth-century houses, is home to a medieval citadel so large that it almost constitutes a city in its own right, with a castle, a forbidding keep, several towers, and numerous dwellings set on the ramparts.

Don't miss the castle's Logis Royal, which was home, in the fifteenth century, to Agnès Sorel, Charles VII's infamous mistress and the grandmother of Louis de Brézé, husband of Diane de Poitiers (see pp. 142–143). Agnès entered the court as the queen's lady-in-waiting after being nicknamed the Dame de Beauté, both for her looks and because the king gifted her the estate of Beauté-sur-Marne as well as the Château de Loches. Having become the king's mistress, she was said to have cured him of his depression. In return, and against all royal etiquette, he treated her like a princess, allowing her to keep her own retinue.

Agnès became notorious for her extravagance, which was exemplified by the length of the trains of her robes. These indulgences would make her many enemies, including the pope. As recently as 2005, a forensic examination of her remains revealed that she may have been murdered—the cause of death was ascertained to be mercury poisoning, not dysentery as was previously thought. One theory to explain the twenty-eight-year-old mistress's murder was that Charles's estranged son, the future Louis XVI, arranged her death because of her undue influence over his father. Agnès died pregnant with the king's fourth child, having already borne him three daughters.

The royal lodgings also house a copy of a well-known portrait of Agnès by Jean Fouquet, in which she is shown with one breast protruding from her robe. The alabaster tomb within which she was laid to rest is also newly located within the Logis, after a three-century battle to have it removed from the church in Loches. The tomb is marked with the symbol of the two *agneaux* (lambs), a symbolic play on Agnès's Christian name. Lastly, the Logis is also home to the sumptuous private chapel of Anne of Brittany (see p. 151), a love token from her third husband Louis XII, as well as a grand hall where Joan of Arc was hailed after liberating Orléans from the English.

A GARDEN OF LOVE: VILLANDRY

About fifty miles from Montrésor is **Villandry**, an impressive chateau with formal Renaissance gardens that are considered some of the world's most beautiful. They are the legacy of Dr. Joachim Carvallo, an eminent Spanish scientist who gave up his career to save Villandry from demolition with the support of his American-born wife, Ann Coleman.

These gardens include one of Loire's romantic highlights, Les Jardins d'Amour. These four ornamental "gardens of love" were designed as extensions of rooms within the chateau. For a proper view of the amorous motifs that decorate them, which are based on the symbols of medieval chivalry, you will need to look out from the belvedere. The first garden, L'Amour Tendre (Tender Love) features hearts that are separated by flames and domino masks, which reference the masked balls of the day. L'Amour Passionné (Passionate Love) also incorporates heart motifs, but they are broken up with box hedges to denote the violence of passion and the movement of dance. Following in theme is L'Amour Volage (Fickle Love), where volatile feelings are symbolized by the color yellow, by four fans interspersed by a cuckold's horns, and by *billets doux* (love letters) sent by a duplicitous lady. The grouping ends with L'Amour Tragique (Tragic Love), in which the aforementioned rivalry brings death.

FROM CASTLES TO CAVES

While most visitors come to the Loire to experience the opulent castles, the region is also home to a much humbler form of architecture that is uniquely romantic—the *caves tuffeaux* (cave dwellings) that were hewn out of rocky outcrops.

Although troglodytes are not exclusive to the Loire, the predominance of the soft white tufaceous limestone in the region—especially between Saumur and Angers—encouraged those whose wallets couldn't stretch to a moated and turreted chateau to dig out cave dwellings throughout the countryside. Incredibly, up to half of the local population is believed to have lived in caves during the twelfth century, and much of the stone that was quarried to provide space for them was transported and reused as building materials for the chateaus.

Rochemenier, an entire troglodyte village about fifty miles west of Villandry, has been preserved as it was at the beginning of the twentieth century, complete with dwellings, barns, stables, wine cellars, and an underground chapel. Inside of the dwellings is evidence of old bread ovens, furniture carved from stone, and tiny alcoves that served as bedrooms—a new hole was chipped out of the wall as each new child arrived.

In nearby Dénezé-sous-Doué, **Les Caves aux Sculptures** are embellished with scenes from what appear to be Satanic versions of the mystery plays. Where medieval mystery plays were based on Biblical episodes, these works satirize the state and the ruling class, as well as Christianity and morality in general. Thought to be the work of a clandestine sixteenth-century sect of libertarians, many of the four hundred cartoonlike, diabolic, often deformed figures are engaged in erotic acts.

More romantically, **Doué-la-Fontaine** to the south of Dénezé-sous-Doué is famous for its roses and for Les Arènes, an old quarry that was turned into an amphitheater, complete with rows of seats carved from the rock, in the fifteenth century. In fact, Les Arènes hosts an annual flower show showcasing Doué's renowned blooms—the Journées de la Rose (Rose Days) in mid-July, when the structure's atmospheric cellars are filled with more than one hundred thousand roses arranged in stunning displays.

Alternatively, seek out some of the region's restaurants and bars that are atmospherically situated within caves, or even spend the night in a cave. **Les Hautes Roches** (www.leshautesroches.com) by the Loire at Rochecorbon is a plush hotel offering troglodyte rooms inside a former dormitory for the monks of the abbey of Marmoutier. The hotel's Passion package includes a dinner in its gourmet restaurant.

Several annual events center on these remarkable gardens, including the highly romantic Nuits des Mille Feux—two evenings in early June when the gardens are lit by two thousand candles and attended by costumed actors and acrobats. These fairy-tale evenings culminate in fireworks displays, mirrored in the lake of the water garden.

The austere **Château de Langeais,** located just along the river from Villandry, is one of the best examples of late medieval architecture in the area. It was in this castle's great hall that Charles VIII married fourteen-year-old Anne of Brittany in 1491, ensuring the annexation of Brittany by France. This was not a marriage made in heaven—Anne showed her unwillingness to relinquish Breton independence by having her entourage deliver two beds from Nantes via barges. Another complication was that Anne was already married to Maximilian of Austria, although the pope would subsequently annul this first marriage. If you visit the castle today, you will see a wax re-creation of the wedding scene, and occasionally, guided tours include costumed actors who explain the details of the secret wedding. Curiously, given Anne's objection to the pairing, she spent a fortune on her dress—one of the first ever in white—dressed her attendants in silk and velvet, and even trimmed her horses in crimson-and-black finery.

AMBOISE AND THE CLOS LUCÉ

North of Montrésor and Chenonceau, on the southern bank of the Loire, lies **Amboise,** once home to the royal court. This very pretty market town with its narrow winding alleys lined with half-timbered houses, quirky one-off shops, pâtisseries, and wonderful markets lies in the shadow of the dramatic Château d'Amboise, which looms over the river from its promontory. A former medieval fortress, the castle was reconstructed and became a favorite dwelling for French kings. It was the place where François I was raised, and where Henri II and Catherine de Médicis (see p. 138) brought up their children, together with Mary Stuart, the juvenile queen of Scotland, who was promised in marriage to their son, the future François II.

The court eventually left the castle during the French Wars of Religion. The chateau was subsequently used as a prison, and large parts of it were demolished during the French Revolution and in the early nineteenth century. However, you may still visit the Royal Apartments, which are furnished with Gothic and Renaissance furniture, as well as tour the maze of underground passageways and towers that lie beneath the Renaissance castle—relics of the medieval fortress. One of the best times to visit the Château d'Amboise is late on a Friday night during high summer, when the gardens are opened up for starlit strolls and the castle and park are beautifully illuminated.

The true gem of Amboise, however, is the pink-brick and tufa manor house where the Italian polymath Leonardo da Vinci spent his final three years. The **Château du Clos Lucé** first became a royal estate in 1490, when it served as an annex of the castle, to which it is reputedly linked by an underground passage. Charles VIII purchased the chateau for his wife, Anne of Brittany (see p. 151), and added a chapel in which she could mourn her children, who had died in infancy. François I subsequently spent time here, as did his sister Marguerite de Navarre, who started writing her *L'Heptaméron*—seventy-two erotic short stories on themes of love, lust, and cuckoldry—within its walls.

During their residency here in the early sixteenth century, the siblings transformed the manor into a haven for the Renaissance movement, inviting painters, poets, and architects. Chief among their guests was Leonardo da Vinci, who was invited by the king to create a stable base at the chateau. Up until this time, the Renaissance genius had been flitting around Florence, Milan, and Rome, hiring himself out as an engineer, architect, and artist to the rulers of the time. Leonardo traveled across the Alps to the Loire by donkey, carrying with him three paintings (the *Mona Lisa* and the uncompleted works *St. Anne* and *John the Baptist*).

Formerly known as the Manoir du Cloux, the Clos Lucé is a dreamy estate—especially in the evening, when visitors are fewer in number and the house is illuminated. Within the old manor, you may visit the bedchamber where Leonardo died, as well as his former workroom, his kitchen, and the Renaissance halls where he received François I and visiting artists. Also on display are forty of the machines that he invented, which have been constructed with the materials that would have been available in his day. Other big draws for visitors include Anne of Brittany's chapel with its frescoes, and the salons of the D'Amboise family, who took over the chateau in the eighteenth century. Before their arrival, the chateau served as home to several courtesans, including François's favorite mistress Marie Gaudin Babou de la Bourdaisière, the great-great-grandmother of Gabrielle d'Estrées (see p. 144). If you're looking for an atmospheric and historical place to get married, the Clos Lucé might fit the bill.

Even more enchanting than the interiors are the Clos Lucé's extensive grounds, in which scale models of many of Leonardo's creations and inventions are tantalizingly hidden away amid the trees and watercourses. Among them are translucent silk screens bearing outsize reproductions of some of Leonardo's paintings, which flutter from trees in a secret grove by a waterfall. Music or narration pervades the air when you press the buttons of the audio-stations set up to explain Leonardo's thoughts, inspirations, and teachings—in this case, how he achieved psychological and emotional depth in his art.

For something more irreverent, head back to the river and cross the stone bridge taking you to the Île d'Or (Golden Island), which replaced a wooden bridge originally erected by Julius Caesar. It is here that you will find a statue of Leonardo sprawled naked against a medusa's head. The island also has canoes for rent, for those who would like to explore the Loire; if that's too energetic a plan, arrive on the Île d'Or by late afternoon or early evening to sip cocktails or a *kir Vouvray pêche* (peach kir with local white wine) at the pub until the wee hours and watch the moonlight bathe the Château d'Amboise across the water.

Or instead, head across the bridge to Amboise's Place Michel-Débré, where musicians may serenade you as you sit on the terrace of a brasserie in the shadow of the castle walls. If you're hoping to find an unusual souvenir or gift, **Midi au Soleil** (57 place du Château) is a quaint gift shop selling wooden toys that resemble some of the inventions by Leonardo on view at the Clos Lucé. You may also like to seek out the old-fashioned Pâtisserie Bigot/Le Fournil, which is the best place in town to stock up on *pavés d'Amboise*, slabs of chocolate, praline, and nougat, as well as *amboisines*—chocolates filled with a local grape liqueur.

Venture into the forest surrounding Amboise to **La Pagode de Chanteloup**, a whimsical, pyramidal 140-foot tower built from six decreasing circles and reflected in a half-moon-shaped pool. It was built by Étienne-François de Choiseul, duc de Choiseul, who served as a minister to Louis XV. The duke retired to the Château de Chanteloup, which once stood at this site, after the king's new mistress, Madame du Barry (see p. 126), had him banished from the royal court.

Climb the pagoda's inner staircase for glorious views over the Amboise forest and the Loire Valley as a whole. This is also a romantic spot for a picnic—if you haven't brought your own, the on-site restaurant sells Paniers de Chanteloup (Chanteloup Baskets) filled with fresh

regional fare. Walk off your feast with a stroll around the estate's parkland, or with a round of *quills* (bowling), croquet, or *pétanque*; the estate offers about fifty such games that were once popular pastimes of the royals and aristocracy. You can also take a rowboat out on the water. If you fall in love with the pagoda and the castle grounds, you can even marry here (see p. 221).

THE PASSION OF POETS: BEAUGENCY AND AROUND

A memorable place to end this condensed tour of the Loire's romantic highlights is **Beaugency**. Well off the tourist trail, it's incredibly picturesque, with cobblestoned and flower-filled streets, and quays lined with lovely waterfront houses. Beaugency has had a tumultuous history for such an idyllic town and it's a wonder that anything has survived. Yet it is the architectural relics—an eleventh-century keep and church, a twelfth-century abbey, a fourteenth-century bridge, and a fourteenth- or fifteenth-century lock—that make Beaugency so charming. Its Romanesque church of Notre-Dame was the setting for two meetings that took place in efforts to resolve royal marriage crises. The first was in 1104, when a council decided to excommunicate Philippe I, called the Amorous after he abandoned his wife Berthe for Bertrade de Montfort, the wife of Foulque IV, count of Anjou and Tours. The Catholic Church's order of excommunication was reversed several times after the king promised to renounce Bertrade, but he always returned to her; eventually she produced three of his children.

A second council met in the church in 1152, this time to annul the marriage of Louis VII and Eleanor of Aquitaine, partly because she was suspected of committing adultery while the king was fighting the Second Crusade, and partly because she had not produced a male heir. Eleanor went on to marry Henri Plantagenet, who would become Henry II, king of England—the dowry that she brought to this second marriage could be considered a factor in the centuries of warfare that ensued between France and England.

There are two towns near Beaugency that are replete with associations with romantic poets. The first is **Talcy** to the north, complete with a stern-looking castle that was purchased in 1517 by Bernardo Salviati, a Florentine banker with connections to the Medici. While attending a ball in nearby Blois in 1545, Salviati's fifteen-year-old daughter Cassandre caught the attention of the twenty-one-year-old lyrical poet Pierre de Ronsard. His forbidden love would produce the 183 sonnets that comprise *Les amours de Cassandre*. Although Cassandre was quickly married off to another man, rumor has it that she carried on an affair with the poet and bore him a child.

Cassandre's niece Diana followed in her aunt's footsteps by capturing the heart of Théodore-Agrippa d'Aubigné when she tended to his wounds during the Wars of Religion. The nurse became the Huguenot poet's muse, inspiring his first work, *Printemps* (*Spring*). Sadly, Diana's Catholic family would never allow her to wed a Protestant, and D'Aubigné broke her heart by marrying another woman. However, he never forgot her; Diana's death would inspire him to write another collection of poetry entitled *Les tragiques*.

Meung-sur-Loire to the east also has a history that is entwined with two famous medieval poets. The first, wild and occasionally criminal François Villon, is believed to have been locked up in the *oubliettes* (dungeon) of the town's chateau. The second, local poet Jean de Meun, was one of the main authors of the *Roman de la rose*, a medieval best seller. Meun wrote his courtly poem to instruct readers in the art of love as well as entertain them. The first 4,058 lines—which were written by Guillaume de Lorris (another native of the Loire)—depict a courtier's attempts to woo a lady. The next 17,722 lines—those written by Meun—are noticeably bawdier and even misogynistic, depicting the heroine Rose as more earthy and sexual than Lorris had painted her. In spite of—or perhaps because of—controversy over its imagery and language, the poem remained one of France's most widely read works for three centuries. A statue by the river of Jean de Meun clutching a rose commemorates this local poet and his most famous work.

Not too much is known of Meun himself, save that he was born Jean Clopinel, or Chopinel, and that he probably spent most of his life in Paris—on the rue St-Jacques in the 5th. He is also credited with having produced the first French translation of the love letters exchanged between Abélard and Héloïse (see p. 85).

Coups de Coeur

EATING

Auberge du Bon Laboureur
6 rue du Bretonneau, Chenonceaux
+33 (0)2 47 23 90 02

This snug former postal inn has a light-flooded, flower-filled dining room dating back to 1786, and a delightful terrace. Many of the ingredients used in its traditionally French fare come from the inn's own garden, overseen by resident gardener Claude, who welcomes guests wishing to inspect his fruit, vegetable, and herb plantations. He's also very happy to let you pick some of his roses, lilacs, tulips, and other blooms to create your own bouquet. Specialties of the house include creamed crayfish with tomato and basil, red mullet, calf's head, sweetbreads, and chocolate *millefeuille* with allspice. This inn is a charming place to stay, with rooms in five old village houses throughout its gardens as well as a pool on-site.

Auberge du Prieuré
2 rue de Clos Lucé, Amboise
+33 (0)2 47 57 69 01

If your lover has a hankering to taste the kind of food that was enjoyed at the royal court in days of old, take him or her to this gorgeous fifteenth-century priory on the grounds of Leonardo da Vinci's Clos Lucé (see p. 152). Whether you dine within the impressive Renaissance rooms or on the shady terraces of the Auberge du Prieuré, you will be able to try a wide range of dishes that you'd be hard-pressed to find anywhere else on the planet—the chef, who greets guests in period costume, is a historical food consultant. Main courses you might sample include scallop flan with dill, pork with sage butter and marrow, and Beggar's Pouch (salmon with basil on a bed of leeks). Leave room for the truly seductive desserts: pear with bitter orange and tropical vanilla, blancmange of figs preserved in sweet honey, and a compote of pineapple with Jamaican spice and butter biscuit. The unique wines include strawberry with pepper and the beautifully refreshing sage and mint.

Auberge Saint-Jacques
60 rue du Général de Gaulle, Meung-sur-Loire
+33 (0)2 38 44 30 39

Meung-sur-Loire (see p. 155) is the setting for this cozy inn where Alexandre Dumas, père, had D'Artagnan, hero of *The Three Musketeers*, wounded in a fight, after which he was comforted by the beautiful but ultimately treacherous Milady de Winter. One of the writer's favorite haunts, the Auberge Saint-Jacques offers well-priced regional specialties such as foie gras with fig compote, fricassee of snails with green cabbage and shallots, and duck roasted in honey. The place is especially renowned for its *pithiviers*, a puff-pastry dessert with an almond-paste filling. The handful of inexpensive guest rooms on-site include the romantic all-pink Rose Nuptiale.

STAYING

For Les Hautes Roches hotel with its troglodyte rooms, see p. 150.

Les Roulottes de la Grangée
1 Les racinaux, La Chapelle Blanche St. Martin
+33 (0)2 47 92 03 44
www.lagrangee.com

Perfectly located for visiting lovely Loches (see p. 148), these old Romani caravans are perfect for adventurous couples who would like to get back to nature. Constructed of wood with brightly painted detailing, the *roulottes* are snug little nests with double beds in cute alcoves. Modern distractions such as TV sets are only provided upon request, and although each caravan has a kitchen, you can be as lazy as you like—breakfast can be delivered to you at any hour that suits, and suppers of local specialties and wine are served by the owners inside their blue-shuttered cottage a short distance away. Packages include two nights for the price of one, along with a dinner in the cottage or a gourmet picnic for an intimate supper in your *roulotte*. Special care is taken to create a romantic ambiance in *roulottes* that are part of this Romantique package. The grounds boast a small fishing lake, hiking trails, and a *pétanque* court, and you can also rent bikes or take a trip by horse-and-carriage—or even learn to drive one.

Hôtel-Restaurant George Sand
39 rue Quintefol, Loches
+33 (0)2 47 59 39 74

This old postal inn dating from the fifteenth century took its name from local history—novelist George Sand (see p. 212) once stopped to change horses in Loches en route to Paris. Tranquil and intimate in ambiance, the hotel offers just nineteen rooms—all basic but well maintained and quite pretty. Downstairs, the excellent restaurant spills out onto a charming terrace, open during the summer months, which juts out over the river. Sit here and you will feel as if you're floating on the water as you feast on local treats like gazpacho with tomatoes and white asparagus, and roast filet of zander with dill.

Le Choiseul
36 quai Charles Guinot, Amboise
+33 (0)2 47 30 45 45
www.le-choiseul.com

The star option among several good hotels in the central Loire town of Amboise (see pp. 151–153), Le Choiseul is nestled at the foot of the dramatic chateau. Its thirty-two guest rooms and suites are spread across several residences set within the hotel's Italian-style gardens with their stunning statuary. Some rooms offer views over the Loire, which runs alongside several of the buildings. The interiors are charming, with vivid floral wallpaper and, in many cases, sloping ceilings and oak beams. Guests are welcome to use the outdoor pool, and have the option to dine at the gastronomic restaurant with its terrace for fine weather, or at the more casual bistro.

Grand Hôtel de l'Abbaye
2 quai de l'Abbaye, Beaugency
+33 (0)2 38 45 10 10
www.grandhoteldelabbaye.com

Gorgeous Beaugency (see p. 154) sets the scene for this atmospheric hotel within the walls of a seventeenth-century abbey. Though the reception area and guest rooms retain an ecclesiastic feel from the flagstone floors, wrought iron, heavy dark-wood furniture, and candelabra, the effect is not at all pious. In fact, you might just feel the frisson of sin when you bring a lover to this monastic setting, as the decor is enlivened by racy touches such as heart-motif cushions, gilt-framed mirrors, and frothy bouquets of flowers. Most of the rooms have unforgettable views over the medieval bridge straddling the Loire, including the breakfast room, which is heated by a vast hearth in the cooler months. Although there isn't a full restaurant on-site, there is a tempting bar with a riverside terrace that may lure you with the promise of glasses of fizz, light meals, and perhaps a game of chess. Otherwise room service is available until 11 p.m.

Champagne

Le champagne est le seul
vin que la femme
peut boire sans s'enlaidir.

Champagne is the only wine
a woman can drink
and remain beautiful.

—MADAME DE POMPADOUR

Champagne is a wine for romantics—an inspiration that has served everyone from lovers and writers to great statesmen. The novelist and gourmet Alexandre Dumas, père, claimed that a glass of champagne beside his inkwell lent his fiction added brilliance, while writer and philosopher Voltaire declared the frothy stuff to be "the sparkling image of us, the French." When the composer Frédéric Chopin embarked on his love affair with the novelist George Sand (see p. 212) in Majorca, he drank champagne to seem witty and more attractive, while Sand herself noted that "champagne helps bring about a state of wonder." Another composer, Richard Wagner, found that champagne alone could renew his "zest for life" and reconcile him with France after his opera *Tannhäuser* was poorly received in Paris.

Champagne has been a hit in show business as well. One of the greatest fans of the fizz was Marlene Dietrich, who claimed that her favorite meal consisted of hot dogs and champagne. She also quipped that champagne "gives you the impression that it's Sunday, that the best days are still to come." In the Leslie Caron film *Gigi* (see p. 57), there's an entire song devoted to the romantic associations of bubbly, "The Night They Invented Champagne," that expresses the happy lovers' wish to "fly to the sky on champagne."

La Champagne, the region to the east of Paris, is the homeland of this most life-affirming of drinks. A must at weddings and other celebrations around the globe, champagne could only come from a place that is as inviting, evocative, and headily romantic as the wine it produces. The preserve par excellence of couples seeking a retreat from the world, the Champagne region is a place to savor slowly, just as you savor a *flûte* or *coupe* of champagne itself.

The art of good living is key to this region, so marry your champagne with some of the fabulous local cuisine, whether it be salmon or snails poached (or soused) in the local bubbly, or the hearty, earthy, sensual dishes stemming from the local *terroir* (produce of the land). Make sure to try Langres, a creamy, slightly crumbly, rinded cheese with an indentation at the top into which you can pour champagne or Marc de Champagne (a brandy made during champagne production from leftover grape skins, seeds, and stalks).

Most visitors to this region of France begin at the city of Reims (pronounced "Rance"), forty-five minutes from central Paris by the express TGV and only thirty minutes from Paris's Charles de Gaulle airport. A historic city, Reims is full of character. French

kings were crowned in its cathedral for more than a millennium. The city and its surrounds are also blessed with the ideal temperature, rainfall, and sunshine for growing vines and ripening grapes for champagne. After spending a day or two exploring the city, your best course of action is to rent or hire a car and tour Champagne's rolling countryside of fertile vineyards and sinuous waterways, punctuated by idyllic villages, half-timbered medieval churches half-hidden amid the hedgerows, and castles from another time. Keep a loose schedule and you're guaranteed to chance upon countless secret corners of the countryside and enjoy many unexpected experiences, whether it's chatting with a champagne farmer as he pulls up on his tractor, joining in a game of *boules* with villagers, or having an impromptu picnic of local foods from the market among the vineyards.

The Champagne region is generally crisp and bright in spring and balmy in the summer. It's best visited, however, in early autumn during *les vendanges*, when the grapes are harvested by hand and the air is filled with their intoxicating aroma. Exact dates of the harvest differ year to year, and even by vineyard according to the ripeness of the grapes, but generally the harvest begins in mid-September. In celebration of the 340 million-or-so bottles that are produced from each harvest, many vineyards host special events, including tours, tastings, grape pickings, and champagne breakfasts or lunches. For further details, contact the Comité Régional du Tourisme en Champagne-Ardenne (+33 (0)3 26 21 85 80; www.tourisme-champagne-ardenne.com).

WINE COUNTRY: REIMS, ÉPERNAY, AND IN BETWEEN

Reims, a compact city but the largest in this region, may have lost most of its medieval buildings to World War I bombs, but the 1920s Art Deco structures that replaced them makes it a pedestrian's joy to discover. Most of the region's champagne is produced around this city—the majority of the vineyards unfurl between Reims and the towns of Épernay and Ay to the south. As a result, Reims finds itself home to the headquarters of many of the *grandes marques* (big brands, or champagne-producing houses; see p. 163). Hence, an education and appreciation of this finest of wines is most appropriately begun in Reims.

To the French, Reims is important not only as the center of the champagne industry but also as the place where, for more than a thousand years, nearly all of their kings were crowned, inside the imposing Gothic cathedral of **Notre-Dame**. Along with the city's Abbey Saint-Rémi, and archbishops' Palais du Tau, this cathedral has been named a UNESCO World Heritage site. Its fine medieval facade has an assortment of quirky and often gruesome detailing, from a rhinoceros gargoyle supported by a hunchback to a carving of wealthy locals, bishops, and kings depicted being hurled into vats of boiling oil on Judgment Day.

Wander inside the cathedral to admire Biblical carvings and thirteenth-century stained glass alongside the twentieth-century windows designed by the artist Marc Chagall (see pp. 195–196). Chagall's windows extend beyond religious themes to highlight the lives of the French kings, including the baptism of Clovis and the coronation of Charles VII, with Joan of Arc beside him.

The most fascinating window of all, however, is the stained-glass window by Jacques Simon in the south transept, which depicts various stages in the production of champagne and the Benedictine monk Dom Pierre Pérignon. The French claim that it was Pérignon who invented champagne, but this is not true if, by "invent," one means that he deliberately created a sparkling wine from a process that could be repeated. Historical documents, in fact, suggest that the English beat the French to the production of champagne by at least twenty years; and it is mentioned by the English dramatist Sir George Etherege in his comedy *The Man of Mode* of 1676.

Dom Pérignon's experiments went on for several decades in the eighteenth century and were fairly haphazard in nature, although the monk did make some important discoveries: most notably, that a late harvest of the grapes in September would result in a fresher-tasting, more elegant wine, and that blending different types of grapes (usually, pinot noir, pinot meunier, and chardonnay) improves quality. It may seem strange that a religious ascetic devoted much of his life to wine, but he was not the first; monks tended the vines in this region, which date back to Roman occupation, until medieval times. The wine that resulted from their harvest was both blessed and consumed during Mass. Clovis I, France's first king, was anointed with wine during his baptism in Reims in 496, inside the basilica at the site where the cathedral now rises. It was Clovis's baptism here that would begin the tradition of the coronation of twenty-five French kings within Notre-Dame de Reims, although the cathedral you see now was built after the first one burned down in 1211.

You may venture inside the Palais du Tau to see where the kings readied themselves for coronation, and where they celebrated them at lavish post-ceremony banquets at which locally produced wines flowed freely. It was the strong association between champagne and royalty that led to its modern connotations of luxury, prestige, power, celebration, and rite of passage—a relationship that has been exploited by the champagne houses since their inception, both in their advertising and packaging. Always eager to demonstrate upward mobility, the middle classes of Europe took to champagne with relish. In the nineteenth century there was a particular effort to make champagne more attractive to women through package design; and, in fact, labels bearing images of marriage, romantic love, and family events such as a child's baptism are characteristic of the champagne bottles from this period.

LES GRANDES MARQUES
CHAMPAGNE TASTINGS AND CELLAR TOURS

Several of the world's most distinguished champagne houses open their doors for multilingual tours of the atmospheric Roman-era chalk caves and *crayères* (tunnels) in which their sparkling wine is stored and aged, followed by a sampling of their champagne. Such tours often require that you make an appointment several days ahead; if you're feeling particularly extravagant, request a private tour culminating in a tasting in a sequestered salon.

The following champagne houses are in Reims. A tip for tasters: don't wear perfume or aftershave, as it will alter your palate.

- **Ruinart**, 4 rue des Crayères, +33 (0)3 26 77 51 51, www.ruinart.com. By appointment only. Founded in 1729, Ruinart was the first champagne house in the region. This house boasts the region's loveliest chalk cellars, and depending on the tour guide's mood, you may be lucky enough to sample a glass of the prestigious "R" or a 1990 vintage at the end.
- **Lanson**, 66 rue de Courlancy, +33 (0)3 26 78 50 50, www.lansoninternational.com. By appointment only; closed in August.
- **G. H. Martel**, 17 rue des Créneaux, +33 (0)3 26 82 70 67, www.champagnemartel.com.
- **G. H. Mumm**, 29 rue du Champ de Mars, +33 (0)3 26 49 59 69, www.mumm.com.
- **Veuve Cliquot Ponsardin**, 1 place des Droits de l'Homme, +33 (0)3 26 89 53 90, www.veuve-clicquot.com. By appointment only.
- **Vranken-Pommery**, 5 place Général Gouraud, +33 (0)3 26 61 62 55, www.pommery.fr. Closed from mid-November to early April.
- **Taittinger**, 9 place Saint-Nicaise, +33 (0)3 26 85 45 35, www.taittinger.fr. Closed from mid-November to mid-March.

Those who have visited the Château de Chenonceau in the Loire Valley (see pp. 141–147) may be interested to learn that the cathedral of Notre-Dame de Reims also hosted the wedding of Louise de Vaudémont and Henri de Valois. Dubbed the "White Queen," Louise was famed for her lugubrious and protracted grieving after the assassination of her husband, who had become Henri III, king of France and Poland. Henri first fell for sweet, blonde Louise because she reminded him of the married woman he adored, Marie de Clèves, the princess of Condé, but he grew to adore Louise in her own right, fussing over her like a child. In fact, their wedding in the Reims cathedral was delayed until evening because the groom—who had personally designed the bride's dress and the costumes of her entourage—spent so long dressing his soon-to-be wife's hair.

Before you leave Reims, seek out some of its unique souvenirs and gifts: champagne flutes with stained-glass designs, chocolate-champagne corks filled with Marc de Champagne, or even champagne sabers, traditionally used to "decapitate" bottles. This technique—not for the fainthearted—is called *sabrage* and is often see at weddings (see p. 221).

ON THE WINE TRAIL

The champagne vineyards are located a few minutes outside of Reims, unfurling to the west and to the south. You are free to tour them at will, but it can be very rewarding to follow the well-signposted trails, or *routes touristiques*. These paths will take you through the heart of the vineyards, past picturesque slope-side villages, and to the front doors of champagne houses. Growers are usually happy to welcome you inside and to share their industry secrets over a taste of their bubbly.

The best route is the forty-five-mile **Montagne de Reims**, which guides you from Reims to Épernay, through an idyllic landscape of hillside vineyards, some of which are part of a regional natural park. Highlights along the way include the **Musée de la Vigne**, a wine and vineyard museum set inside an ancient lighthouse—built as an advertising gimmick by a champagne house and once home to a dance hall—in Verzenay, and the town of Ludes, which is home to six champagne houses.

Beyond Épernay, the **Côte des Blancs** route takes you to Villenauxe-la-Grande via chardonnay-growing territory, with villages formed into amphitheaters dotting the hillsides along the way. The road is crossed by the Marne River with its charming little locks just waiting to be explored by boat. The must-see site here is the **Musée du Mariage et du Champagne Henry du Vaugency** (1 rue d'Avize) in Oger. Set within a fragrant garden, the museum displays more than six hundred objects relating to French marital customs from 1820 to 1940, including glittering tiaras and ornate wedding wreaths, plus more than a thousand champagne-bottle labels dating as far back as 1800. A visit culminates with a tasting of the house champagne in the cellar, amid displays of old winemaking tools.

The other two routes are the picturesque **Massif de St-Thierry**, which takes you west of Reims, and the **Vallée de la Marne**, which passes through riverside towns to the west of Épernay. Good stops on the Vallée de la Marne circuit include **La Cave des Filles** (463

avenue du Général Leclerc) at Dizy, a charming all-women-run cellar, whose aim, in part, is to remove the mystique from wine-buying for other women, and the family-run **Joly-Champagne** (16 route de Paris) at Troissy, with its warm and welcoming tasting room.

Not far from Troissy, at Condé-en-Brie, be sure to stop at the handsome **Château de Condé**, where amid the sumptuous seventeenth- and eighteenth-century interiors and artwork, you can see the bedroom of the infamous Olympe Mancini, who is believed to have been a mistress of Louis XIV during her teens. Mancini was later married to Eugène-Maurice of Savoy, comte de Soissons, whose family owned Condé. Appointed head of the queen's household in the mid-seventeenth century, she quickly became involved in courtly intrigues. Most notoriously, she devised a plot to poison a lady-in-waiting, Louise de la Vallière (see p. 126), with whom the King had fallen in love.

This incident became enmeshed in the wide-reaching Affaire des Poisons, during which the midwife and suspected witch La Voisin (Catherine Deshayes) implicated several people in the French court, including Olympe Mancini and Françoise-Athénaïs de Rochechouart, marquise de Montespan, the king's mistress, as conspirators in powder peddling. According to La Voisin, the Marquise had procured aphrodisiacs and performed Black Masses in her company to gain Louis XIV's favor. La Voisin was publically burned in Paris, while Olympe was expelled from France, never to return.

Condé's castle is no stranger to infamy—until quite recently, it was owned by descendants of the libertine novelist the Marquis de Sade. The castle, however, is an undeniably romantic setting and a great venue for those looking to get married (see p. 227).

The town of Épernay is notorious as the place where Napoléon I stocked up on champagne to take on his military campaigns. The emperor chose this town because he was close friends with its mayor, Jean-Rémy Moët, whose family champagne house Moët & Chandon remains one of the world's most famous to this day. Napoléon would later award Jean-Rémy Moët with the Légion d'honneur for his assiduous promotion of champagne around the world—a promotion that extended as far as the Russian troops who plundered the Moët cellars after Napoléon's abdication. In response to this theft, Jean-Rémy Moët merely uttered: "I'm letting them drink all they want. They will be hooked for life and become my best salesmen when they go back to their own country."

Épernay has its very own **avenue de Champagne**, where several champagne houses welcome visitors. The various tours available allow glimpses of 150 miles worth of cellars containing millions of bottles of fizz. Moët & Chandon is arguably the loveliest among the champagne houses, with flower gardens and an orangery on-site, in addition to the cellars themselves. Its sumptuous gift shop is also a great place to find an extra-special treat for the love of your life.

FINDING YOUR FIZZ

Champagne should not be drunk, it should be tasted. One should not swallow it greedily. One should taste it slowly in narrow glasses, in well-spaced, thoughtful sips.

—COLETTE

The novelist Colette (see p. 21) spoke as wisely about the appreciation of champagne as she did about other sensual matters. Champagne, as with almost everything in life, is a matter of personal taste, and finding your favorite brand of bubbly—mine is Taittinger—can be the most delightful of quests. The following hints will give you some idea of what to look out for.

The words "grand cru" on a label mean that the champagne within the bottle comes from vineyards fulfilling a certain number of criteria that, together, are believed to result in a better quality of grape. A large percentage of such vineyards are clustered around the north- and southeast sides of the Montagne de Reims, where the TGV line makes a loop to spare the precious land. Below the grand cru vineyards in rank are the premier cru, followed by the cru normal. But it's not always simple to work out what cru you are dealing with, since most of the big brands, such as Krug and Roederer, do not disclose on their labels whether exclusively grand cru grapes are used—customers are expected to know the calibre of the wine they are buying.

Then there's the vintage, which simply means the year in which the grapes were grown—nonvintage champagnes incorporate wine from two or more different harvests. Consulting vintage charts may be helpful, but always remember that the charts are based on averages, and that both superb and terrible wines can be produced in any given year. Furthermore, the charts have been compiled by people whose tastes may differ widely from your own.

Concerning the age of a bottle of champagne, the rule of thumb is that, up to a point, the longer it is aged, the more flavorful and refined it will become. Generally speaking, nonvintage champagnes are aged for two to three years, vintage champagnes for three to five years, and luxury, specially blended cuvées de prestige for six or seven years; however, there are wide variations between producers. Some vintage champagnes and most cuvées will benefit from a further two to four years of aging after purchase.

Lastly, champagne comes in different designations, according to the amount of sugar it contains, with the least sweet being brut naturel or brut zéro, running up through extra brut, brut, extra sec, sec, and demi-sec to doux. Most modern champagnes are brut. Other phrases worth looking out for on labels are blanc de blanc (white from white), meaning the champagne is made from 100 percent chardonnay grapes, and blanc de noir (white from black), meaning it's made from black pinot noir or pinot meunier grapes, or a mixture of the two. Most champagnes are made from a combination of both white and black grapes.

When you've identified the right champagne for you, you're confronted with another dilemma—how best to drink it. Until the middle of the twentieth century, bubbly was usually served in coupes—wide, shallow glasses with a saucerlike shape that is said to have been modeled after the breast of Marie-Antoinette (see pp. 126–127) or Madame de Pompadour (see p. 137), depending on which account you read. These days, tall, thin, long-stemmed flûtes are preferred, because their smaller surface area allows the bubbles to dissipate more slowly. Industry insiders and professional tasters, however, favor regular wine glasses as they allow adequate room for swirling the liquid to release its aromas without spilling a drop.

In any event, for all the discussions of the right vintage, cru, grape combination, and drinking vessel, how much you enjoy a particular glass of champagne may often have more to do with whom you're drinking it, where, and why than with the wine's technical excellence.

Coups de Coeur

EATING

Le Colibri
12 rue Chanzy, Reims
+33 (0)3 26 47 50 67

Within a five-minute stroll of Reims's historic cathedral (see p. 161), Le Colibri is a cozy and convivial spot with warm colors—scarlet, burnt orange, and eggplant—gleaming wooden floors, and an odd assortment of erotic artwork and light installations that serve to enliven the mood and provide conversation starters. Lunchtime specials, including a champagne cocktail, make for a good-value gourmet break between sightseeing sessions. Otherwise, the à la carte menu features regional specialities such as rabbit with Reims mustard and cream, alongside Italian-influenced dishes such as carpaccio of beef with pepper-infused vinegar and Parmesan. That said, lovers may be tempted by the options for sharing, including *caquelons*, a type of fondue that involves plunging raw seafood (scallops, prawns, salmon, and monkfish) into a stock made with champagne and then dipping the cooked morsel into a sauce of your choice. Another option meant for two is the chocolate fountain, a dessert that requires you to dip seasonal fruits into melted milk chocolate.

Restaurant L'Assiette Champenois
40 avenue Paul Vaillant-Couturier,
Tinqueux, Reims
+33 (0)3 26 84 64 64

Set within its own extensive grounds in the Tinqueux district of Reims, L'Assiette Champenois is a chic hotel that boasts a restaurant serving bold and challenging cuisine to adventurous foodies. Dishes have been known to include black Gascon pork with guacamole, tacos, and lemon cream; ravioli of blue lobster; wild sea bass with cucumber and pistachios; and a pigeon tart with spinach and tomato. If everything on the menu sounds alluring—and you're unable to make up your mind—opt for one of the tasting menus offering a smaller sampling of house specialties. The modern dining room is outfitted in white linen, with shimmering glass chandeliers, and blood-red roses, and its huge bay windows offer views of the gardens. In summer the tables spill out onto an idyllic terrace where, on sunny days, you may also enjoy aperitifs. At all other times of the year there's a snug bar in which to sample Krug Grande Cuvée and other champagnes. In keeping with the modern style of the fifty-five guest rooms, the bar's hip decor forms an interesting counterpoint to the building's quaint half-timbered exterior. There is also a sparkling swimming pool on the premises for hotel guests.

Restaurant Le Théâtre
8 Place Pierre Mendès, Épernay
+33 (0)3 26 58 88 19

Fresh local produce is the keystone of this smart, spacious restaurant, which is presided over by a Flemish chef. The specially selected Le Terroir

menu features cauliflower soup with squid and scallops, gilthead bream with local sweet pink lentils, and frozen nougat with exotic fruit. For utter bliss, share a dish of the tiramisu, which is made with the rose cookies native to Reims. Accompany your meal with a bottle or two of Brut Impérial from the star local champagne house Möet & Chandon (see p. 167). The waitstaff strike a great balance between friendliness and discretion—perfect for diners on a date.

STAYING

Château Les Crayères
64 boulevard Henry Vasnier, Reims
+33 (0)3 26 82 80 80
www.lescrayeres.com

There are many reasons to stay at this regal hotel located on its own parkland in the outskirts of Reims. One of the most compelling has to be the ease with which the staff is able to organize invitations to the frighteningly exclusive Veuve Clicquot Ponsardin champagne house in the village of Verzy, about twenty minutes from the city. A VIP trip to Veuve Clicquot's ivy-swathed "cottage" is nothing short of extraordinary, including as it does a three-course lunch of dishes that have been chosen to complement a selection of wines. Another perfect reason to stay at the chateau is that your reservation for any of the twenty rooms (three of which are located in the cottage on the grounds) will guarantee you a table in the hotel's stunning, Michelin-three-starred restaurant. Here, you may indulge in the extravagant Tradition de Champagne menu, featuring nine courses, each with a different pairing of Moët & Chandon (or Dom Pérignon). In February look out for Valentine's Day packages, which include a bottle of champagne, dinner for two, and a room overlooking the interior courtyard. For honeymooners, the hotel offers a package that combines accommodation in a super-deluxe room with champagne, chocolates, and flowers, as well as dinner and a visit to one of the local champagne houses.

Hôtel de la Cathédrale
20 rue Libergier, Reims
+33 (0)3 26 47 28 46
www.hotel-cathedrale-reims.fr

Proof that you don't need a fortune to score yourself a romantic bolt-hole, the Hôtel de la

Cathédrale is a typically French provincial hotel offering charming rooms at bargain prices just a few steps from Notre-Dame de Reims. The accommodations are basic, but over the past few years, much effort and imagination has gone into updating and freshening the decor. There's a bright, gaily decorated breakfast room, or you can choose to have your Continental treats brought up to your room for a couple of extra euros.

Château de Fère
Route de Fismes, Fère-en-Tardenois
+33 (0)3 23 82 21 13
www.ila-chateau.com/fere

The setting of this sixteenth-century castle located forty-five minutes west of Reims is beyond romantic—hidden within a tranquil forest, the château lies in the shadow of a second, ruined medieval castle, which you can admire as you enjoy drinks or dinner on the terrace. Arrive in the evening, when the ruins are floodlit, and you may think that you've walked right into a fairy-tale. The twenty-five guest rooms and suites vary widely (an ongoing process of restoration will mean that certain rooms may be a little rough around the edges). As is often the case with old French chateaus, there are squeaky floorboards, strange layouts, and drafts. If this old-fashioned charm doesn't appeal to you, ask for one of the rooms that have been given a makeover—the suites that offer velvet sofas and freestanding tubs are especially inviting. In summer you may make use of a tennis court and an outdoor pool on the grounds, and the friendly staff can organize a hot-air ballooning excursion over the vineyards.

Royal Champagne
Bellevue, Champillon
+33 (0)3 26 52 87 11
www.royalchampagne.com

An impossibly romantic nook hidden among the grand cru vineyards north of Épernay, this former coach house is where Napoléon I and his entourage used to stop on the way to Reims. Practically made for honeymooning couples, the Royal Champagne is discreet and refined, offering twenty-five rooms and suites with private terraces on which to sit and enjoy the sunset over the valley's vineyards with a glass of bubbly. Deep sofas and sumptuous fabrics give you the feeling that you're cocooned in unadulterated luxury, while the chefs in the restaurant will pamper your palate with such delights as foie gras and sweet potato *millefeuille* presented with a chutney of exotic fruits, or red snapper with chorizo and green-tea noodles. The Royal Champagne is particularly atmospheric in the colder months, when a cellist often plays beside the crackling hearth.

Normandy and Brittany

L'amour, c'est l'espace et le temps
rendus sensibles au coeur.

Love is space and time
measured by the heart.

—MARCEL PROUST

Northwest of Paris, France extends to the Atlantic coast through a landscape of lush valleys and forests dotted with the occasional city or large town and pinpricked by tiny villages that seem lost in time. Where the land meets the English Channel—or La Manche (The Sleeve) as the French call it—the coastline offers numerous surprises, from the unspoiled harbors and chic resorts of Normandy to the wilder, wind-lashed, and invigorating terrain of Brittany.

Normandy, which abuts the Île-de-France region surrounding Paris, is known for its turbulent history. Long fought over by England and France, the region was also the scene for many crucial battles during World War II. And yet Normandy has largely remained the rural idyll of green fields that it has long been, interspersed with towns and villages with quaint half-timbered houses. The Seine, which winds lazily through the landscape, has drawn many artists to the region, including Claude Monet. Its coastline, meanwhile, became fashionable among aristocrats from Paris in the nineteenth century, encouraging the development of a string of remarkable seaside resorts. With modern transportation, this Norman Riviera is a mere two hours from the French capital.

The cuisine based on the fruits of the fertile countryside of Normandy is rich, creamy, sensual, and deeply satisfying. The region's well-fed cows produce milk for world-famous local cheeses such as Camembert, Pont l'Evêque, and Livarot, as well as for the rich butter and cream that is used plentifully in Norman cuisine. Meat dishes are rustic and visceral, but those who prefer lighter fare will be delighted with the local seafood, including Normandy's famous oysters, mussels, scallops, and turbot.

Whatever you eat, be sure to give in to the temptation offered by the produce of Normandy's orchards, especially famed apple- and pear-based tipples such as cider, perry, calvados (apple brandy, often drunk as a *trou normand*, literally a Norman "hole" or pause between the courses of a meal), or *pommeau* (unfermented cider and apple brandy). A *kir normand* is a measure of *crème de cassis* (black currant liqueur) topped with cider instead of the standard champagne or wine. Normandy's apples are also used extensively in local dishes such as *moules à la normande* (mussels cooked with apples and cream), pigeon with apple, *bourdelots* (apples baked in pastry), and *flan normand* (apple tart).

Normandy segues into Brittany at the Mont-St-Michel and its abbey, one of the world's most atmospheric attractions and a designated site on UNESCO's World Heritage List. It is here that the Channel coast begins to become more dramatic, with jagged outcrops, suggestively shaped rocks, and in many places pink stone that was, according to legend, stained that color by the spilled blood of persecuted saints.

As with Normandy, gastronomy is an important part of discovering Brittany, whether you visit one of the traditional crepe houses, dine on the famous local lamb (*agneau pré-salé*) raised on the rich salt marshes around the Bay of Mont-St-Michel, or buy oysters fresh from their beds offshore at a seafront stall. Cider, preferably served in a sandstone *bol*, is the tipple of choice in Brittany as well as in Normandy.

Brittany is a vast region, so for this guide I've limited myself to the most romantic of *départements*—the Ille-et-Vilaine, just west of the Mont-St-Michel, and the neighboring Côtes-d'Armor, where the seaside resorts are generally less developed than those on the Atlantic coast of Brittany, and where the ports are more picturesque.

GIVERNY: AN ARTIST OF THE FLOATING WORLD

Were it not for the Paris-born artist Claude Monet, Giverny would be an unremarkable, albeit scenic, village just within the Normandy border, fifty miles northwest of central Paris. The most famous of the Impressionist artists, Monet decided to move to Giverny after he caught a glimpse of the village from a train window in the early 1880s. In 1883 he rented a house here that he would later purchase, and where he would plant the extraordinary gardens that he portrayed in many of his most famous paintings.

Monet moved to Giverny with Alice Hoschedé and their combined family of eight children. At the time that they met, Alice was still married to the wealthy department store owner Ernest Hoschedé, an arts patron who had commissioned a few wall panels from Monet. Alice fell in love with Monet after the artist and his first wife Camille moved in with the Hoschedés.

Camille died in 1879, but Monet and Alice didn't marry until 1892, after Alice's estranged husband's death. Alice suffered from Monet's frequent and lengthy absences as he traveled far from home to paint the effects of different lighting on various landscapes and monuments. She must have complained of these trips to Monet, for in one letter he writes: "If you only knew how much it pains me to see you suffer like this. Your letter this morning upset me so much I wondered whether I shouldn't come back to you."

Over the years, it seems that Alice was successful in persuading Monet to spend more time at Giverny. She became, according to the Monet expert Paul Hayes Tucker, "a lifeline for him, a source of solace, and strength," running the household and family affairs efficiently so that he was free to lose himself in his work. Touchingly, the relationship between Claude and Alice was reprised in the next generation, when their offspring, Claude's eldest son Jean and Alice's daughter Blanche, married. Blanche was Monet's favorite among Alice's children, so it must have been a great comfort to him that, after Alice died in 1911, closely followed by Jean in 1914, it was Blanche who cared for him as he began to succumb to old age and the loss of his sight. Monet found Alice's death terribly difficult to withstand; his productivity declined dramatically, and he told one art dealer friend: "I cannot make anything out of my sad existence."

You can still wander Monet's riotously colorful gardens, where the water lilies that he painted so compulsively continue to float on the tranquil pond crossed by a Japanese-style footbridge. You may see many of these incredible water lily canvases in the Musée de l'Orangerie (see p. 19) in Paris. Unfortunately, there aren't any original paintings on the grounds of the **Fondation Claude Monet**, which comprise the gardens, Monet's pink house, and the studio (now a gift shop) that he had built in order to work on his massive-scale paintings. However, there are copies of some of his works on display in the house with its restored period interiors, as well as some of his personal effects, including his collection of Japanese woodcut prints. Drop in at the village cemetery if you wish to pay homage to the Monet family, including Claude and Alice.

THE NORMAN RIVIERA

Like the French Riviera in southern France (see pp. 193–199), the "Norman Riviera" is an Anglophone term that doesn't mean much to the French. The natives refer to the same stretch of coast sweeping east to west from Honfleur to Sallenelles as the Côte Fleurie (Flowery Coast). The shoreline is part of the *département* of Calvados, which is most famous for the products of its orchards, most notably the fiery apple brandy of the same name. The seaside resorts of Calvados only came into vogue in the mid-nineteenth century, with the arrival of the socialite Marie-Caroline de Bourbon-Sicile, duchesse de Berry, who began inviting fellow Parisians to dip their toes in the chilly waters of the English Channel in Dieppe, a port not far along the coast in the *département* of the Seine-Maritime.

Honfleur, which lies eighty miles northwest of Giverny and past the picturesque town of Rouen (see p. 177) is a picture-postcard port hugging a gorgeous inner harbor that is lined with beautifully preserved ancient buildings of different heights and colors, and quays where prawns and other seafood can be purchased directly from the fishing boats.

From this heart in the harbor, a network of cobbled streets unfolds, offering charming cafés and idiosyncratic boutiques.

Honfleur boasts several compelling sights that are not to be missed. The first is the **Musée Eugène Boudin** (Place Erik Satie), a museum named for the painter of seaside scenes who was born in the town in 1824 and later lived in Deauville (see pp. 178–180). Boudin, a collaborator and lifelong friend of Claude Monet (see p. 174), helped to set up Honfleur's town museum, which now bears his name. Two rooms are dedicated to his works: several focus on various views of Honfleur and a few take the beach at Deauville as their subject matter. The museum also places Boudin in the historical context of other nineteenth-century artists, including Monet, and showcases several twentieth-century artists also linked with Honfleur.

There are further cultural diversions at the off-the-wall **Maisons Satie** (67 boulevard Charles V). This remarkable venue provides a musical and visual journey into the world of musician and composer Erik Satie, another native son and a key figure in the artistic ferment of early-twentieth-century Montmartre (see pp. 90–96). It was in this section of Paris that Satie had an affair with the artist Suzanne Valadon (see p. 93), which, although it only lasted about six months, was to have a lifelong effect on him. The rooms of the Maisons Satie, the half-timbered house where the eccentric composer was born in 1866, have been transformed into a series of Surrealist stage sets evoking Satie, his works, and his inspirations. Within the exhibition, invisible clocks tick, shadows flit across walls amid a jumble of umbrellas (Satie was obsessed with umbrellas), and a carousel ride reveals itself to be composed of nonsensical instruments. It's the kind of place that defies explanation. Multilingual headsets enhance the mood of this parallel universe of whimsy with everyday noises such as whispers and falling rain, as well as provide a commentary set against a backdrop of Satie's music and writings.

The next stop along the coast is **Trouville-sur-Mer**, which was the first resort to sprout up on what is now known as the Norman Riviera, inspired by nearby Dieppe after the Duchesse de Berry and her aristocratic chums came to bathe there. Bathing is perhaps somewhat of a misnomer for the activity in which these visitors actually engaged. Swimming in the sea was considered somewhat risqué at the time, so the aristocrats were carried in sedan chairs, fully clothed, to dangle their toes at the water's edge.

But where neighboring Deauville (see pp. 178–180) feels like an expensive resort, Trouville still feels, at least in parts, like an authentic fishing town. This is partly because the fishing industry is still alive here: fishermen continue to sell their catch on the quay, and a fishmarket is held daily. Like Honfleur, Trouville is a good place in which to wander along winding lanes bordered by one-off cafés and shops, and along its beach of sugar-fine sand. It was on this beach in 1836 that the novelist Gustave Flaubert

THE ROUEN AFFAIR

Fans of Gustave Flaubert should make a stop in the delightful medieval city of Rouen, Normandy's historic capital. It was here in 1821 that the novelist was born, and the city features prominently in the novel widely regarded as his masterpiece, *Madame Bovary*. The tale of an adulterous provincial doctor's wife, *Madame Bovary* earned Flaubert a public obscenity trial in his day, but is now held to be one of the most influential novels ever written.

In the novel, Emma Bovary and her husband Charles live near Rouen, and it is while attending an opera in town that Emma becomes reacquainted with Léon, a young law student on whom she'd had a crush a few years earlier. The pair arranges to meet in the city's cathedral, and from here they take a passionate ride in a closed carriage through the cobbled streets of the city—a scene that has become one of the most famous in western literature.

After the crazed ride, Léon and Emma meet secretly each week in a hotel room in Rouen that they come to see as their "home." You may take a horse-and-carriage ride through the town of Rouen as they did, as well as visit Rouen's cathedral, where they engaged in their psychological foreplay. This cathedral is also infamous for having been obsessively painted by Claude Monet (see p. 174) as he sought to capture the effects of different lighting on its facade. One such painting can be seen in Rouen's delightful Musée des Beaux Arts (esplanade Marcel-Duchamp).

(see pp. 208–209) met his first love at the tender age of fifteen, while he was on vacation with his family. Flaubert had noticed a fur-lined cape that was getting wet on the sand. He returned it to its owner, twenty-six-year-old Elisa Schlésinger, and was invited by her partner Maurice to accompany the couple and their young daughter on boat trips and walks. It was then that Flaubert fell madly in love with Elisa. Although his passion was never consummated, he wrote about the encounter in his first finished work, *Mémoires d'un fou* (*Memoirs of a Madman*), a year or two later. Flaubert made another pilgrimage to Trouville in 1853 and went on to base many of his female characters, including Marie Arnoux in his *L'éducation sentimentale* (*Sentimental Education*), on Elisa, with whom he kept in touch until her death. As late as 1859 Flaubert wrote movingly to a friend of his feelings: "Each one of us has in his heart a royal chamber. I have had mine bricked up, but it is still there."

These days, a statue of the writer in Trouville's port bears witness to the town's importance to Flaubert, who began his own sentimental education here. Another writer who helped to popularize the town is Marcel Proust (see p. 179) who stayed in the glamorous Hôtel des Roches Noires. This hotel is no longer standing but was immortalized in a painting by Monet while he was honeymooning in Trouville with his first wife Camille (the newlyweds actually stayed in the cheaper Hôtel Tivoli, which stood on the rue des Bains).

It was while he was staying in Trouville that Napoléon III's half-brother, Charles-Auguste-Louis-Joseph, duc de Morny, was inspired to transform the next village along the coast, **Deauville**, into a "kingdom of elegance." Within four years, Parisian and international aristocrats were flocking to Deauville's beach, racecourse, casino, and grand hotel. The town was so snooty that a local joke held that wealthy men kept their wives in Deauville while their mistresses were relegated to working-class Trouville.

Depending on your take (and taste), Deauville is either wonderfully glamorous or overpriced and snobby. Prices are certainly stratospheric during the two weeks each September when the town hosts its world-renowned Festival du Cinéma Américain. The names of an array of American movie stars who have attended this film festival since its inception in 1975 can be seen painted on the wooden bathing cabins on the promenade stretching alongside the fabulous beach.

Aside from this vast and spectacular beach, Deauville is a place for taking afternoon tea in a luxury hotel, spending a day at the horse races or watching a polo match at one of two racecourses, the Hippodrome de Deauville La Touques and the Hippodrome de Deauville Clairefontaine, or fluttering at the seafront Grand Casino. Architecturally inspired by the Petit Trianon at the Château de Versailles (see p. 126) and the Restoration theaters of Paris's Champs-Élysées, the Grand Casino is France's third largest casino and one of the biggest in Europe. It's believed to have been the model for the Casino de Royale-les-Eaux in Ian

Fleming's first James Bond novel, *Casino Royale*—Fleming is known to have played at Deauville as a young man. The Deauville casino was also where novelist Françoise Sagan, the precocious author of *Bonjour Tristesse* (see p. 192), won the fortune that allowed her to buy her house in Equemauville near Honfleur. She purchased the property that very night and in cash.

Like Honfleur, Deauville abounds with romantic associations, both fictional and otherwise. In F. Scott Fitzgerald's *The Great Gatsby*, Deauville gets a brief mention as one of the places newlyweds Tom and Daisy Buchanan stayed during their year in France. In real life, Coco Chanel used to vacation here with her lover Arthur "Boy" Capel, a British polo player. It was Capel's blazers that inspired Chanel's classic suit designs, and his fortune that allowed her to set up her third boutique, on Deauville's rue Gounaut-Biron, in 1913. It was from here that Chanel moved from millinery—avant-garde cloche and pillbox hats—to clothing. To learn more about Coco's life and humble beginnings, watch the 2009 movie *Coco avant Chanel* (*Coco Before Chanel*), starring Audrey Tatou of *Amélie* fame (see p. 57). The film was partly shot in Deauville, where, taking up Chanel's couture baton, the late designer Yves Saint Laurent also had a house. High-end clothing and accessories shopping has unsurprisingly remained one of this town's big draws.

But the town is perhaps best known as the setting for the Oscar-winning 1966 movie *Un homme et une femme* (*A Man and a Woman*), about a young widow, Anne (Anouk Aimée), and a widower, Jean-Louis (Jean-Louis Trintignant), who meet at their children's boarding school in Deauville. Over several trips back to Deauville, they fall in love, despite Anne's feelings of loss and guilt about her late husband. The director Claude Lelouch is said to have been inspired to make the film when he was sitting on the beach at Deauville at 6 a.m. one morning, and upon seeing a young woman and her child nearby, tried to imagine what circumstances had brought the mother to that moment of her life.

Trouville and Deauville provided elements for the fictional resort of Balbec in Marcel Proust's semiautobiographical masterpiece *À la recherche du temps perdu* (*Remembrance of Things Past*). However, a third resort, **Cabourg**, west along the coast from Deauville, provided the greatest inspiration for the novelist, especially its Grand Hôtel, where you can still vacation in classic French seaside style (see pp. 187–188). It is in Balbec that the narrator meets Albertine Simonet with her "brilliant, laughing eyes and plump, matte cheeks," who will replace his first love Gilberte Swann in his affections. The narrator's romance with Albertine, one of a group of "*jeune filles en fleur*" ("young girls in bloom") whom he sees on Balbec's beach, provides much of the material for this expansive, multivolume work.

Although Cabourg's promenade has since been named for Proust and a number of informational panels with quotes from the novel are exhibited along the walkway, this is a charming, gentle resort with a vast, flat beach that you may have all to yourselves in the

off-season. Don't miss the sight of the *trotteurs*—French trotting horses pulling riders in chariots-training on the beach. Cabourg's beach is nicknamed the Plage aux romantiques (the Romantics' Beach) after a beloved song of 1966 by Pascale Danel, the final line of which is a marriage proposal.

Like Deauville, Cabourg is also the setting for a film festival, which is held each July. Much more relaxed and intimate than the Deauville festival—to the extent that you can mingle with the directors and stars on the beach, in the town's streets, and at restaurants and musical events—the Journées Romantiques, Journées Européennes focuses on romantic films. The film festival's current patrons are the actress Sandrine Bonnaire and her actor/scriptwriter husband Guillaume Laurant, who married in Cabourg after meeting and falling in love at the Grand Hôtel, when Bonnaire was there in 2001 to receive the title of best actress in a romantic movie, for her role in *Mademoiselle*.

THE MONT-ST-MICHEL AND A TASTE OF BRITTANY

The most-visited French site outside of Paris, the **Mont-St-Michel** near the Norman border with Brittany is no insider's secret. But approaching it, as it rises magnificently from its surrounding bay of quicksand, you will understand why this is one of the world's most photographed structures. This rocky islet topped with a Benedictine abbey and steepled Romanesque church is truly awesome.

Once on the Mont, you are almost certain to feel disappointed by the crowds of tourists who throng the steep, cobbled streets and the masses of trinket shops that cater to them. However, you may experience the true mystery and magic of this historic monument without the crowds by staying in a hotel on the Mont. Booking a room here will mean that you can explore the islet's attractions at sunset or after dark, when the majority of people have left for the day (see p. 188).

On the islet, you can visit the abbey and its spooky crypts, or venture within various museums, including a historical museum, a maritime museum, and a multimedia space with a *son-et-lumière* show on the church's history, construction, and legends. You can also attend a service led by the handful of monks and nuns who still live here. All are enjoyable. But best, by far, is simply climbing to the upper ramparts of the Mont and drinking in the amazing views its higgledy-piggledy rooftops in one direction and over the shimmering sand flats in the other.

As you gaze over the immense bay, you'll spot figures walking on the sand. You may join them, but only as part of a guided walk (www.mont-saint-michel-baie.com), as the tides have been likened by writer Victor Hugo to "a galloping horse," and even today people are drowned or swallowed up by the quicksand just as many medieval pilgrims to the abbey once were. These tours center on a variety of themes, from night outings and storytelling, to picnics and fishing on foot, to excursions focusing on "literature in nature." The area around the mount is also good for coastal bike rides and horseback riding, or you can float over the bay in a hot-air balloon, sail across it in a restored *bisquine* (traditional fishing boat) from the working port of Granville, or even ride out onto the sandbars in a tractor-drawn cart to see local mussels growing on *bouchots* (wooden poles).

Many people in Brittany challenge the Norman ownership of the Mont-St-Michel—the mount was historically located in Brittany, in fact, until the Couesnon River, which forms the border between Normandy and Brittany, changed course. Most of the Baie du Mont-St-Michel is in Brittany, including such charming spots on its shore as the oyster-farming town of Cancale and its resort, Port Mer. Stop in **Cancale**—at one of the Channel coast's most intimate retreats, Les Rimains, or the neighboring Gîtes Marins (see p. 187)—and feast on oysters with wedges of lemon served on plastic plates at seafront stalls for a fraction what they cost in the restaurants a few steps away. Enjoy them as the natives do, with a bottle of cider on the beach, tossing the shells back into the ocean while watching the tractors out in the oyster beds just offshore and admiring the distant views of the Mont-St-Michel. Proof that romance doesn't have to mean candlelight and champagne.

Cancale forms the start of the stunning Côte d'Émeraude (Emerald Coast), which takes you almost as far as St-Brieuc. Not far outside Cancale, on the quiet coastal road toward St-Malo, lie a number of glorious, deserted beaches with shimmering rock pools and banks of wild oysters. They include the Plage de la Touesse at St-Coulomb, where the writer Colette (see p. 21) lived in a villa from 1911 to 1926. She drew inspiration from the setting for her novel *Le blé en herbe* (*The Ripening Seed*), the story of the love affair between two adolescents during a family vacation. You may also spot dolphins leaping offshore from these beaches.

Other highlights of the long Emerald Coast are the ancient walled pirates' town of St. Malo and its beach resort of Rothéneuf, and St-Malo's neighboring town, **Dinard**, best known for its associations with the artist Pablo Picasso (see p. 34). Picasso spent the summer of 1922 at the resort, with his wife Olga Kokhlova and their son Paulo. He returned with them in 1928 and 1929, but on these occasions, unbeknownst to Olga, he secretly installed his mistress Marie-Thérèse Walter in a nearby hostel for young women.

In Dinard, Picasso, who Marie-Thérèse later described as a "wonderfully terrible lover," would take his teenage lover to cavort in a cabana on the Plage de l'Ecluse. The artist had been obsessed by the erotic potential of beach huts since adolescence, when he glimpsed a seminude woman on a beach in his native Spain. During their stay in Dinard, Picasso painted Marie-Thérèse daily, often beside the cabana or with the key to it in her hand, or playing ball with her friends or sisters. Olga, meanwhile, was portrayed as a scrawny bather with a reproachful mouth. Sometimes, Picasso even portrayed his wife and his mistress on the same canvas. For instance, *Le baiser* (*The Kiss*) of 1929, which is on display in the Musée National Picasso in Paris (see p. 34), features the artist's wife and his mistress conjoined in one bifurcated head. Located in the same collection and also painted in 1929, *Baigneuses à la cabine* (*Bathers Outside a Beach Cabana*) depicts the two women side by side, both naked. Olga, again, is bony and grim-faced, her arms linked above her head in a travesty of a ballet pose (she had been a dancer before injury curtailed her career), while the sporty Marie-Thérèse is fit and serene.

Fans of Picasso's work or those intrigued by his amorous adventures can rent the hilltop gabled house in which his family stayed during their third visit here in 1929—the Villa Bel-Event. This four-bedroom property featuring a large garden and inspiring sea views was where Picasso painted many of the *Baigneuses* (*Bathers*) paintings that remain his legacy of the Breton coast. The villa lies on the Promenade Clair de Lune (Moonlit Promenade), a coastal walkway scented by palm trees and other tropical plants. The path is best experienced on summer evenings, when music is piped onto it and the gardens bordering it are illuminated.

The Promenade Clair de Lune offers the best views of many of Dinard's belle-époque villas, which were built by British aristocrats who popularized the resort in Edwardian times. Even today, the resort retains something of a genteel British feel—an impression enhanced by the fact that it plays host to the Festival du Film Britannique each October. This festival awards two prizes named for Alfred Hitchcock, of whom there is a statue in the

town. Some people claim that the British director was inspired by one of Dinard's angular villas when he designed Norman Bates's house for the 1960 film *Psycho*.

The seascapes of Dinard and the delightful fishing village of **St-Lunaire** nearby are said to have inspired part of *La Mer* (*The Sea*), one of the most famous works of the French composer Claude Debussy. St-Lunaire, with its gorgeous beaches and English-style houses, is another popular summer retreat for Parisians. From this fishing village, it's a twenty-mile drive to the fortified medieval castle of **Fort la Latte**. Set on top of a 230-foot cliff against a clear blue sea, the fort—where Kirk Douglas and Tony Curtis shot the final scenes of *The Vikings* —provides one of the Breton coast's most dramatic sights. Take a trip to the Cap Fréhel on another prong of the same peninsula and climb the steps of the 1950s Phare du Fréhel, a lighthouse offering views over nearby islands and even as far as Normandy.

PRETTY IN PINK: THE CÔTE DE GRANIT ROSE

It's ninety miles from Dinard to Pors-Hir, which is roughly the midpoint of Brittany's northernmost stretch of coastline, named the Côte de Granit Rose (Pink Granite Coast) for its rare pinkish-brown rocks. Legend has it that the rocks were stained by the blood of persecuted saints. Many of these rocks, eroded by the elements over the course of millions of years, are contorted into odd formations named by locals after the objects they are said to resemble, such as *sorcière* (witch), *tas de crêpes* (pile of crepes), and *tortues* (tortoises), which makes them fun to spot.

Suggestively shaped rocks aside, this is a breathtakingly beautiful stretch of coast with turquoise water, white sand, and tranquil boat-filled bays. Avoid major resorts such as Perros-Guirec and instead seek out the quieter spots, such as the *sentier de douaniers*, a former coastguards' footpath that runs between the sea and the low hills covered with pine trees, lavender, mimosa, heather, and other wildflowers. Alternatively, around Pors-Hir, follow the signposted coastal route named the Côte des Ajoncs (Gorse Coast) around a series of tiny bays inhabited by even tinier villages, including Gouermel Plage, with its gorgeous view of the sea and brasserie-crêperie, and Buguélès, where you can see houses that have been built between mighty boulders, often so tightly that they appear to be wedged in. At night, red, green, and white lights pulsing from lighthouses and the violent rocking of the buoys will remind you of the treacherous nature of the coast.

Get hold of a *horaire des marées* (tide table)—free from the Comptoir de la Mer, a chain of stores in Brittany—if you want to venture out to one of the many offshore islands on your own. There are, however, regular boat trips to the seabird and seal sanctuary of the Sept Îles. Alternatively, venture inland from the pink coast to discover menhirs, dolmens, and other prehistoric remains amid the unspoiled towns and villages.

Those interested in the romantic legends of the area should head east of Pors-Hir, via Tréguier and Lézardrieux, to the **Sillon de Talbert**. This natural formation is a breathtaking and even perplexing sight: a thin spit of land curving out a full two miles into the sea that is seemingly resistant to the tides that ought to wash it away. (In fact, this peninsula is stretching northeast and will eventually break away from the coast.) Among the numerous myths associated with the Sillon are those of the magician Merlin, of Arthurian legend, who is said to have placed the millions of pebbles here to allow him get closer to the fairy Viviane—his student with whom he fell in love. Another myth holds that King Arthur himself fell in love with the sorceress Morgan Le Fay, after seeing her sitting on a rock in the middle of the sea combing her long hair. Morgan, equally smitten, threw one pebble after another in front of her to form a pathway through the waves to the king. Today, those who venture to the tip of the spit are rewarded with a view of the Héaux-de-Bréhat lighthouse, splendid and awesome in its isolation about six miles out to sea.

For an atmospheric conclusion to your visit to the pink coast, head for the ruined Gothic **Abbaye de Beauport** in its stirring position on a bay close to Paimpol. Guided tours take visitors through the cellars, kitchen, church, and cloister filled with Mediterranean plants. For the ultimate romantic effect, visit the abbey on a Wednesday or Sunday in July or August for an Escale de Nuit, a nighttime walk (10 p.m. to 1 a.m.) during which dreamlike scenes from the monks' daily lives are projected onto the abbey ruins, along with other quirky images such as a maze made of roses and a library illuminated by fireflies.

COUPS DE COEUR

EATING

La Petite Chine
14–16 rue du Dauphin, Honfleur
+33 (0) 2 31 89 36 52

A favorite haunt of the late fashion designer Yves Saint Laurent whenever he visited the port of Honfleur (see pp. 175–176), this chic tearoom is perfect for a brunch or lunch date. Set in a quaint house just a few steps from the town's inner harbor, La Petite Chine offers coffee and cakes alongside light fare such as soup, tarts, *tartines* (open sandwiches), and pasta. Alternatively, if you've skipped lunch while sightseeing, indulge in an afternoon tea of *clafoutis* (a fluffy, custardlike dessert from the southwest of France), a brownie with cream, a bowl of crumble, a scone, or a serving of *fromage blanc* (a yogurtlike cheese) accompanied by cinnamon, honey, and almonds. Fine teas from India, Taiwan, and elsewhere may be enjoyed with your meal or purchased in leaf form in the adjoining shop, which also sells pretty teapots and other tea-making accoutrements, along with luscious pastries, jams, and old-fashioned candies.

Dupont avec un Thé
6 avenue de la Mer, Cabourg
+33 (0)2 31 24 60 32

Breakfast to a soundtrack of opera or Sunday brunch accompanied by live piano music are just two of the highlights of this award-winning pâtisserie only a five-minute stroll from Cabourg's Grand Hôtel and seafront (see p. 179). But you can come throughout the day to enjoy hot and cold savory treats, including salads, sandwiches, tarts, *croques* (melts), and luxury pies. Chocoholics will think they've died and gone to heaven when they see the chocolate specialties, which include a dark-chocolate fondue for two with dips of seasonal fruits, homemade cookies, and chocolate macarons. Or celebrate Cabourg's literary links with the Heures du Proust afternoon tea, comprising two madeleines (the shell-shaped cakes that trigger the narrator's spasm of involuntary memory in *À la recherche du temps perdu*) and either a Brazilian or Caribbean hot chocolate or your selection from more than forty types of tea. Wines and aperitifs are also served. There are branches of this patisserie in Trouville-sur-Mer (see p. 176) and Deauville (see pp. 178–179).

Le Moulin de Jean
La Lande, Cuves
+33 (0)2 33 48 39 29

If you're traveling west to the Mont-St-Michel (see pp. 180-181), it's well worth timing your journey to coincide with lunch or dinner at this former watermill just east of the town of Avranches. Stunningly beautiful, Le Moulin de Jean is the brainchild of superstar chef Jean-Christophe Novelli and despite his departure has remained a top-notch eatery. In summer, eat on the terrace to enjoy sunset views and the sounds of birdsong and gurgling water; in winter a fire crackles invitingly in the hearth. Menus change frequently, but typical *plats de résistance* are pollack with mushroom risotto and vermouth sauce, roast duck with potato-and-chestnut mash and cider sauce, and a *controversy* of white and dark chocolate. After your meal, you're free to wander on the lovely restaurant grounds alongside the small lake.

Le Blue B
Grand Hôtel Barrière
46 avenue George V, Dinard
+33 (0)2 99 88 26 26

Sumptuous in decor and boasting incredible bay views, this restaurant within the Grand Hôtel Barrière—part of a small group of exclusive hotels in France that include the Hôtel Fouquet's Barrière in Paris (see p. 73)—is a seductive spot for a special *dinner à deux*. Numerous gourmet menus are offered, among them L'écailler, comprising a vast seafood platter with oysters from nearby Cancale (see p. 181) followed by apple tart with vanilla ice cream, or—for unashamedly hedonistic couples—L'épicurien, which includes foie gras with dessert wine, roast lobster with spices, fillet of beef with port, a selection of cheeses, and dessert. Note that a meal with drinks in Le Blue B is included in this classic seaside hotel's Be My Love in Dinard package, as are a bottle of champagne, flowers, and use of the indoor pool, hammam, and other leisure facilities.

Le Surf
Plage de Longchamp, St-Lunaire
+33 (0)6 80 26 08 58

This unassuming shack, with its humble terrace and line of tables and chairs arranged along the seawall overlooking the best of St-Lunaire's beaches (see p. 183), could well be the surprising setting for one of the most romantic meals of your life. Within the ramshackle building, a minuscule kitchen miraculously produces an amazing diversity of dishes, from *croques*, crepes, waffles, and panini featuring anything from peanut butter to smoked salmon, steaks, *moules de bouchot*, whole lobster (requiring twenty-four hours' notice), and salads both simple and more elaborate. Don't miss the Indonesian salad, with grilled king prawns, seaweed butter, basmati rice, rocket, and shallots cooked in lemon juice. Prices are an absolute steal. If you're not hungry, you can kick back and watch the surfers on the beach or the children fishing in the rock pools as you enjoy a kir, cider, or hot chocolate.

STAYING

Le Grand Hôtel de Cabourg
Les Jardins du Casino, Cabourg
+33 (0)2 31 91 01 79
www.mercure.com

The very image of a French seaside palace-hotel, the Grand is famed for its connections to the novelist Marcel Proust, who stayed here every summer from 1907 to 1914 and drew inspiration from the town of Cabourg for his fictional resort of Balbec (see p. 179). Although now owned by the Mercure chain and recently renovated, Le Grand Hôtel de Cabourg has retained its belle-époque decor. One room is furnished according to the novelist's descriptions of the room in which he used to stay (the actual room is now the manager's office), but all of the rooms have a chintzy charm that harkens to a more refined age. You can choose between garden and sea views;

some rooms with a sea view also have a balcony. The old-world ambiance extends to Le Balbec, the hotel's formal seafood restaurant, and its bar, which features live music. Cabourg's Grand Casino stands beside the hotel, should you fancy a spin on the roulette table or a hand or two of poker.

La Maison du Vert
Ticheville, Vimoutiers
+33 (0)2 33 36 95 84
www.maisonduvert.com

For those who don't mind getting away from the coast, this hotel and vegetarian restaurant within a scenic green valley about forty miles south of the Norman Riviera is perfect for couples looking for a retreat from the modern world. Consisting of just three simple guest rooms within a former redbrick bakery of a tiny village, this hotel is surrounded by organic flower and vegetable gardens, in which you are free to wander at will, and where you can take aperitifs (including organic local cider, beer, and wine) on fine days. There's also a terrace on the grounds for alfresco dining in summer. The restaurant itself has garnered a good reputation for its global vegetarian and vegan cuisine—a real rarity in France. Dishes run the gamut from Indian *thalis* to *rösti* (pan-fried potato and onion cake).

La Mère Poulard
Grande Rue, Mont-St-Michel
+33 (0)2 33 89 68 68
www.mere-poulard.fr

It's not easy to find a good hotel among the tourist traps of the Mont-St-Michel (see pp. 180–181), but La Mère Poulard provides the historical atmosphere conducive to spending a night or two at this iconic sight. The hotel's twenty-seven guest rooms offer views of the abbey, which is illuminated by night, or of the awesome bay that surrounds the Mont. The rooms are simple, uncluttered, and pleasant. The on-site restaurant is famous for its omelets, which are still prepared according to the secret recipe of Mère Poulard, who was once the chef here. Indeed, a whole ritual is devoted to the omelets, which are whisked and prepared in front of a crowd of tourists. Also on offer is the famed *agneau pré-salé* (lamb that derives its intense flavor from feeding on the local salt marshes) as well as Brittany lobster and other seafood. The hotel's piano bar, with its old photos, is the perfect place to snuggle up and take in the splendid bay views. Guests are advised to bring minimal luggage due to the length of the walk from the parking lot to the Mont and the hotel's narrow and winding staircases.

Cottage Les Rimains/Gîtes Marins (Maisons de Bricourt)
62 rue des Rimains, Cancale
+33 (0)2 99 89 64 76
www.maisons-de-bricourt.com

The most delightful and intimate of retreats, Cottage Les Rimains comprises just four romantic rooms within a tiny cliff-top cottage overlooking the oyster beds of Cancale (see p. 181), with a communal terrace for breakfast. The rooms form part of Les Maisons de Bricourt, a mini-empire owned by local boy–turned–celebrity chef Olivier Roellinger and his wife, Jane. The Maisons also comprises the nearby Gîtes Marins, a small collection of luxurious self-catering "seaside cabins" decorated in a New England style and accommodating from two to eight people. Guests

who stay in the Gîtes are free to gather vegetables and herbs from the kitchen garden on the grounds; the fabulous cabin kitchens feature ovens designed by Roellinger himself. Both Les Rimains and the Gîtes afford easy access to the old *chemin des douaniers* (coastguards' path), which is so romantic that it's also known as the *chemin des amoureux* (lovers' path). You can follow it down to Cancale's harbor, or, if you're feeling reckless, in the other direction, to the very limits of the Breton coast. Elsewhere in Cancale, the Maisons offer the Château Richeux, a 1920s villa containing eleven guest rooms, two suites, and Le Coquillage, a "marine bistro" serving contemporary takes on classic Breton and Norman seafood dishes. Also in the village is Roellinger's Cuisine Corsaire culinary school, Les Entrepôts Epices-Roellinger spice, salts, and aromatic oils shop, and the truly heavenly Grain de Vanille tearoom and ice-cream parlor.

La Maison des Lamour
La ville Guerfault, Plélo
+33 (0)2 96 79 51 25
www.lamaisondeslamour.com

A half-hour's drive inland from the Côte de Granit Rose (see pp. 183–185), the Lamour family's domain comprises a handful of enchanting, eccentric B and B rooms just perfect for couples wishing to get away from it all, as well as a few self-catering houses (one of them for two people). The B and B rooms are idiosyncratically furnished with tasteful bric-a-brac—if you like their funky-meets-rustic style, the grounds hold an *artisanat-brocante* where you can buy into the same junkshop chic (and stock up on homemade cider and rhubarb jam). The family, who has lived here for generations, is devoted to green tourism, and the accommodations are part of a working farm that spreads across a scenic valley. The vast grounds include an old mill housing an inn famed for its hearty pork stew and sweet and savory pancakes. Prices for food and lodging are exceptionally reasonable, but a special Weekend en Amoureux (Lovers' Weekend) package will give you even more of a reason to discover this truly original destination.

Southern France

L'amour est le plus grand
rafraîchissement dans la vie.

Love is the greatest
refreshment in life.

—PABLO PICASSO

Where the north could be characterized as largely cerebral, France's Mediterranean coast—less than an hour's flying time from the capital—is a full-on assault of the senses. The first pleasurable sensation that you will notice is the intoxicating light: intense and dazzling, it has inspired many famous painters to both live in the region and to record it for posterity in many of their best-known works. Then there are the bewitching smells of the Mediterranean: lavender, lemon, mimosa, jasmine, thyme, tarragon, basil, fennel, and other flowers, fruits, and herbs that result in a heady mix of perfumed air when combined with the salty tang of the ocean and the exotic spices used by the North Africans who have settled in southern France.

Matters of taste are central to life in the south, perhaps even more so than in the rest of France. But with the astonishing quality and variety of the local produce grown in this region, who could resist the voluptuous pleasures of the table? To visit the south of France is to embark on a culinary adventure that will most likely change your taste buds forever and awaken you to a whole new world of flavors, textures, and even colors. Oil from the silvery olive trees that swathe the hillsides is central to Mediterranean cuisine, while other mainstays include anchovies, red mullet, bream, sea urchins, and zucchini flowers. A dish that is most associated with Marseille but is presented all over southern

France in various guises is bouillabaisse, a soup so pungent and sensual that it has its own erotic legend.

But even the humblest *soupe de poisson* (fish soup) served here is paired with a fiery chili aioli (garlic mayonnaise), croutons, and melted cheese. *Soupe au pistou,* another regional concoction, consists of beans and vegetables lifted to ecstatic heights by the addition of garlic paste, basil, Parmesan, and tomatoes. Other pastes are often served beside evening aperitifs, on toast, or alongside raw vegetables for dipping. The most notable are a combination of olives mashed in their ever-present oil with garlic or capers into tapenade, or with anchovies into *anchoïade*. Drinks are similarly full-bodied, from the dry, intensely fruity rosés de Provence and robust red côtes de Provence wines, to the aniseed-flavored, knock-your-socks-off spirit, pastis.

Mediterranean France—especially the region known as Provence—can be a land of clichés, as is the fate of many of the world's most beautiful places. Yet it's possible here, amid the tourist crowds, to find moments of peace and harmony, where the scene before your eyes does indeed resemble something from an artist's canvas. Life *can* happen at a slower pace, if you let it. It's a question of discovering those lesser-known places—those secret corners—in which time seems suspended. If you don't believe me, seek out any town or village square and watch, spellbound, as local men (and occasionally women) gather under the orange trees to play a round or two of *boules* or *pétanque,* lost in concentration as they spin their well-worn silver balls.

MOVIES ON THE MED

Head to La Ciotat near Marseille to admire L'Eden movie theater, said to have hosted the world's first public motion picture screening in 1896. Suffused with the light and ambiance of the Mediterranean, the following movies will also help get you into the mood for your exploration of the south of France.

- MARIUS (1931). Alexander Korda's cinematic rendering of Marcel Pagnol's play by the same name (see p. 207), set in Marseille and concerning the love affair between Fanny, a fishmonger's daughter, and Marius, a café owner's son who dreams of going to sea. The film was reinvented as the Oscar-nominated *Fanny* (1961), directed by Joshua Logan and starring Leslie Caron.
- LES VISITEURS DU SOIR (*The Devil's Envoys*; 1942). An allegory of the struggle between good and evil, largely shot around Tourrettes-sur-Loup (see pp. 198–199) by director Marcel Carné (see p. 56). It was in this very town that its scriptwriter, Jacques Prévert, hid with friends during the Nazi occupation. The plotline of the fifteenth-century lovers' defiance of the devil is actually a parable of the occupation and of Prévert's personal experiences of it.
- BONJOUR TRISTESSE (1958). Otto Preminger's screen adaptation of the classic French novel by Françoise Sagan, who oversaw the film script. Jean Seberg stars as Cecile, a seventeen-year-old whose sexual awakening is accompanied by her compulsion to intervene in the love affairs of her playboy father Raymond, played by David Niven, as they holiday on the French Riviera.
- LA BAIE DES ANGES (*Bay of the Angels*; 1963). The story of a love affair between two lost souls over the roulette tables of Nice. Jeanne Moreau stars as the gorgeous divorcée who catches the eye of a toy-boy thrill-seeker. Agnès Varda, widow of the director Jacques Demy, restored the print to bring the film back into circulation in 2000.
- LA LUNE DANS LE CANIVEAU (*The Moon in the Gutter*; 1983). An underrated offering from Jean-Jacques Beineix, starring Gérard Depardieu as a Marseille man seeking to avenge his sister's death and also torn between his passion for a rich amateur photographer played by Nastassja Kinski and his poor but beautiful girlfriend.
- TROIS PLACES POUR LE 26 (*Three Places for the 26th*; 1988). Another Jacques Demy film, this time a musical romantic comedy set in Marseille, starring the legendary Yves Montand (see p. 88) as himself. Returning to the city of his adolescence to star in an autobiographical musical, Montand spends his free time searching for his first love, Mylène.

- Marie Baie des Anges (*Marie from the Bay of Angels*; 1997). Manuel Pradal's scarred idyll of wild Romani girl Marie and her boyfriend Orso amid Vespa gangs on the French Riviera, described by one *New York Times* reviewer as a "dizzying paganistic ode to Eros."
- Marius et Jeannette (1997). Directed by Robert Guédiguian, the story of a relationship between the guard of an abandoned cement factory near Marseille and a checkout operator and mother of two whom he catches trying to steal paint from the plant. Both must open themselves up to happiness again if their love is to have a chance.
- A Good Year (2006). Ridley Scott's beautifully shot foray into Provence, starring Russell Crowe as a British banker who, having inherited his uncle's chateau and vineyard, rediscovers love, friendship, and trust. Marion Cotillard of *La vie en rose* fame (see p. 88) plays the love interest, Fanny Chenal.

NICE: FINDING PARADISE IN THE BAY OF ANGELS

France's fifth largest city, Nice has one of the country's busiest airports, with several flights a day from Paris, which average around ninety minutes, as well as easy international connections to many other cities. Six hours from the capital by express TGV—for those with the inclination and the leisure to discover the French countryside from their windows—Nice is also one of the most popular cities outside Paris among foreign visitors. But don't worry: this is a place big enough and with enough off-the-beaten-track attractions to entice couples seeking a dose of privacy.

Nice is one of France's—and indeed the world's—oldest settlements, dating back to around 350 BC, when it was founded by the Ancient Greeks based in Marseille (see pp. 207–212). Its name is probably a derivation of "Nike," the name of the Greek winged goddess of victory, strength, and speed. Today, Nice is a sparkling Mediterranean city with a subtropical feel that stems from its heavily imported vegetation of palm, eucalyptus, and citrus trees. Rising from the cobalt waters of the Bay of Angels—named after an extinct species of local shark that, according to legend, became half-angel after an angel fell in love with one of them—the city is infused with a light that has attracted many artists across the decades, from Henri Matisse and Marc Chagall (see pp. 195–196) to Niki de Saint Phalle.

Art collides with history in the **Cimiez**, an area high up in the city, where it climbs sharply away from the coast. Amid olive groves and the remains of an independent Roman

city, which includes thermal baths, an amphitheater, an ancient road, and a museum depicting ancient Roman life, sits the **Musée Matisse de Nice** (164 avenue des Arènes de Cimiez), which houses some of Henri Matisse's greatest depictions of the region. The painter and sculptor first came to Nice from Paris in 1917, hoping to escape the rain and to cure his bronchitis. Falling in love with the city, he spent most of the remainder of his life here.

In addition to many of the artist's studies of the female back, the collection includes several scenes that were inspired by his new home. These works include *Tempête à Nice* (*Storm in Nice*) and a poster entitled *Nice, travail et joie* (*Nice, Work and Joy*). Across the road from the museum is the glorious apartment building that was originally the **Hôtel Regina**, which was built in part for Queen Victoria, whose retinue of about one hundred people required her to take over the whole west wing. A statue of the queen in front of the building commemorates this royal connection. After staying in several of the city's hotels, Matisse lived and worked in the Regina for a long period in his career, returning to it late in his life after seeking refuge from the bombs of World War II in nearby Vence (see pp. 197–198). Though in poor health, Matisse insisted on working from his bed, using charcoal affixed to long poles to draw on the walls and ceiling of his suite. He died in 1954 and is buried in the cemetery of the nearby **Monastère de Cimiez**, where you can pay respects at the tomb that he shares, rather strangely, with his estranged wife of forty-one years, Amélie Noellie Parayre.

Although Amélie seldom came to Nice with her husband, it wasn't until 1932 that that the real rift occurred. The fracturing of the relationship began when Amélie sacked their housekeeper Lydia Delectorskaya, a Siberian refugee who had also begun to work as Matisse's model and assistant. Amélie did this not out of jealousy, but because in her eyes, Lydia had taken over the household. As a result of the dismissal Lydia shot herself in the chest, but amazingly she survived her injury. She would return to nurse Matisse when, newly divorced, he discovered he had cancer, and remained his devoted companion and manager throughout his productive final two decades. After his death, she wrote an eyewitness account of his painting methods, *L'apparente facilité* (*Apparent Ease*).

The grounds surrounding the Matisse museum are dotted with statues of eminent jazzmen such as Louis Armstrong, and music buffs will be glad to know that this park is the setting for the world-renowned **Nice Jazz Festival**. The pathways are similarly named after many famous musical legends. The annual open-air festival takes place in Cimiez over eight days in July.

Down from the hill and past the Regina, the **Musée National Marc Chagall** (avenue Docteur Ménard) is one the most compelling museums devoted to an individual artist in southern France. The Russian-born painter and sculptor Marc Chagall, regarded as both a precursor to Modernism and one the world's foremost Jewish artists, was involved with the museum from the start and actively helmed its activities until his death in 1985. Although Chagall's oeuvre wasn't exclusively religious or spiritual, this museum was conceived as the home for seventeen joyful, brightly colored canvases of various scenes from the Bible to which he gave his own poetic interpretation. The museum also holds a few stained-glass windows, mosaics, and engravings.

Of the Biblical scenes, twelve depict stories from the Old Testament, while the remaining five illustrate Le cantique des cantiques (Song of Songs), each one of which depicts a variation on the overall theme of love. *Le cantique des cantiques IV,* for instance, shows Bathsheba, the wife of Uriah the Hittite, fleeing with King David, her new love, on a winged horse. Chagall imported the winged horse, a figure from ancient Russian legend, into the Biblical story to symbolize the lovers' impetuous desire, as well as David's youth

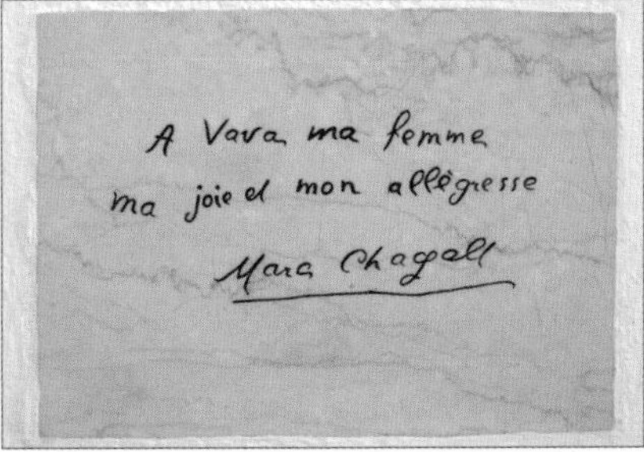

and fertility (he has impregnated Bathsheba). But flying figures are a recurrent motif in Chagall's work, one that the artist himself attributed to his feelings for his mother, "her breasts so warmly nourishing and exalting me, and I feel I could swing from the moon."

It's also fitting that these five love-themed paintings are dedicated to Chagall's wife Valentina, known as Vava. As a dedication transcribed onto a plaque on the wall testifies: "A Vava ma femme, ma joie et mon allegrèsse." ("To Vava my wife, my joy, and my lightness.")

It was Vava Brodsky who restored Chagall to happiness and creativity after a fallow period following the death of his first wife, muse, and confidante Bella in 1944—an event that, according to the artist, made "everything turn black." Vava, a Russian milliner living in London, was hired by Chagall's daughter Ida to be his housekeeper. Vava was the second of Chagall's housekeepers with whom he began a relationship: after Bella's death he had a son with his unhappily married assistant Virginia Haggard McNeil.

Vava and Chagall met in Vence (see pp. 197–198) and married within three months of Virginia's departure in 1952, when Vava was forty years old and Chagall was sixty-five. Vava reawakened the artist from the long depression that had dogged him ever since Bella's death by encouraging him to take on major artistic projects such as the Biblical series at this museum, the ceiling of the Palais Garnier opera house in Paris (see p. 76), and the stained-glass windows for Reims' cathedral (see p. 161). Vava also appeared in many of his paintings. The couple lie together in the cemetery in St-Paul-de-Vence (see p. 198), in a grave they share with Vava's brother, Michel Brodsky.

Despite the sprawl of this city, Nice is surprisingly manageable on foot—aside from the heights of the Cimiez district, most of what you will want to see and do is located in the old town by the waterfront, an area called **Vieux Nice**, where everything is within a walking radius of no more than twenty minutes. Here, a picturesque labyrinth of alleyways and narrow pedestrian streets are bordered by charming houses and punctuated by pretty squares. The old town will lure you to browse its charming boutiques and markets, especially the daily flower and produce market in the **Cours Saleya**.

As Nice is so close to Italy, the ice cream available is wonderful. Pick up a cone from one of the specialty stores or stalls that are particularly abundant in Place Rossetti; **Fennochio** is famed far and wide for its incredible flavors, including locally inspired orange blossom, jasmine, lavender, verbena, and violet. The enclosed pedestrian square of the Place is the hub of the old town—home to the Ste-Réparate cathedral, a fountain, and several handsome red and ocher buildings. The old town is best enjoyed at night, when the facades are beautifully illuminated and street music permeates the air.

One thing that Nice does *not* offer the best in is sand, as most of its public beaches are made up of *galets* (large, flat stones). Unless you're staying at a plush hotel with its own stretch of sand or feel like shelling out the fee to enter a private beach, you're better off heading to Antibes (see pp. 204–207) to swim and sunbathe. On the other hand, Nice's **Promenade des Anglais**—so named because the city was a popular wintering spot for wealthy English people in the late eighteenth century—is the venue for one of the world's most stunning seafront walks.

Along the promenade you'll spot the iconic **Hôtel Negresco** with its perky pink dome—a palace-hotel dating back to 1912 and listed among France's historic monuments. It was outside of this hotel that the legendary dancer Isadora Duncan met her tragic end, after her long scarf became caught in the wheels and rear axle of the car in which she was traveling. The driver was a handsome French-Italian mechanic, and Duncan's last words are said to have been "Je vais à l'amour" ("I am off to love").

AROUND NICE: VENCE AND ÈZE

Before heading north for some artistic inspiration, take a scenic detour east of Nice, to the medieval village of **Èze**, for heart-stirring views of the sea and the surrounding landscape. Located in an "eagle's-nest" position atop a tall hill in the shadow of a ruined fortress, this spot is said by some to have been the site of a Phoenician temple honoring Isis, the goddess of motherhood and fertility, due to the Egyptian cross that resides within the village church, Notre-Dame de l'Assomption. In tribute to this legend, Èze's botanical gardens with their collection of cacti and other succulents also contain sculptures of earth goddesses by the artist Jean-Philippe Richard, who conceived of these sensual figures as descendants of Isis. Contemplative spaces—terraces that jut out over the sea—provide visitors with ergonomic seating and gorgeous views. Reserve one for yourselves and let the astonishing watery landscape transport you to paradise.

Northwest of Èze, two close-knit towns in the hills of Nice's *arrière-pays* or back-country, Vence and St-Paul-de-Vence, long served as magnets for creative figures. British writer D. H. Lawrence spent his last years in **Vence**, while artists Raoul Dufy and Henri Matisse (see pp. 194–195) also lived here for a time. Although Vence has a reputation for the purity of the springwater that gushes up through its fountains and for the Roman relics and pretty medieval architecture in its center, its two key sights are religious buildings with artistic connections. The first is the tiny **Cathèdrale de la Nativité de la Vierge** (Place Godeau), which has a lovely mosaic by Chagall depicting Moses in the bulrushes. The second, the small **Chapelle du Rosaire** (466 avenue Henri Matisse), set on a hillside just outside of town, was the result of the unlikely relationship between Henri Matisse and a nun who was his muse for a time. Step inside and you'll be blown away by the chapel's blend of exuberant color and chaste serenity.

A few steps from the Chapelle du Rosaire, Matisse's colonial-style Villa le Rêve (Dream Villa) is often rented by artists, therapists, or those simply looking for a beautiful place to stay. With eight bedrooms, the villa is too large for one couple, but those thinking of tying the knot in the region will be interested to know that it can be rented for celebrations such as wedding receptions (www.villalerevevence.com).

It's possible to walk from Vence to **St-Paul-de-Vence**, either along the road or by a ravine and through some woods. This stunning medieval hilltop town is encircled with ramparts and offers wonderful views over the Mediterranean and the southern Alps. It began attracting artists and celebrities in the early twentieth century: Chagall, Pierre Bonnard (see p. 68), Amadeo Modigliani (see p. 114), Robert Doisneau, André Gide, and Jean Cocteau are just a few of the many artists and writers who came here. Later, American author James Baldwin spent his final years in the town. This is a spot so beautiful that the aged and infirm Matisse, while working on the Chapelle du Rosaire (see p. 197), would visit just to sit under the orange trees and take afternoon tea in his car.

Head for the wonderful **Foundation Marguerite et Aimé Maeght** on a wooded cliff where the ravine path from Vence leads into St-Paul. This private museum devoted to modern and contemporary art includes many works by Marc Chagall, who lived in St-Paul for nearly twenty years and is buried in its cemetery with his second wife Vava (see p. 196). One such work is the mosaic *Les amoureux* (*The Lovers*) on the exterior wall of the museum building, which the artist dedicated to his dealer Aimé Maeght and his wife Marguerite, who set up the museum.

What is perhaps most charming about the Fondation is the way its nine thousand works of art spill out into a wonderful setting of lawns, pools, and fountains. In fact, many of the fountains and other outdoor features were designed by artists, contributing to the mood of lighthearted playfulness. The most striking is the Spanish artist Joan Miró's *Labyrinthe*, a stone maze filled with sculptures and ceramics. The maze has been interpreted by some as symbolizing a rite of passage; the large sculpture entitled *Oeuf* (*Egg*) emerging from a pool within the piece is probably intended to be symbol of motherhood or fertility. The front sculpture garden, meanwhile, has an unmistakeably priapic figure by Miró.

St-Paul is one of the *villages perchés*—literally, perched villages—that grace the hilltops of Nice's backcountry. Another such village is **Tourrettes-sur-Loup**, where you can admire one of the region's trademark bell towers, which were constructed of wrought iron so that the strong *mistral* (wind) would pass through them rather than topple them over. Packed with medieval and Romanesque buildings and artisans' workshops, Tourrettes is perhaps

best known for its cultivation of violets, the scent of which pervades the village from October to March. In early May and late July, the leaves of the plants are torn off and transported to nearby Grasse (see pp. 200–203), where they are used to make perfume essences.

One of the best times to come to Tourrettes is in early March (the exact date varies according to the state of the blossoms), when the end of the violet-picking season is celebrated with a violet festival featuring local music and dancing in the streets, which are strewn with flowers. There is also a special Mass in the church, a flower procession, and most notably, the Battle of the Flowers, during which crowds lining the streets are showered with blooms thrown from passing floats. If you can't make it to Tourrettes in the spring, inquire at the tourist office in town to arrange a visit to a local producer.

The sunny terraces surrounding Tourrettes are also employed in growing orange blossoms, cabbage roses (*Rosa centifolia*), and jasmine—all of which are used at the famous local candy factory, the **Confiserie Florian des Gorges du Loup** (Pont du Loup). Free guided tours of the factory will enable you to witness the production of tart fruit candies in Provençal flavors; flower and citrus-fruit marmalades; crystallized flowers; glazed fruits; and chocolates such as *orangettes* (strips of candied orange peel dipped in chocolate). It is a scenic, sinuous drive in the shadow of the ruined viaduct of the Pont du Gard to other *villages perchés* in this vicinity, including Gourdon and Bar-sur-Loup at the entrance to the Gorges du Loup (Wolf Pass).

GRASSE, MOUGINS, AND THE LIFE OF THE SENSES

Travel west of the trio of hilltop villages clustered around the Gorges du Loup to find the remarkable town of **Grasse**, which has been justly dubbed the perfume capital of the world. It's here that more than two-thirds of France's natural aromas are produced (both for perfume and for culinary flavorings), and also where many of the great noses of the perfume industry have been trained. Lovers of the novel *Perfume: The Story of a Murderer* (see p. 121), by German author Patrick Süskind (or the 2006 movie adaptation), will recognize Grasse as the city to which the "gifted and abominable" apprentice perfumer Jean-Baptiste Grenouille heads in his quest for the ultimate scent—one that will make people love him. Read the book before coming to Grasse, not just for the setting and compelling plot but for *Perfume's* descriptions of perfumery techniques such as maceration and enfleurage.

The perfume industry in Grasse took root in the eighteenth century, when the suitability of its microclimate for flower farming, including the cultivation of jasmine, was first appreciated. Today three major perfumeries have factories, museums, and shops in Grasse and host workshops where you can learn to create your own perfume. The most famous of the houses is **Fragonard**, whose perfumery in the center of town (20 boulevard Fragonard) has a museum with a collection of perfume-related artifacts that date back five millennia.

The second, **Galimard** (73 route de Cannes), began as the supplier of perfumes, pastes, and olive oils to Louis XV, the Beloved (so called because of his initial popularity with the public). This perfumery has a *studio des fragrances* where you can create a personal scent and then have it stored on a database should you wish to order it later in the guise of eau de parfum or body cream, among other products. The third producer is **Molinard** (60 boulevard Victor Hugo), which has a display on-site of antique René Lalique and Baccarat perfume bottles as well as vintage scent labels that are displayed amid Provençal furniture dating from the sixteenth to eighteenth centuries.

As if that wasn't enough, Grasse reopened its **Musée International de la Parfumerie** (International Museum of Perfume; 2 boulevard du Jeu de Ballon) in late 2008. Now doubled in size, the museum has an impressive collection covering perfume and its manufacture as well as the history of soap and cosmetics. Exhibits range from the hand and foot of a three-thousand-year-old Egyptian mummy, which was perfumed as a means of preservation, to a cosmetics case that belonged to the French queen Marie-Antoinette (see pp. 126–127).

The artist Jean-Honoré Fragonard, who is now recognized as one of the masters of French painting, had nothing to do with perfume. The artist's name was simply appropriated by the entrepreneur Eugène Fuchs when he opened Fragonard in 1926, as a way to link

Eaux
d'Ange
Rouge
d'Espagne

his products with local tradition. Jean-Honoré himself was born in Grasse in 1732, and the **Villa-Musée Jean-Honoré Fragonard** (23 boulevard Fragonard) now displays many of his works within an elegant late-seventeenth-century house surrounded by palm trees.

The artist began his career painting religious and classical subjects but made his name with scenes of love and voluptuous goings-on that members of Louis XV's bawdy, pleasure loving court commissioned from him. He was also asked to provide artworks for the apartments of Louis's last mistress, Madame du Barry, in Louveciennes (see pp. 108–109). A replica of the intimate and subtly erotic *Les progrès de l'amour dans le coeur d'une jeune fille* (*Progress of Love in the Heart of a Young Girl*) series of four paintings that Fragonard under took for Madame du Barry, beginning with *The Pursuit* and running through *The Meeting* (also known as *The Surprise*) and *The Love Letter* to culminate in *The Lover Crowned*, are on view at the museum.

There have been suggestions that Fragonard himself was no stranger to romantic entanglements: some sources insist that he fell in love with his sister-in-law, Marguerite Gérard, who became his pupil and assistant when she was just fourteen. The fact that Marguerite never married only heightens speculation that this beauty had an affair with her brother-in-law, with whom she collaborated on a number of genre scenes. You can see a selection of her solo works on display within the Villa-Musée Jean-Honoré Fragonard, as well as view some trompe l'oeil wall paintings by Fragonard's son, Alexandre-Évariste, who went on to become a renowned painter and sculptor in his own right.

Among Grasse's beautiful gardens is the **Jardin des Plantes**, which reflects local heritage and industry with its focus on the fragrances of Provence—in particular, jasmine, rose, and tuberose, the three flowers that are indispensable when building a perfume. If you feel like rolling up your sleeves, local producer Hubert Biancalana of **Le Domaine de Manon** (36 chemin du Servan) will take you out to see his rose and jasmine fields and may even let you help pick the blooms.

One of the highlights of the year in Grasse is the Battle of the Flowers. This floral "fight" was adored by Queen Victoria, a frequent visitor to Grasse, and is still practiced as part of La Jasminade, also called the Fête du Jasmin (Jasmine Festival), that is held each August. The event also features folk music, fireworks, street performances, and open-air parties. If you'd prefer to avoid the heat and crowds of August, visit Grasse in May during the Expo Rose—an exhibition of more than fifty thousand roses made into bouquets.

Given its sweet-smelling industry, and its beautiful museums and gardens, Grasse is a surprisingly gritty and down-to-earth town that stretches haphazardly but scenically across a hillside. The obligatory touristy trinket shops do exist, but you can also find warrens of dark medieval alleys lined with ancient houses with crooked open stairwells, and colorful, shabby North African groceries and cafés. In fact, Grasse's palm trees and

the red and ocher houses with their peeling shutters evoke the feeling that you have landed somewhere quite exotic—a sensation only reinforced by the absence of supermarkets and the presence of charming *brocantes* (antique-cum-junk shops) such as **Quatre Mains** (12 rue Amiral de Grasse). There are also tiny pâtisseries that lure you in to sample their *fougassettes*—pastries gorgeously scented with locally grown orange blossom.

Indeed, the gourmet is in luck in Grasse. Aside from the numerous bistros and restaurants around town, particularly on the arcaded **Place des Aires**, Grasse and its environs produce some of the world's best olive oil. The town's traditional oil mill, the **Huilerie Sainte-Anne** (138 route de Draguignan), is a good spot to stock up on bottles of the unctuous green-gold liquid and luxurious olive-based soaps. There are tours of the mill available daily.

For true foodie heaven, head out of Grasse to **Mougins**, just a few miles to the southeast. This pretty town with its medieval heart has been famous for its cuisine since the 1930s, when local fisherman Célestin Veran made his name cooking bouillabaisse (see p. 209) for visiting celebrities such as the Duke of Windsor. Mougins's fame as a gastronomic mecca truly began in 1969, when the superstar-chef Roger Vergé opened **Le Moulin de Mougins** (424 avenue de Notre Dame de Vie) restaurant in an abandoned olive-oil mill. It now holds two Michelin stars and also offers twelve sumptuously themed guest rooms where diners can sleep off their excesses. Since it was launched, other gastronomic establishments have sprung up in the town to rival it: the one-Michelin-starred **Le Candille** (part of Le Mas Candille luxury hotel; see p. 218), **Le Jardin** (205 avenue du Golf), and **Le Park de Mougins** (144 avenue St-Basile).

Mougins has plenty of more budget-friendly—but still welcoming—traditional restaurants in which you may dine equally memorably on Provençal cuisine. In September, the town hosts **Les Étoiles de Mougin Festival International de la Gastronomie et des Arts de Vivre** (International Festival of Gastronomy and the Art of Gracious Living), featuring demonstrations from famous chefs from around the world, together with tastings and gala dinners.

Mougins is more than the sum of its world-class eating opportunities: visit the **Musée de la Photographie de Mougins** (by the Porte Sarrazine medieval gate) for its exhibition of images of Pablo Picasso (see p. 34) by Robert Doisneau and other eminent photographers. The Spanish artist lived in the village from 1937 to 1939 with his muse Dora Maar, and then spent the last thirteen years of his life in a hilltop *mas* (old farmhouse) called **Notre-Dame-de-Vie**, about two miles from the village.

This farmhouse is forever marked by tragedy—the artist's grief-stricken widow and final muse, Jacqueline Roque, committed suicide there after his death in 1973. For three decades, the villa remained untouched—scattered with original artworks and personal effects—right down to an unopened bottle of champagne in the fridge and a pair of Picasso's reading glasses left on a dresser in the couple's bedroom. This bizarre neglect was the result of ongoing family feuds caused by Picasso's failure to leave a will.

In 2008 the villa was finally rescued from oblivion by a Belgian art dealer, who renamed it L'Antre du Minotaur (Minotaur's Lair), in reference to the half-bull, half-human of Greek mythology with whom, in his later years, Picasso identified himself. This identification was multilayered and included Picasso's acknowledgment of the voraciousness of his sexual appetite and the sacrifices he demanded from his lovers—often extending to their peace of mind and even sanity.

ANTIBES AND THE CAP D'ANTIBES: ARTISTS AND LOVERS

Heading back down to the coast to the west of Nice, you'll find more works by Picasso at the **Musée Picasso** in the resort town of **Antibes**. Occupying part of the Château Grimaldi, which once belonged to the eponymous Genoese family who rule Monaco, the museum was established to hold all of the town's art. When Picasso was visiting the area in 1946, he was invited to live and work in the castle for two months. In gratitude, he donated sixty-seven works to the town, and its museum became the first in the world named for the Spanish artist. The collection now includes about two hundred and fifty pieces by Picasso—many of which were donated by his widow Jacqueline Roque (see above).

Picasso's donation included *Ulysse et les sirènes* (*Ulysses and the Sirens*), a work based on the Homeric myth of the bird-women who lured mariners to their deaths with their seductive singing. Ulysses and his crew escaped this fate thanks to the intervention of the sorceress Circe, who loved Ulysses. Picasso's twelve-foot work depicts the hero tied to his ship's mast to withstand the sirens' song. There's also his *Joie de vivre* (*Joy of Life*) a luminous beach bacchanal inspired by the end of World War II and by his contentment with his lover at the time, the painter Françoise Gilot.

Picasso painted on canvases but also on the walls of the Grimaldi castle. One of the walls still bears his famous *Les clés d'Antibes* (*The Keys to Antibes*), which consists of three fawns' heads. This painting has been preserved throughout a gigantic restoration project that was completed in the middle of 2008. The newly expanded space also displays photos by Michel Sigma of Picasso and Françoise together, ceramics that Picasso produced at the Madoura pottery workshop in nearby Vallauris, and several works by other twentieth-century artists.

Picasso first came to Antibes in July 1924 with his wife Olga Kokhlova and son Paulo. He returned in 1931 with Olga, but this time he secretly installed his mistress Marie-Thérèse Walter nearby (just as he did in Dinard in Brittany; see p. 182). The Picassos were among the artistic celebrities who helped transform the Côte d'Azur into a summer resort—previously, it had been a place to visit in winter. Other fashionable figures who contributed to its popularity were the composer Cole Porter and his wife Linda, and the writers F. Scott and Zelda Fitzgerald.

F. Scott Fitzgerald used the **Hôtel du Cap-Eden-Roc**, which still stands at the tip of the Cap d'Antibes headland stretching south from the town of Antibes itself, as a model for the Hôtel des Étrangers in *Tender Is the Night*, his novel about a failing marriage not entirely dissimilar to his own. With its ornate, often floral, rather old-fashioned decor, the hotel is not to everyone's tastes, but it is a classic choice for those in search of luxury and privacy. Guests who have sought seclusion there include Marlene Dietrich, and the Duke and

Duchess of Windsor. Elizabeth Taylor and Richard Burton, who had an affair at the hotel, returned to it for their honeymoon. This is also the place to which A-list stars flock after flaunting themselves at the film festival in nearby Cannes each May.

THE START OF THE AFFAIR

Since the nineteenth century, Antibes's beautiful setting and the fifty or so beaches surrounding it have made it a popular spot with artists, including novelist Guy de Maupassant, painter Claude Monet (see pp. 174–175), and the poet and screenwriter Jacques Prévert.

One improbable figure on the streets of Antibes was the British novelist and part-time spy Graham Greene, who fled here in 1966 after he was implicated in a financial scandal in the United Kingdom. Greene chose Antibes as his place of exile partly because he had spent time on a yacht in its marina twenty years earlier, and partly to be close to Yvonne Cloetta, a woman he had met in Cameroon in 1959. Although both were still married (Greene was separated from his wife Vivien and Cloetta's marriage was an unhappy one), they embarked on an affair that was to last until Greene's death in 1991. Greene once remarked that if "[Yvonne] didn't exist, I'd put a bullet through my head."

It is Yvonne who is said to have finally ended Greene's emotional attachment to Lady Catherine Walston, another married woman with whom he had an affair—one that provided the basis for his novel *The End of the Affair*. Yvonne lived in Juan-les-Pins, the town adjoining Antibes, with her daughters; her husband worked in Africa.

A plaque at the back of the Résidence des Fleurs, the apartment block on rue Sadi Carnot in which Greene wrote seven novels and a number of stories—some of them set in Antibes—pays tribute to the novelist. Fans of Greene—or lovers seeking to emulate his intimacy with Cloetta—can still dine at **Chez Félix au Port** (50 boulevard Aguillon), the modest café and restaurant where they often lunched together after an aperitif of a dry martini without lemon. The café is mentioned in Greene's story "Chagrin in Three Parts," and was used as the location for the filming of a scene from the Dirk Bogarde TV adaptation of another Greene story, "May We Borrow Your Husband?" The latter—the tale of a honeymooner "borrowed" from his new bride by two gay men—also includes a mention of **L'Auberge Provençale** (61 place Nationale), which is another place where Greene and Cloetta liked to dine. The **Hôtel Royal** (16 boulevard du Maréchal Leclerc) is yet another of their hangouts that you can still visit.

It was F. Scott Fitzgerald who coined the term "Jazz Age" to designate the hedonistic period that lasted for roughly ten years from the end of World War I. Those who love the music that inspired this era will feel at home in Antibes's neighbor Juan-les-Pins, which hosts the world-famous Festival International Jazz à Juan each July.

Antibes was built at the site of the ancient Greek port of Antipolis, and the foundations of the Grimaldi castle reach down into its ruins. The chateau's protective walls were added in the tenth century, after numerous assaults by the barbarian tribes who came in the wake of the fall of the Roman Empire. An archaeology museum showcases these layers of history in a collection of artifacts wrested from local digs and shipwrecks.

The castle is linked via a secret passageway to the basement of **Balade en Provence**, a seemingly inoffensive shop located by the half-timbered town market and specializing in local olive oil. Within its cellar lurks the region's only licensed absinthe bar, which sells glasses of the "green fairy" that inspired—and often ultimately ruined—so many artists around the turn of the twentieth century. This space, with its Roman well, marble bar, and rickety wooden tables and chairs, doubles as a sort of museum, filled with vintage absinthe paraphernalia, including old posters and artworks portraying the drink as a semi-naked, green temptress. The patron of the bar is happy to chat about how the emerald spirit is made from herbs, including the hallucinogenic wormwood, and how it can best be savored—a ritual involving a perforated spoon, a sugar cube, and ice water.

MARSEILLE: PLEASURE THROUGH EVERY PORE

Earthy and often shabby—or even downright dirty—Marseille is Paris-on-Sea meets North Africa: contradictory, dizzying, intoxicating, *real*, with a spicy ethnic mix of Corsican French, North Africans (Arabs and Berbers), Comorians, Armenians, Turks, Chinese, and Vietnamese. When you've had your fill of the region's lavender fields and sleepy *villages perchés*, come to this white-hot city for a dose of urban romance alongside the glittering blue waters of the Mediterranean.

A little over three hours by express TGV from Paris, Marseille is a far cry from the bucolic Marcel Pagnol novels and Cézanne paintings that constitute the popular image of Provence. On the other hand, one of Pagnol's lesser-known works, his play *Marius*, depicts much of the charm of Marseille in its slice of life set in a sailors' bar in the old port, where the heroine Fanny works at a shellfish stall. In 1931 Alexander Korda popularized the story in a Paramount movie (see p. 207).

Before Pagnol, the novelist Gustave Flaubert (see pp. 176–177), who was among those smitten with Marseille's eclecticism and hedonism, described the city as: "... a babel of all the nations, where one sees blond hair ... black beards ... blue eyes, black looks ... the turned-down collars of the English, the turban and wide trousers of the Turks ... People are taking in pleasure through every pore, in every form, as much as they can ... crowding into the cabarets, laughing with the girls, turning over jugs of wine, singing, dancing, love-making at their ease."

Flaubert's rapture was partially inspired by his affair with Eulalie Foucaud, who ran the Hôtel de Richelieu on rue Francis-Davso (then rue de la Darse), where he stayed with his family on the way to Corsica. Age thirty-five, Creole, and "magnifique" (according to Flaubert's literary friends the Goncourt brothers), Eulalie had recently returned to France from Peru. This voluptuous widow was responsible for the eighteen-year-old writer's sexual initiation when she visited his hotel room after he smiled (or, according to another account, blew a kiss) at her.

After a tearful separation and a six-month exchange of letters, Flaubert lost touch with Eulalie, and when he returned to Marseille years later, he found the hotel abandoned. On his final visit to the city, he discovered a bazaar occupying the first floor of the hotel and a wig-maker and barbershop on the second floor. Going upstairs for a shave, he recognized the wallpaper from the room in which he had slept with Eulalie, and wrote later to a friend, "It had been a long time since I had so deeply thought or felt, I don't know which."

Some aspects of Flaubert's novella *Novembre* (*November*), published two years after he met Eulalie, are believed to be based on his four-day erotic idyll with the hotel-keeper in Marseille. Eulalie is said to have informed the character of Marie, a prostitute who longs for acceptance and romance.

STEAMY STUFF

Marseille's greatest fame does not come from any of its historically rich buildings, but instead from its most widespread contribution to French cuisine: a seafood soup called bouillabaisse. This rich, delectable broth is made with a different recipe in every restaurant and home across the city, meaning there's no such thing as an authentic, definitive bouillabaisse. That said, most versions include garlic, fennel, thyme, bay leaf, and orange peel, which are often supplemented by pistils of saffron. This spice, long held to harbor medicinal properties, was also used by the Persians as an aphrodisiac, while Cleopatra would add it her baths with the belief that it made lovemaking more pleasurable.

The orange-gold soup is served in a bowl and topped by grilled slices of country bread slathered in rouille, a mayonnaise comprised of saffron, garlic, olive oil, and cayenne pepper. Your waiter will set a plate of at least three types of fish by your bowl, featuring most typically *rascasse* (scorpion fish) from the nearby calanques (see p. 210), *grondin* (sea robin), and conger eel, plus a variety of seafood (mussels, crabs, octopuses, sea urchins, and—in the most expensive versions—langoustines), and several kinds of vegetables. Beware that this may not be the kind of soup you want to eat in front of someone with whom you don't feel familiar or comfortable—the gelatinous quality of the broth is a result of the dense bones and cartilage of the *rascasse*, which make for a lot of spitting into one's napkin!

As is often the case with classic dishes, the origins of bouillabaisse are steeped in legend. Many locals will tell you that this was the soup made for the god Vulcan (or Hephaestos) by his consort Venus (or Aphrodite), to send him into a deep sleep while she frolicked with Mars (Ares); the combination of seafood and saffron is held to be soporific. The prosaic will insist that bouillabaisse was developed from *kakavia*, a simple fish stew that was eaten by the ancient Greeks who founded Marseille. This basic recipe is said to have been elaborated on by the city's fishermen who, returning to shore after a long day at sea, rigged up cauldrons of seawater on wood fires and threw in the fish that were too bony to serve in restaurants, along with garlic and fennel.

France's largest commercial port and third-biggest city, Marseille doesn't sound like a romantic destination. But the country's oldest city, founded as a trading port by Greeks around 600 BC, offers a great deal of atmosphere, and, as Flaubert suggested, a life-affirming outlook. A romantic legend about the city's founding has it that Protis, a Greek explorer who was seeking a site for a new trading post, was invited to a banquet that was hosted by Nann, or Nannos, the chief of a local Celtic tribe, to find a suitable husband for his daughter Gyptis. The latter unhesitatingly chose Protis from among her various suitors, and the couple moved to the hill just north of the cove where the explorer had come ashore. It was there that they founded Massalia—now called Marseille.

Relics of the past exist within many of the city's nooks and crannies and form much of its charm. Among these gems are the **Jardin des Vestiges**, which is studded with the remains of the Hellenic port, including ramparts and a necropolis. This garden is accessed via the **Musée d'Histoire de Marseille** (Centre Bourse, Square Belsunce), which documents the city until the eighteenth century. There is also the **Musée des Docks Romains** (Place de Vivaux), which is built on the excavation site of the old Roman harbor, as well as the **Musée d'Archéologie Méditerranéenne** (2 rue de la Charité), which houses collections of Egyptian, classical, and regional artifacts. The museum is one of several cultural venues that inhabit the Vielle Charité building, a seventeenth-century hospice for orphans and vagrants and now a historical monument. It lies at the heart of Le Panier (The Basket), the oldest part of Marseille, to the north of the old harbor. The name "Panier" is derived from a seventeenth-century cabaret that was located here. Also within Le Panier is the **Musée du Vieux Marseille** (rue de la Prison), which reveals the story of Marseille from the eighteenth century on (where the Musée d'Histoire leaves off) and is located within the sixteenth-century Maison Diamantée.

Aside from these and other sights in this vast city, Marseille is also a wonderful place in which to idly wander, although—as with Paris—you will need to choose a specific area to explore to avoid being overwhelmed. One of your best options may be colorful Noailles, with its souk-like market and Arabic and Indo-Chinese stores, or perhaps the Vieux Port (Old Harbor), where fishermen still auction their catch at the daily fish market on the water's edge on the Quai des Belges, or quite possibly the Corniche, an ocean-side walkway and road. From the Corniche you can catch glimpses of the calanques, a beautiful natural formation of jagged and dramatic fjords that begin a short way outside of town and that you can discover by shore (from Callelongue, Luminy, Sormiou, Morgiou, or Cassis) or by boat.

Marseille, as Martin Garrett points out in his book *Provence: A Cultural History*, was, for a long time, primarily a place to pass through. Those who spent time here included the

novelist George Sand and her lover, composer Frédéric Chopin. Fleeing Majorca, they stopped here for three months, staying at what is now known as the Grand Hôtel Beauvau (see p. 219) while Chopin recuperated from illness.

Like Nice, Marseille is not a resort town, although some of its stretches of sand are fine for an afternoon of sunbathing and swimming. Prime spots to get a tan include those beaches between the harbors of La Pointe Rouge and La Madrague to the south of the city. Closer to the center of Marseille, the Escale Borély by the Parc Borély is a good place to find beach bars and restaurants from which to view the sunset. To truly get into the spirit of Marseille, order a glass of pastis, an anise-flavored aperitif associated with southeastern France but especially with Marseille, where the locals have nicknamed it *pastaga*.

The Escale is located at the bottom of the avenue du Prado, near the replica of Michelango's *David*, which was presented to the city by marble sculptor Jules Cantini in 1903. Michelangelo's Renaissance masterpiece *David*, which depicts the nude Biblical king in a contemplative mood prior to his battle with Goliath, attains a height of seventeen feet. The eagle eyed may notice that David is apparently uncircumcised, which contradicts Judaic norms but may be due to the conventions of Renaissance art.

GYPSY FEVER: ARLES AND THE CAMARGUE

From Marseille, you could very well make your escape across the waters of the Med to French Corsica, Italian Sardinia, or even North Africa—all of which are accessible by ferry from the city. But just as exotic is the Romani territory to the west of the city. Arles and the national park of the Camargue, though less than an hour from Marseille, are in essence worlds away.

This said, Arles, like Marseille, is an authentic and resolutely untouristy town—a fact that is quite surprising given its close ties to the artist Vincent van Gogh, who created more than three hundred paintings and drawings here, some of which are among his most famous works, in the years 1888 and 1889. This happy absence of tourist hordes is no doubt due to the fact that Van Gogh's work now commands such high prices that none of the originals have remained in the city of their inception—there is no museum dedicated to Van Gogh in this region. Still, armed with a book depicting his paintings, you can have a lot of fun retracing his steps around town.

His most recognizable work is *Café Terrace at Night*, depicting the terrace of Le Forum coffeehouse by night. The yellow-painted venue still exists, although it's been re-christened, perhaps inevitably, as the **Café Van Gogh** (10 Place du Forum). From the Place du Forum it's a short stroll northeast to Place Lamartine, where Van Gogh once lodged. He painted his residence at 2 Place Lamartine from inside (*Bedroom in Arles*) and outside (*The Yellow House*). In his painting *The Poet's Garden*, two lovers are depicted walking in the small park across from the yellow house. This work was originally painted for his guest room when his friend and fellow artist Paul Gauguin came to stay.

Van Gogh himself dubbed the park the Poets' Garden in reference to the Italian poets and friends Giovanni Boccaccio and Petrarch, both of whom spent time in southern France. Each poet wrote about love, Petrarch most famously in his *Rime Sparse* (*Scattered Verse*), which was inspired by his passion for a woman he referred to as Laura, whom he had glimpsed in a church in Avignon, to the north of Arles. Laura may have been Laura de Noves of Avignon, the wife of Count Hugues de Sade, an ancestor of the famous libertine writer the Marquis de Sade. In his *Posteritati* (*Letter to Posterity*), Petrarch wrote of how he "struggled constantly with an overwhelming but pure love affair—my only one."

Although the café and house no longer exist—the yellow house was destroyed by a bomb during World War II—it's only a few steps from the Place Lamartine to the river Rhône, which served as the setting for what must be the most romantic work that Van Gogh undertook in Arles. Within his *Starry Night*, two lovers stroll by the inky waters that reflect both the glittering stars overhead and the gaslights glowing on the opposite bank. In this instance, the view has hardly changed since Van Gogh set up his easel here, on the quay that has since been named the Quai du 8 Mai 1945.

Arles is not all about Van Gogh, however: its Roman and Romanesque monuments have earned this city a place on the UNESCO World Heritage List. These monuments include the thermal baths of the Roman emperor Constantine I, and the Alyscamps, an ancient necropolis that Van Gogh once painted. There's also the Arènes, a Roman amphitheater that regularly hosts *courses camarguaises*—Provençal bullfights in which the bull wears a tassel (attached to its horn) that athletic men try to remove without getting injured (or killing the bull). Occasionally there are also Spanish-style corridas, when bulls are allowed to run through the streets before being killed by a matador.

There's also the **Museon Arlaten** (29–31 rue de la République), a museum of regional folklore that was set up by the Nobel Prize–winning poet Frédéric Mistral. Mistral was born in 1830 in Mallaine, a town just north of Arles, and one of his most famous works, "Lou pouèmo dóu Rose," describes a voyage on the Rhône River to Beaucaire, near Mallaine. In the poem, a romantic Dutch prince boards a barge and falls in love with the daughter of a poor ferryman. Unfortunately the lovers drown when the barge takes on water after a lethal hit by a steamboat.

More recently, Arles has spawned the Gipsy Kings, whose members are descended from *gitanos* (Spanish Romanis). Three of the group are sons of the famous flamenco singer José Reyes, who began singing *cante jonde* (deep chant), a style of song that is laced with themes of love, passion, and death. The Gipsy King's musical style, *rumba catalana*, is a pop-inflected version of flamenco. It can be heard on albums such as *Cantos de Amor* (*Love Songs*) or performed live by local groups and artists in many of the cafés and restaurants of the region.

Between Arles and the Mediterranean to the south stretches the **Camargue**, the largest river delta in western Europe, much of which is a protected regional park and nature reserve. This area's biggest draw is the incredible wildlife, including pink flamingos, black Camargue bulls, white Camargue horses, and wild boar. This region is still considered a wild marshland, and within it you may see *gardians* (French cowboys) astride Camargue horses rounding up bulls for corridas in Spain.

Of the few small towns that dot this almost eerie landscape, the fishing port of **Saintes-Maries-de-la-Mer** on the southern coast is where Romanis from all over Europe flock each year to venerate Saint Sarah, their patron saint. There's a lot of discussion as to who Sarah actually is. To many French, she is the daughter of Mary Magdalene, one of the three Marys for whom the town is named (the other two are Mary Salomé and Mary Jacoby).

According to legend, this trio of women, who were the first to see Jesus's empty tomb after his resurrection, fled from the Holy Land to this part of France. Sarah, who is also known as Sarah-la-kali (Sarah the Black) for her dark skin, is contended by others to have been a local queen who welcomed the refugees, an ancient pagan goddess, or the Egyptian servant of Mary Magdalene. This site may have also once served as home to an Eygptian fortress dedicated to the sun god Ra.

Avoid the summer in Saintes-Maries, when the town becomes a full-blown resort with all the trappings. The best time of year to come is May, when Rom, Manouches, Tziganes, and other Romani groups come to honor Sarah, Mary Salomé, and Mary Jacoby at their shrine in the town's imposing fortified church. The two-day festival includes the baptizing of children, much religious ecstasy, and lots of general feasting and partying in the streets. On the first day, a colorful procession takes Sarah's statue—which is clad in a brightly hued dress and jewels—from the church to the sea and back, accompanied by traditional music and the ringing of church bells. The following day, the statues of the other two Marys are carried through the streets in a boat and then cast out to the sea. There's another pilgrimage in late October, specifically for Mary Salomé.

Even outside of these busy but deeply atmospheric rituals, you can visit Sarah's statue in the crypt of the church. The thirteenth-century structure is also the setting for the final scene of the Occitan poem "Mirèoi" by Frédéric Mistral. In this, another doomed love story

by the poet, the daughter of a wealthy farmer falls for a poor basket maker's son, but her parents intervene and she dies in the church of Saintes-Maries, after the saints appear to her and tell her that happiness lies in Heaven.

Romani culture has influenced this region in many ways, including with the live music that is played in many cafés and restaurants. Indeed, the world-famous flamenco guitarist Manitas de Plata began his career playing in Saintes-Maries during the annual pilgrimage. There's also a 1930s bullring that hosts bull-related sports, like the Arènes in Arles, including *courses camarguaises* and the more bloodthirsty corridas. These sports are no doubt what drew writer Ernest Hemingway here in 1927, while on his honeymoon with his second wife Pauline Pfeiffer, a fashion reporter for Paris *Vogue*.

Outside the crush of summer, Saintes-Maries is a fine town of narrow streets, uncrowded beaches, and unpretentious little fish *cabanes* in which to enjoy local *tellines* (small clams), squid, or the catch of the day as the sun sets over the Mediterranean. Aside from fish, a local specialty available in most restaurants is *taureau sauvage à la gardiane*, a hearty bull stew that is enriched with red wine. The **Brasserie La Siesta** (10 avenue Van Gogh) with its facade of neon flamingos is a popular spot to try this and other *specialités camarguaises*.

Saintes-Maries is a stepping-stone to the Camargue as a whole—the wild plains of which are perhaps most romantically experienced on horseback. Many local *mas*—estates founded in the sixteenth and seventeenth centuries by wealthy landlords from Arles—have been modernized and converted into luxurious hotels, some of which offer riding excursions and vacation packages (see p. 219).

COUPS DE COEUR

EATING

L'Amandier de Mougins
Place du Vieux Village, Mougins
+33 (0)4 93 90 00 91

While Le Moulin de Mougins draws the crowds to the gastronomic pilgrimage site of Mougins (see pp. 203–204), L'Amandier, set up by the same celebrity chef, Roger Vergé, in the 1970s, may seduce you. Though Vergé is no longer at the helm, L'Amandier is easier on your wallet and doesn't require booking months in advance. For dining, choose between the timeworn interior with its cozy fireplace and antique machinery from its former incarnation as an olive mill, or the lush rooftop terrace. The food is correspondingly soul-satisfying: think tomato tart with tapenade, thyme sorbet with a quinoa tabouleh, and braised sea bass with zucchini flowers. You can learn how to create these or similar dishes in the cooking school above the restaurant.

Auberge de la Vignette Haute
370 route du Village, Auribeau-sur-Siagne
+33 (0)4 93 42 20 01

Tucked away on the edge of a thirteenth-century village in the hills west of Grasse, this inn is like something out of a dream, with nineteen delightful medieval-themed guest rooms (three in the village itself), a Roman-style outdoor pool and fountains, and the Curiosa, a private museum that traces the history of love through the ages with erotic and courtly artworks and artifacts. The restaurant is similarly rarefied, with tables lit by oil lamps and tableware made out of pewter. Each of the four separate dining areas has its own ambiance: a former barn, a tower, a discreet *petit salon* that is made for lovers, and a terrace beside the pool lit by flaming torches and offering views over mimosa-covered hills. The adventurous cuisine takes its cues from the Provençal landscape: pressed foie gras with figs and gingerbread, dried-tomato mash and truffle oil, and roast pigeon with a lavender-infused sauce and roast potatoes.

Le Petit Nice-Passédat
Corniche J. F. Kennedy, Marseille
+33 (0)4 91 59 25 92

This restaurant and hotel located within a neo-Greek villa on the stunning Corniche road that snakes around Marseille's shoreline offers sunset views alongside its two-Michelin-starred cuisine. Sliced octopus held captive in a silky jelly and a dessert of tomato sorbet are among the standouts. Don't miss the bouillabaisse (see p. 209), described by chef (and hotel proprietor) Gérald Passédat as his poetic take on the tradition, as well as a re-creation of the emotions that the dish inspired in him when he first tasted it as a child. This bouillabaisse is served in three courses to form an entire meal: in addition to the traditional two courses of fish and soup, Passédat has added a starter of a shellfish carpaccio with fried strips of *girelle* (rainbow wrasse). If you're not hungry enough for a full meal, come for the substantial bar menu, which runs the gamut from an omelet or fish soup to roast chicken with roast potatoes, all best accompanied by a flute or two of champagne. Guest rooms are modern and chic, and there's a twinkling gem of an outdoor pool.

La Cave à Huitres
38 avenue Theodore Aubanel,
Saintes-Maries-de-la-Mer
+33 (0)4 90 97 96 60

Among many touristy restaurants in Saintes-Maries-de-la-Mer, La Cave à Huitres (The Oyster

Cellar) with its healthy contingent of locals is a blast of fresh sea air. Although the lay of the land on the road skirting the coast dictates that this simple fish café and wine bar is *sans* ocean views, taking a seat on its charming sidewalk terrace, with its marine-blue wrought-iron chairs and wooden tables, will immediately put you in a vacation frame of mind. Although the ambiance is seaside rustic and the prices are competitive, there's nothing second rate about the seafood on offer, which includes local oysters, mussels with *frites*, crab, and lobster fresh from the water and simply prepared.

STAYING

Château de la Chèvre d'Or
rue du Barri, Èze
+33 (0)4 92 10 66 66
www.chevredor.com

Gracing the hillside of medieval Èze (see p. 197), the Château de la Chèvre d'Or (Chateau of the Golden Goat), with its magical views over the shimmering waters of the Mediterranean, has been favored by names as illustrious as Marlene Dietrich, Lauren Bacall and Humphrey Bogart, Elizabeth Taylor, and Robert de Niro. The thirty rooms and six suites that comprise this castle are scattered around the village, and hence quite literally provide a hideaway for lovers. Some of the rooms are classical in feel, while others are coolly modern. If money's no object, the Presidential Suite has a two-person sunken indoor Jacuzzi, plus an outdoor Jacuzzi and private infinity pool on its sundeck. Alternatively, check out the Romeo & Juliet packages, each of which includes champagne and a candlelit dinner on a private terrace, which are specially created for wedding nights, anniversaries, and other loving occasions. Of the four on-site eateries, the contemporary Mediterranean restaurant was, at the time of writing, expected to be awarded its third Michelin star. The private terraced gardens contain quirky classical and animal statuary and a pool where you can swim beside ocean views. Private yoga classes are also available in the gardens, and you can round them off with an ayurvedic massage rooted in traditional Indian medicine.

Mas Candille
boulevard Clement Rebuffel, Mougins
+33 (0)4 92 28 43 43
www.lemascandille.com

A driveway lined by silvery olive trees and pines sweeps down to this fabulous hotel, restaurant, and Japanese-style spa on a hillside at the edge of Mougins (see pp. 203–204), with glorious views over the Provençal landscape. Many people come here solely for the Michelin-starred restaurant, where you can feast on exquisite confections such as scallop tartar with vodka cream and Aquitaine caviar, or orange-saffron artichokes with nasturtium petals. But it's also worth booking one of the luxurious guest rooms in this eighteenth-century farmhouse, which profits from the peace and calm of its voluptuous surrounds. Its steeply tiered grounds provide two great pools (one is for adults only), an outdoor Jacuzzi with valley views, and a Shiseido spa complete with its own gardens, a plunge pool, and decadent hammocks. There's also a poolside restaurant in which you can breakfast and dine alfresco in summer. And in the off-season, this cozy retreat offers roaring log fires to console you about the absence of the

sun. For loving bliss, book a Romance package with a mountain-view room, complete with red roses and champagne, an eight-course gastronomic extravaganza, and one ninety-minute spa treatment per person.

Grand Hôtel Beauvau Marseille Vieux Port
4 rue Beauvau, Marseille
+33 (0)4 91 54 91 00
www.mgallery.com

Although it's now part of a chain, this hotel retains the personal, even quirky charm that has pervaded its facilities since it hosted a number of famous writers and musicians who visited Marseille in the nineteenth and early twentieth centuries. Among the great names to grace the hotel were George Sand and her lover Frédéric Chopin (see p. 212), Alfred de Musset, and Jean Cocteau. Some of the charming duplex suites, which extend into the mansarded eaves of the building, are named after these famous guests and feature artwork that relate to them or bear romantic quotations from their writings. Such details share space with antique furniture and a warm Mediterranean decor. Travel paraphernalia—old suitcases and vintage travel guides—dotted about the hotel are reminders of Marseille's role as a stopover between Europe and more exotic climes. The city's oldest and best-situated hotel, the Beauvau offers views over the old port and up to the basilica. There isn't a restaurant on the premises, but room service is available around the clock, and the prime location is just steps away from the bustling eateries at the port.

Grand Hôtel Nord-Pinus
Place du Forum, Arles
+33 (0)4 90 93 44 44
www.nord-pinus.com

A flash of flamenco passion and a haven for romantics in the heart of untouristy Arles (see pp. 213–214), this hotel exudes character, history, and charisma. The interiors include one-off antiques bought at auctions, hot Romani colors, old mosaics, witty black-and-white photographs of Africa by Peter Beard, and vintage bullfighting posters. There are also a few fading images of Jean Cocteau, who stayed here. Other illustrious visitors have included Henry James, Pablo Picasso (see pp. 204–205), Ernest Hemingway, and famous matadors who appeared at the local arena. The second-floor, split-level suite, accessed via its own spiral staircase, offers extra space and privacy. There's a decadent, crumbling, and mysterious feel to the Nord-Pinus that only enhances its eccentric and intense charms, which extend into the brasserie and bar.

Hôtel les Arnelles
Route d'Arles, Saintes-Maries-de-la-Mer
+33 (0)4 90 97 61 59
www.lesarnelles.com

Although there are more luxurious options in the national park of the Camargue (see p. 214), Les Arnelles stands out for its laid-back feel. The hotel blends seamlessly with its surroundings, making you feel as if you've truly escaped from the modern world. Even the swimming pool has been designed to appear to meld with the landscape, while the serene restaurant—which serves hearty Mediterranean cuisine including local bull stew—is actually set in the midst of the marsh and accessed by wooden boardwalks. Bulls' heads and bull motifs enliven the decor, from the bar to the sixteen guest rooms and solitary suite. These are refreshingly simple, each with its own wooden deck terrace on which to sit and soak up the silence. For those keen to see some of the famed local wildlife, the hotel has its own riding school, which hosts trips on the Camargue's white horses, believed to have been introduced to the region by Arabs. The most romantic of these trips are taken at sunrise or sunset and include either breakfast or an aperitif on the beach.

5€ la botte
Tournesol
4,60€ la botte
Roses "Akito"
5 € la botte
Rose High Magic
5€ la botte

GETTING MARRIED IN FRANCE

Getting Married in France

"Un marriage heureux est une longue conversation qui semble toujours trop brève."

"A happy mariage is a long conversation that always seems too short."

—ANDRÉ MAUROIS

France is famous for its bureaucracy, which extends to all of life's twists and turns, so it should come as no surprise that marriage in this beautiful country requires a good deal of paperwork and planning. Don't let this put you off: France's glorious architectural heritage—from grand hotels to sumptuous chateaus—as well as its well-priced food and drink and accommodations make it a thoroughly romantic and affordable setting in which to tie the knot.

That said, you will save yourself a lot of time and trouble by signing your official marriage documents in a city hall or equivalent in your home country before traveling to France for a religious or nonreligious ceremony or blessing followed by a reception. There are strict marriage procedures in France that require all couples to wed in a civil ceremony held in a *mairie* (city, town, or village hall) before the marriage is considered legal. Crucially, for this to take place, either the bride or the groom must reside in the *commune* (administrative division) in which the ceremony is to be performed for at least forty days before the wedding.

Some couples limit themselves to the civil ceremony, which is generally restrained and solemn in tone, although guests are welcome to attend, and some *mairies* offer a special room that may be personalized for the event. Most couples follow up the civil ceremony with a religious or a nonreligious ceremony or blessing, during which they can symbolically demonstrate their love by exchanging vows. Since the religious ceremony is not legally recognized in France, you will need to present your certificate of civil marriage—whether from France or your home country—to the minister, priest, or rabbi before he or she will provide a blessing.

The sheer range of exquisite French venues for your post-wedding party is almost dizzying, from fairy-tale chateaus or Parisian riverboats to villas overlooking the glittering waters of the Mediterranean or hot-air balloons. You can also expect the food and wine to be simply superb. Among my favorite venues in which to get married in Paris are the Four Seasons Hôtel George V (see p. 67) just off the Champs-Élysées, which offers a romantic wedding package, and the luminous Salle Gustave Eiffel at the top of the Eiffel Tower (see pp. 64–65). In the Champagne region, the Château de Condé (see p. 165) stands out, while the Loire Valley—home to many of the world's most gorgeous chateaus—is a wonderful place to celebrate your nuptials. Atmospheric venues in the Valley of the Kings include the Château de Villesavin (see p. 140), the Clos Lucé (see pp. 152–153), and the Pagode de Chanteloup (see pp. 153–154). Or head south, to the palm-tree-fringed, colonial-style Villa le Rêve (see p. 198) with its spellbinding views of the Mediterranean and the hills of Provence that once provided inspiration for Henri Matisse, who lived in the villa for a time.

Authentic French wedding receptions tend to be surprisingly bawdy affairs that are often accompanied by racy speeches and jokes. After some receptions—and sometimes well into the wedding night—friends of the bride and groom will bang pots and pans, ring bells, sound horns, and sing loudly outside the newlyweds' window. The couple is expected to greet their noisy guests in their wedding clothes and invite them in for a drink and treats. This traditional prank is called *chiverie*.

Of course, you may not wish to emulate the French at your wedding reception, but you may want to participate in some of their less invasive traditions. For instance, after the toast, many newlyweds drink from a double-handled goblet known as a *coupe de mariage* (often a family heirloom), which is sometimes symbolically filled with wine taken from two vineyards. At many weddings, champagne bottles are theatrically "decapitated" using the technique of *sabrage* (see p. 164). After the meal, there's usually dancing—either traditional French dances such as the *rond* from Brittany, or modern disco.

If organizing a wedding abroad seems too much for you, or if your lack of fluency is getting in the way, then a wedding-planning service (see p. 226) can take the headache out of planning. Wedding planners provide seamless help in overcoming the legal hurdles to getting wed in France or take care of practicalities such as finding a reputable photographer and caterer.

FRENCH WEDDING SUPERSTITIONS AND TRADITIONS

The custom of wearing a white wedding dress began with Anne of Brittany (see p. 151), when she wed her third husband, Louis XII, in 1499. At that time, most brides wore red as a symbol of virginity. Anne, a recent widow, wed in white because it was, at the time, the color of mourning among the nobility and royalty.

It wasn't until the nineteenth century that white wedding robes came into vogue among the general public. Many fashion historians assert that the modern style of white wedding gown, with its elaborate detailing (perhaps gold or silver embroidery), was inspired by the dress that was worn by Eugénie when she married Napoléon III in 1853.

In small villages, the groom continues the tradition of calling on the bride on the morning of the wedding. The bride may have taken a ritual bath, purifying herself of evil, and possibly also of memories of previous partners.

As they process from the bride's house to the chapel, the bride—who walks with her father, behind the musicians—cuts white ribbons that local children have stretched across the road. Such obstacles are symbols of the couple's willingness to forge a common path through life.

Traditionally, for weddings, churches are filled with incense and flowers, and a silk canopy is erected by the altar. A square of silk (called a *carré*) is held over the bride's and groom's heads as they receive the priest's final blessing to protect them from malice. (This same scarf is later used to wrap their children when they are baptized.)

When the couple leaves the church, guests scatter aromatic laurel leaves in their path, and the pair may also pass through an arch of flowers. As they walk, the newlyweds are showered with rice or wheat, symbols of prosperity and fertility, and the bride may be given a loaf of bread. In some areas of the south, children gather on the chapel doorstop to catch coins or *dragées*—almonds covered in chocolate, nougat, or sugar—which are thrown as symbols of happiness and celebration.

French wedding cakes are usually in the form of a traditional *croquembouche*, a pyramid of cream puffs topped with a caramel glaze and spun sugar. This confection has its origins in the Middle Ages, when guests would bring small cakes and pile them in the center of a table—if the bride and groom could kiss over them without knocking the pile down, they would have a prosperous life.

The reception may conclude the following morning with French onion soup, served as a pick-me-up after the long night of celebration. The bride and groom may also host a brunch for their guests before embarking on their honeymoon.

Last but not least, there's the honeymoon—so much more than just the icing on the cake. Again, a wedding planner can provide an invaluable service in helping to find the honeymoon destination of your dreams. Or take the hands-on approach and simply browse the chapters of this guide, which features delectably French destinations and hotel accommodations in which to spend this most precious of times; many of the hotels listed offer special packages specifically designed to celebrate your wedded bliss.

WEDDING RESOURCES

INFORMATION:

www.ambafrance-us.org

http://france.usembassy.gov/root/pdfs/paris-marriage.pdf

www.ukinfrance.fco.gov.uk/en

www.mariages.fr (French-language)

WEDDING SERVICES AND PACKAGES:

www.weddingsinfrance.com

www.getmarriedinfrance.co.uk

www.piecemontee.com

www.mariage-concept.com

www.loveandlord.com/france

www.feteinfrance.com

CIVIL WEDDINGS IN FRANCE: THE RED TAPE

Most *mairies* require four to six weeks to process an application to marry on-site, and you may need to get married or at least publish the banns (the announcement of a forthcoming marriage) within three months of receiving the documents. You can only make the first publication of the banns (a compulsory step) after the bride or groom has resided in the *commune* for at least thirty days. The banns must be posted at the appropriate *mairie* no less than ten days before the marriage date.

If you need a translator to be present, the *mairie* may be able to provide details; if not, you can look in the French yellow pages, the *Pages Jaunes* (www.pagesjaunes.fr), under "Traducteur Assermenté." You will also need one or two witnesses per spouse, but representatives of the *mairie* can serve this role if you don't have your own witnesses.

The following documents (originals or officially certified photocopies) are required by most *mairies*, but **it is crucial that you check for their exact requirements**:

- A French resident permit or valid passport from your native country
- A birth certificate (translated by an official translator)
- A certificate of celibacy (less than three months old). This document can be prepared by a consular officer in France.
- An affidavit/certificate of law, certifying that you are free to contract marriage in France and that the marriage will be recognized in your home country. This document should be produced in French by your embassy.
- A medical certificate (less than three months old)
- Proof of residence in the *commune* of the *mairie* (such as an electricity bill)
- A *certificat du notaire* by a French solicitor if you opt for a prenuptial agreement.

The embassy can also translate the marriage certificate and have it forwarded to the authorities in your own country, although this is not a legal requirement.

ESSENTIAL FRENCH WEDDING VOCABULARY

attestation/acte de mariage (marriage certificate)
extrait de naissance (birth certificate)
carte de séjour (French residency permit)
attestation de célibat (certificate of celibacy)
certificat de coutume/certificat de capacité matrimoniale (affadavit/certificate of law)
certificat medical (medical certificate)
justificatif de domicile (proof of residence)
mairie (town hall)
maire (mayor)
adjoint au maire (deputy mayor)
conseiller municipal (town councillor)
officier de l'etat civil (French civil authority)
témoin (witness)
publication des bans (publication of banns)
lune de miel (honeymoon)

LOVE AND FOOD

Love and Food

"… la gorgée mêlée des miettes du gâteau […] m'avait aussitôt rendu les vicissitudes de la vie indifférentes, ses désastres inoffensifs, sa brièveté illusoire, de la même façon qu'opère l'amour."

"… the mouthful of tea mixed with cake crumbs […] had immediately made the vicissitudes of life unimportant to me, its disasters innocuous, its brevity illusory, acting in the same way that love acts."

—MARCEL PROUST

Food, like love, can change your life. No one forgets where he slurped his first oyster or took his first sip of champagne—just as no one forgets her first kiss. Nor can one deny the mood-enhancing properties of a slab of good dark chocolate and its miraculous ability to chase away the blues. Food and drink can be as life affirming as sex, and people with a good appetite tend to have a healthy libido. Preparing and sharing a meal with a partner, moreover, can be one of the most tender acts of love.

The pairing of food and love can be positively earth-shattering. Since the dawn of humanity, food has had an important role in foreplay—mental and physical—and in the whole glorious ritual of the erotic exchange. The *Kama Sutra*, the classical Indian treatise on the art of making love, contains a selection of recipes for external and internal use: in part seven "Means of Attracting Others to Yourself," you'll find ointments and preparations featuring edibles such as black pepper, honey, milk, ghee (clarified butter), fennel bulbs, shatavari (a relative of asparagus), and licorice.

In France, food is a way of celebrating life. From sourcing the best local produce while browsing in colorful markets filled with intoxicating fragrances to breaking bread with your loved one—whether in the intimacy of your home or hotel room or in a Michelin-starred restaurant in the heart of Paris or on a hilltop overlooking the hills of Provence or the Mediterranean Sea—the pleasures of the table are an essential part of any romantic stay in the land of amour.

GARLIC—L'AIL

A mainstay of French cuisine, garlic is a "hot" plant with a long-standing reputation as an aphrodisiac: the ancient Greeks and Egyptians embraced its sexy effects, while Jewish leader Ezra the Scribe decreed that it be eaten on Friday nights to "promote love and arouse desire." Modern research has suggested that garlic may indeed help sexual performance in men.

CHILI PEPPERS—LES PIMENTS

Chili peppers, which are related to the *Kama Sutra*–endorsed black pepper, contain heat-giving capsaicin—a chemical that stimulates the nerve endings and raises the pulse, affording a natural endorphin high. In the Basque country of southwest France, the Espelette chilies are strung in garlands from the farmhouses to dry in the sun, before being used in fiery local dishes such as the erotically charged oyster brochette with Bayonne ham.

ASPARAGUS—LES ASPERGES

The suggestive shape of asparagus and the sultry opportunities for flirty consumption have endowed it with a reputation that seems to be backed up by science: it contains vitamin E, which is thought to stimulate sex hormones and thus increase sexual potency. French asparagus is often white because it is harvested before the shoots push up through the soil. It's at its most sexy when topped with a sauce of butter, lemon juice, parsley, and truffle shavings, as is traditional in the cuisine of Normandy (see pp. 172–189), or simply drenched in butter so you can pick it up with your fingers and suck it into your mouth.

PARSLEY—LE PERSIL

This most popular of garden herbs has been shrouded in myth and superstition since cultivation of it began about two thousand years ago. Some link this fragrant plant with devilish dealings, while others—among them the ancient Greeks—have used the seeds to spark arousal in women. Whether the Greeks were right or not, parsley comes in very handy on dates, as a breath freshener for those who have overindulged in garlic.

TRUFFLES—LES TRUFFES

"The truffle reeks of sex," asserts British food journalist Elizabeth Luard, who devoted a whole book to the highly prized—and highly priced—fungi. This is quite literally true, since truffles emit musky pheromones that make them irresistible to sows—hence the instinctive way the creatures seek them out in the ground. In his *Physiologie du goût* (*Physiology of Taste*) of 1825, the gastronome Jean Anthelme Brillat-Savarin asserted that the woodsy, earthy, peppery smell of *truffes* "awakens lustful and erotic memories among the skirt-wearing sex and lustful and erotic memories among the beard-wearing sex." Live dangerously by imbibing a truffle and champagne cocktail featuring truffle liqueur.

OYSTERS—LES HUÎTRES

Slippery, salty, and glistening, the oyster seems to have the sole purpose of conjuring up images of sex. An erotic favorite since the time of Aphrodite—the Greek goddess of sensuality and love who inspired the term "aphrodisiac"—the oyster is now known to be a source of zinc, which is essential in the production of testosterone, which is known to increase libido.

The high zinc content of oysters is also characteristic of other shellfish. Head to Marseille for a bowl of bouillabaisse, a golden-orange seafood broth steeped in romantic myth.

RABBIT—LE LAPIN

Like other animals known for their mating prowess and virility, rabbit has sometimes been considered an aphrodisiac. It's a popular delicacy in France, where it is often cooked in a similar way to chicken. Romantic recipes include rosemary-skewered rabbit on a champagne-and-truffle risotto.

CHOCOLATE—LE CHOCOLAT

The natural high we get from chocolate is partly due to the stimulant phenylethylamine, which emulates the effects of endorphins. It may also contain chemicals that affect the brain's neurotransmitters to make you feel weak in the knees as people in love often do. A classic French chocolate dessert is *petits pots au chocolat*—little ramekins, coffee cups, or glass tumblers filled with rich, silky-smooth dark chocolate dotted with crème fraîche and a dusting of cocoa powder.

VANILLA—LA VANILLE

Vanilla was listed as an aphrodisiac in old medicinal literature, and modern studies have shown that it raises adrenalin levels in the blood, increasing lustful feelings. The flavor of vanilla is derived from tropical orchids that, according to the mythology of the Totonac people who first cultivated them, sprang into existence where the blood of two ill-fated lovers touched the earth. Place a couple of vanilla pods in a jar of granulated sugar to add a sensual touch to your dessert recipes.

FIGS—LES FIGUES

This erotically fleshy plant—one of the oldest in the world—is believed to have been Cleopatra's favorite fruit. In ancient Greece, figs were a sacred food associated with love and fertility, and each new crop meant a celebration that included ritual copulation. Like asparagus, the reputation of figs as a sexual stimulant may stem from their appearance—splitting a fig and devouring it in front of your lover may put you in an erotic frame of mind.

The figs grown in France's Mediterranean region are more intensely flavored than those hailing from farther north. Serve them cut in half and topped with *fromage frais* flavored with vanilla seeds.

CHAMPAGNE—LE CHAMPAGNE

"Candy is dandy but liquor is quicker," quipped the poet Ogden Nash. If you start your date with a champagne cocktail, you'll be certain to feel less inhibited and more relaxed. Try a pick-me-up highball with champagne, brandy, orange curaçao, and pastis—the French liqueur flavored with aniseed, a plant that the Greeks and Romans claimed had sexual powers.

Drinking champagne or wine can be an arousing experience, but be careful not to overdo it or you might just feel sleepy. If you love the fizz, you must tour the romantic Champagne region of France, where the effervescent bubbly is created (see pp. 158–171).

RECIPES

LAPIN AUX TRUFFES À LA YOLANDE

(Serves 4)

You only need a small amount of truffles for this classic dish that I associate with Yolande "Yoyo" Amaglio, the woman I came to see as my "French mom" and a true goddess of the kitchen. She often served us the wild rabbit that her husband Daniel would hunt on weekends. If you find it hard to source a rabbit, substitute a large chicken, similarly cut into sections.

For optimal fragrance and flavor, wait until the last minute to grate the truffles. Serve the dish with a fresh baguette and haricots verts, steamed until almost soft and then quickly fried in olive oil, bacon fat, or duck fat with minced or crushed garlic. A sprinkling of chopped parsley is optional.

2 medium onions, whole
2 cloves
2 medium carrots, peeled and diced
a pinch or two of a spice blend made up of equal parts nutmeg, cloves, ginger, and cinnamon
1 sprig thyme
2 or 3 whole bay leaves
2 cups water
1 medium rabbit, cut into 7 pieces (front and back feet, chest, saddle, and head)
4 tablespoons duck fat
½ cup bacon, diced
1½ cups small white onions, peeled and diced
3 tablespoons butter
1 tablespoon flour
2½ cups Pineau blanc (a fortified wine; alternatively, use a dry white wine with a splash of brandy)
2 tablespoons truffles, freshly grated
Salt and freshly ground pepper to taste
Chopped parsley (optional)

Preheat the oven to 275°F. Stud the whole onions with the cloves. Place the carrots and whole onions in a casserole dish with a pinch or two of the spice mix, thyme, bay leaves, and water. Bring the mixture to a boil slowly and reduce the heat. Simmer uncovered for one hour to concentrate the stock. Strain the broth and discard the solids.

Wash the rabbit pieces and pat them dry with a cloth. Heat the duck fat in a skillet. Add the rabbit pieces and brown on all sides over a low flame (essential to keep the flesh tender). Remove the browned pieces and keep them warm in a preheated oven. Cook the bacon in the duck fat.

Heat the butter in a skillet. Add the white onions and sauté them. Add the flour to the butter and onions. Cook over a low heat to create a roux. Add the wine to deglaze the pan. Add the rabbit, bacon, and stock. Grate the truffles over the dish and season with salt and pepper. Cook over a low heat for about 45 minutes. Garnish with chopped parsley and serve.

LE TABBOULEH DE RIHAB

(Serves approximately 4, depending on accompaniments)

France's sizeable Arab populations eat versions of this bulgur wheat–based dish, often as part of a meze. The extravagant use of parsley and the inclusion of black pepper make it a sexy addition to any romantic meal. I was introduced to this dish by the beautiful Rihab Kamel, a Syrian doctor who was my roommate while I was a student in Paris.

¼ cup fine bulgur wheat
2 lemons, juiced
1 teaspoon salt
1 teaspoon paprika
3 bunches fresh parsley, finely chopped
½ cup fresh mint, finely chopped
3 scallions or 1 red onion, finely chopped
1/2 white cabbage, finely chopped
4–5 medium cucumbers, finely diced
4–5 medium tomatoes, finely diced
1¾ cup olive oil
Juice of 1 lemon (optional for dressing)
Salt to taste

Soak the bulgur wheat in the juice of two lemons, salt, and paprika in a bowl and chill in the refrigerator for two hours. In a second bowl, combine the parsley, mint, scallions or red onion, cabbage, and cucumbers and chill in the refrigerator until the bulgur has finished soaking. Add the bulgur to the second bowl, then the tomatoes and olive oil. Mix well and salt to taste. Add lemon juice to taste, *et voila!* (If you're not serving immediately, soak the bulgur and prepare the other ingredients, but wait to mix the two until you are ready to eat.)

MARMITE DE POISSON À LA CONRAD

(Serves 2)

My husband often wooed me with this silky fish concoction when we were living in our crumbling farmhouse in the depths of the French countryside. The beauty of the dish is its malleability—you simply make it up as you go along, using whatever seasonings and seafood you are in the mood for, in quantities that suit your hunger. There are few things sexier than a delicious stew thrown together in the spirit of hedonistic abandon.

Serve unadorned in a bowl with crusty rustic bread.

2 tablespoons of extra-virgin olive oil
2 medium potatoes, diced
2 medium carrots, diced
1 medium onion, thinly sliced
2 cloves of garlic, chopped
A pinch of chili, paprika, turmeric or whatever spice you have on hand (to taste)
A pinch of parsley, thyme, or whatever herb you have on hand (to taste)
1 cup white wine
1½ cups fish stock or hot water
Green vegetables (haricots verts or asparagus works well)
Fish and shellfish (salmon, a white fish, and prawns work well)

Heat the olive oil in a sauté pan. Add the potatoes and carrots and cook over low heat for about five minutes. Add the onions, garlic, spices, and herbs. Pour the wine over the vegetables and continue cooking until the alcohol has evaporated. Add the stock or hot water. Simmer for another 15 minutes or until the potatoes are cooked through.

Add the green vegetables and simmer until cooked (about five minutes for haricots verts and two minutes for asparagus spears). Place the fish and shellfish on top of the stew and cover. Simmer until cooked (approximately 5 minutes for fish and shellfish and 1 minute for prawns).

CLASSIC CRÈME BRÛLÉE

(Serves 2)

No collection of French recipes, no matter how small, should omit this divine vanilla-infused dessert. Taste aside, eating a "burnt cream"—cracking its crisp golden shell and plunging your spoon into its creamy innards—is an erotic experience in its own right. Served in one ramekin with two spoons, this is the perfect dish to share with a lover.

1 cup of heavy cream
⅛ vanilla pod, cut across the middle
3 medium egg yolks
4 teaspoons granulated sugar
Confectioners' sugar, for dusting

Put the heavy cream and vanilla pod in a saucepan, and heat to a simmer. Do not allow the mixture to boil. Remove from the heat and set aside for 1 hour to allow the vanilla to infuse the heavy cream.

Preheat the oven to 275° F. Put the egg yolks and sugar in a mixing bowl and whisk until pale and creamy. Strain through a fine sieve. Add the egg yolk and sugar mixture to the heavy cream and vanilla pod mixture and stir. Pour into one large ramekin (or two small ones) set on a roasting pan. Add hot water to the pan until the water level reaches halfway up the side of the ramekin. Bake for about 30 minutes or until the crème is just set but still a little wobbly in the center.

After removing the ramekin from the oven, let it cool. Cover with plastic wrap and chill in the refrigerator overnight.

Just before serving, dust with a teaspoon of confectioners' sugar. Caramelize with a mini blowtorch held about 4–5 inches from the surface. Let harden for a few minutes and serve.

INDEX

ABOUT THE AUTHOR

British-born writer, editor, and translator RHONDA CARRIER lost her heart to Paris—and France as a whole—as a teenager staying with French penfriends through long indolent summers. Later, as part of her degree in Modern Languages at the University of Cambridge, she spent a year gaining a deeper appreciation of Gallic culture in all its guises while studying French literature at the Sorbonne in Paris. More recently, she and her family lived in an old cognac farm in the Charente-Maritime.

Currently based in the U.K., and having spent many years in London reviewing restaurants, bars, hotels, shops, and more for *Time Out*, Debrett's, and other publishers, she still spends several months each year in France. She has written widely about Paris and other French regions, as well as setting much of her award-winning short fiction in the country, particularly the French capital. This includes "Other Lives" in the *French Literary Review*, and "Nine Cubed" in *68: New Stories from Children of the Revolution* (Salt Publishing).

She is married to the novelist and photographer Conrad Williams, with whom she has three young sons.

ACKNOWLEDGMENTS

Thanks to Sophie Amaglio (now Bureau) and her parents Daniel and Yolande for welcoming me into their family and in doing so inspiring an enduring love of France and the French way of life. Thanks, too, to Gemma Hirst, and to my rue St-Jacques roommates Rihab, Azar, Patricia, and Natalie, for sharing Paris with me. Nick Royle, Anne Billson, and Howard Rombough gave me some invaluable Paris tips.

My gratitude to Claire L. Gierczak, Susi Oberhelman, and the rest of the staff at Rizzoli for reigning in this monster to create such a beautiful book. Thanks too to Caitlin Leffel Ostroy for her efforts at the commissioning stage.